IN MEMORY OF:

    Ransom and Ann Oetzel

PRESENTED BY:

  Mr. and Mrs. Terry Oetzel
          and
      Family

Women's Firsts

Women's Firsts

MILESTONES IN WOMEN'S HISTORY

VOLUME 1

Activism
The Arts
Business
Education
Government

Peggy Saari, Tim & Susan Gall, Editors

AN IMPRINT OF GALE

DETROIT · NEW YORK · TORONTO · LONDON

Women's Firsts: Milestones in Women's History

Peggy Saari, Tim L. Gall, and Susan B. Gall, Editors

Staff

Elizabeth Des Chenes, *U•X•L Developmental Editor*
Carol DeKane Nagel, *U•X•L Managing Editor*
Thomas L. Romig, *U•X•L Publisher*

Margaret Chamberlain, *Permissions Specialist*
Shalice Shah, *Permission Associate*

Shanna P. Heilveil, *Production Assistant*
Evi Seoud, *Assistant Production Manager*
Mary Beth Trimper, *Production Director*

Pamela A. E. Galbreath, *Senior Art Director*
Cynthia Baldwin, *Product Design Manager*

Linda Mahoney, *Typesetting*

Library of Congress Cataloging-in-Publication Data

Women's firsts: milestones in women's history/
Peggy Saari and Tim and Susan B. Gall , editors

p.   cm.
Includes bibliographical references and index.

Contents: v. 1. Activism-government v. 2. media-sports

ISBN 0-7876-0653-7 (set: alk paper).
ISBN 0-7876-0654-5 (vol. 1: alk paper)

ISBN 0-7876-0655-3 (vol. 2: alk paper)

   1. Women—History—Miscellanea—Juvenile literature. 2. Women—
History—Chronology— Juvenile Literature. 3. Women—Biography—Miscellanea—Juvenile Literature.

[1. Women—History.]

I. Saari, Peggy. II. Gall, Timothy L. III. Gall, Susan B.
HQ1121.W8858 1997
305.4'09—dc21

97-25479

CIP AC

™ This book is printed on acid-free paper that meets the minimum requirements of American National Standard for Information Sciences–Permanence Paper for Printed Library Materials, ANSI Z39.48-1984.

Printed in the United States of America
10 9 8 7 6 5 4 3 2

Contents

Bold type indicates volume number

Bette Davis (see "The Arts: Film" entry dated 1941)

Volume 2

Reader's Guide

Women's Firsts: Milestones in Women's History provides information on over 1,000 milestones involving women around the world, from early history to the present. Both Women's Firsts volumes are divided into five chapters. Each of the ten chapters focuses on a specific theme: Activism, The Arts, Business, Education, Government, Media, Professions, Religion, Science and Technology, and Sports. Every chapter is divided into subject categories and entries summarize milestones and provide bibliographic information. Sidebar boxes examine related events and issues, while more than 140 black-and-white illustrations help enliven and explain the text. Both volumes contain a timeline of important events, a "words to know" section, and a cumulative index.

Anne Hutchinson (see "Religion: Founders and Leaders" entry dated 1635)

A Note about Researching Firsts

In compiling Women's Firsts, the editors tried to deal with sources critically and honestly to present the most representative and accurate list of firsts by women possible. Some probable firsts could not be included due to a lack of definitive proof. Beyond general error, differences among sources often occurred when there was uncertainty about which date to use or the criteria for claiming a first. Each entry in *Women's Firsts* was researched through multiple sources for accuracy, with the final content reflecting a majority point of view.

Acknowledgments

Special thanks are due for the invaluable comments and suggestions provided by U•X•L's women's books advisors:

Annette Haley, High School Librarian/Media Specialist at Grosse Ile High School in Grosse Ile, Michigan; Mary Ruthsdotter, Projects Director of the National Women's History Project; Francine Stampnitzky, Children's/Young Adult Librarian at the Elmont Public Library in Elmont, New York; and Ruth Ann Karlin Yeske, Librarian at North Middle School in Rapid City, South Dakota.

Additional thanks go to Stephen Allison for his extensive contributions to the book, and to Jon Saari for his continued writing and editing assistance.

Comments and Suggestions

We welcome your comments and suggestions for future editions of *Women's Firsts*. Please write: Editor, *Women's Firsts,* U•X•L, 835 Penobscot Bldg., Detroit, Michigan, 48226-4094; call toll free: 800-877-4253; or fax to: 313-961-6347.

Photo Credits

Clara Barton (see "Professions: Medicine and Health Care" entry dated 1881)

The photographs appearing in *Women's Firsts: Milestones in Women's History* were received from the following sources:

On the cover: Pearl S. Buck (**Courtesy of AP/Wide World Photos. Reproduced by permission.**); Lynette Woodard (**Courtesy of Corbis-Bettmann. Reproduced by permission.**); Juliette Gordon Low (**Courtesy of Girl Scouts, USA. Reproduced by permission.**)

AP/Wide World Photos. Reproduced by permission.: pp. v, ix, xiii, xiv, 26, 40, 42, 43, 52, 58, 60, 61, 64, 66, 68, 69, 71, 90, 98, 113, 114, 122, 171, 188, 191; 197; 201, 208, 211, 269, 272, 275, 309, 312, 313, 320, 321, 328, 334, 337, 339, 340, 341, 343, 361, 371, 408, 413; **Corbis-Bettmann. Reproduced by permission.:** pp. xi, xv, xvii, 82, 89, 110, 116, 120, 126, 237, 255, 291, 300, 356, 374, 383, 395, 409; **EPD Photos. Reproduced by permission.:** pp. 1, 45, 105, 109, 155, 159, 252, 256, 278, 373; **The Library of Congress. Reproduced by permission.:** pp. 2, 44, 50, 115, 241, 331, 332; **Camp Fire, Inc. Reproduced by permis-**

sion.: p. 8; **Girl Scouts, USA. Reproduced by permission.**: p. 9; **The Granger Collection, New York. Reproduced by permission.**: pp. 16, 41, 385; **Cleveland Antiquarian Books. Reproduced by permission.**: p. 17; **UPI/Corbis-Bettmann. Reproduced by permission.**: pp. 28, 314, 335, 405; **Archive Photos. Reproduced by permission.**: pp. 54, 139, 303, 364, 386; **Fisk University Libraries. Reproduced by permission.**: p. 108; **The Whitney Museum of American Art. Reproduced by permission.**: p. 129; **Pepperidge Farms, Inc. Reproduced by permission.**: p. 133; **Benetton, USA. Reproduced by permission.**: p. 137; **Brown Brothers. Reproduced by permission.**: p. 153; **Spelman College. Reproduced by permission.**: pp. 156, 157; **Massachusetts Institute of Technology (MIT) Museum. Reproduced by permission.**: p. 166; **United States Military Academy at West Point. Reproduced by permission.**: p. 169; **Embassy of Iceland. Reproduced by permission.**: p. 185; **Embassy of Pakistan. Reproduced by permission.**: p. 189; **Embassy of Turkey. Reproduced by permission.**: p. 190; **Harry S Truman Library. Reproduced by permission.**: pp. 194, 202; **Women for Military Service for America Memorial Foundation, Inc. Reproduced by permission.**: p. 203; **Ronald Reagan Library. Reproduced by permission.**: 209; **ABC Photography Department. Reproduced by permission.**: p. 225; **United Press International. Reproduced by permission.**: p. 231; **John Carroll University Broadcast Archives. Reproduced by permission.**: p. 233; **Photograph by Lisa Berg. American Bar Association. Reproduced by permission.**: p. 249; **National Archives and Records Administration. Reproduced by permission.**: p. 261; **American Medical Women's Association. Reproduced by permission.**: p. 267; **John F. Kennedy Library. Reproduced by permission.**: p. 274; **Rhode Island Historical Society/Women in Military Service Memorial Foundation, Inc. Reproduced by permission.**: p. 277; **Women in Military Service for America Memorial Foundation, Inc. Reproduced by permission.**: pp. 279, 282; **United States Coast Guard. Reproduced by permission.**: p. 283; **The Salvation Army National Archives. Reproduced by permission.**: p. 285; **Archives of the History of American Psychology. Reproduced by permission.**: pp. 325; **International Swimming Hall of Fame. Reproduced by permission.**: p. 366; **International Tennis Hall of Fame. Reproduced by permission.**: pp. 368, 369.

Women's Firsts: A Timeline of Events

c. 1351 B.C. Hebrew prophetess Deborah was the only female judge in ancient Israel.

Seventh century B.C. Greek physician Hygeia was the first person to teach preventive medicine.

First century A.D. Alexandrine alchemist Maria the Jewess was one of the founders of chemistry.

Early eleventh century Japanese noblewoman Shikibu Murasaki was the first novelist.

1559 Italian artist Sofonisba Anguissola was the first woman to become a famous professional painter.

Golda Meir (see "Government: Prime Ministers" entry dated 1969)

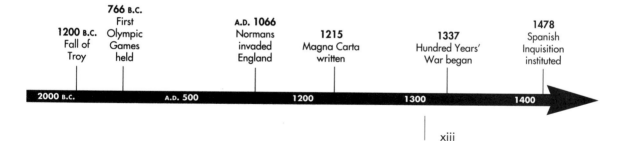

1200 B.C. Fall of Troy

766 B.C. First Olympic Games held

A.D. 1066 Normans invaded England

1215 Magna Carta written

1337 Hundred Years' War began

1478 Spanish Inquisition instituted

2000 B.C.   A.D. 500   1200   1300   1400

Marie Curie (see "Science and Technology: Physical Science" entry dated 1903)

1633 French aristocrat Louise de Marillac founded the Daughters of Charity.

c. 1675 Queen Anne (Totopotomoi) was the first woman to become a Native American chief.

1824 American activists Lavinia White and Louise Mitchell founded the first women's labor union.

1848 American feminists Lucretia Coffin Mott and Elizabeth Cady Stanton organized the first women's rights convention in the United States.

1854 British health care worker Florence Nightingale established modern nursing practices.

1879 American religious leader Mary Baker Eddy founded the Church of Christ, Scientist (also called Christian Science).

1882 Dutch physician Aletta Jacobs opened the world's first birth control clinic.

1896 French cinematographer Alice Guy-Blanché was the world's first female producer-director of motion pictures.

1908 American Annie Smith Peck climbed the north peak of Mount Huascaran in Peru.

1912 Italian educator Maria Montessori introduced her revolutionary teaching method.

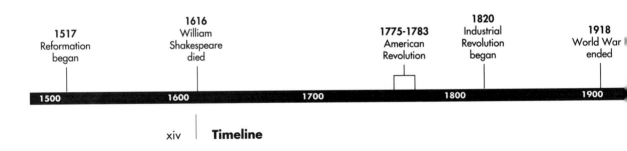

1517 Reformation began

1616 William Shakespeare died

1775-1783 American Revolution

1820 Industrial Revolution began

1918 World War I ended

| 1500 | 1600 | 1700 | 1800 | 1900 |

1916 Canadian lawyer Emily Gowan Murphy became the first female magistrate in the British Empire.

1920 Chinese political activist Jingyu Xiang cofounded the Chinese Communist Party.

1938 Austrian physicist Lise Meitner codeveloped the theory of nuclear fission.

1945 American mathematician Grace Brewster Murray Hopper developed operating programs for the first digital computer.

1951 English molecular biologist Rosalind Franklin helped determine the structure of DNA.

1959 American toymaker Ruth Handler created the Barbie Doll.

1963 Austrian conservationist Joy Adamson founded the World Wildlife Fund.

1966 Indian politician Indira Gandhi was elected the first woman leader of the world's largest democracy.

1970 Danish shoe designer Anna Kalso introduced the Earth Shoe.

1971 American journalist Gloria Steinem cofounded *Ms.* magazine.

1975 Australian pediatrician Helen Caldicott began her campaign against nuclear power and weapons.

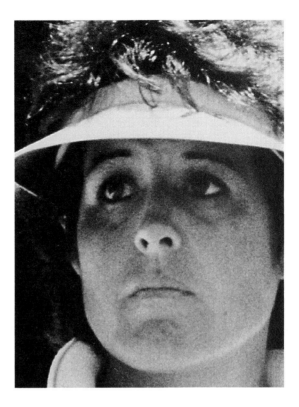

Nancy Lopez (see "Sports: Individual Sports" entry dated 1978)

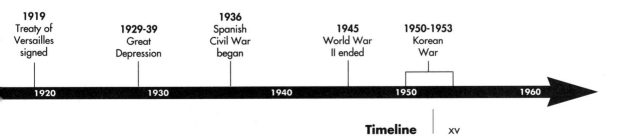

1919 Treaty of Versailles signed

1929-39 Great Depression

1936 Spanish Civil War began

1945 World War II ended

1950-1953 Korean War

1920   1930   1940   1950   1960

1979 English politician Margaret Thatcher became the first female prime minister of Great Britain.

1981 American lawyer Sandra Day O'Connor was appointed the first woman Justice of the U.S. Supreme Court.

1982 Russian cosmonaut Svetlanta Saviskaya was the first woman to walk in space.

1983 American composer Ellen Taaffe Zwilich was the first woman to win a Pulitzer Prize for music.

1986 American chemist Susan Solomon identified the cause of the "hole" in the ozone layer.

1988 Pakistani political activist Benazir Bhutto became the first modern-day female leader of a Muslim nation.

1993 American executive Lucy Salhany became the first woman to head a national television network.

1996 American astronaut Shannon Lucid set a record for spending the longest time in space.

1997 American diplomat Madeleine Albright was appointed the first female U.S. Secretary of State.

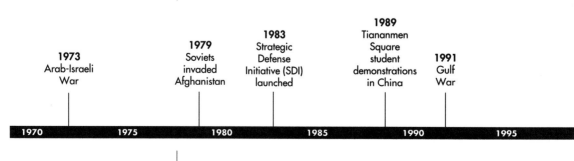

1973 Arab-Israeli War

1979 Soviets invaded Afghanistan

1983 Strategic Defense Initiative (SDI) launched

1989 Tiananmen Square student demonstrations in China

1991 Gulf War

| 1970 | 1975 | 1980 | 1985 | 1990 | 1995 |

Words to Know

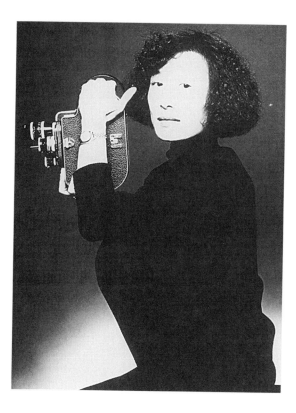

Christine Choy (see "The Arts: Film" entry dated c. 1970s)

A

Abolitionist: A person who supports putting an end to slavery.

Aeronautical engineer: An engineer who designs aircraft.

Anatomist: A scientist who studies the structure of organisms, including the human body.

Anthropologist: A scientist who studies human beings in relation to physical, environmental, social, and cultural characteristics.

Archaeologist: A scientist who studies the fossils, relics, and buildings of past civilizations.

Astronomer: A scientist who makes observations of objects and matter outside the earth's atmosphere.

B

Bacteriologist: A scientist who studies bacteria and their relationship to medicine, industry, and agriculture.

Biochemist: A scientist who studies chemical compounds and processes in living organisms.

Biologist: A scientist who studies plant and animal life.

Biophysicist: A scientist who applies physics to biological problems.

C

Choreographer: A person who creates dance movements and designs dance productions.

Christianity: The religion derived from the teachings of Jesus Christ, based on the Bible as sacred scripture, and professed by Eastern, Roman Catholic, and Protestant followers.

Cinematographer: The principle photographer on a telefilm or motion picture.

Convent: A community or house of nuns belonging to a religious order or congregation.

E

Epidemiologist: A medical scientist who studies the number and distribution of cases of disease within a population.

Exile: Forced absence from one's country or home.

F

Feminist: A person who supports the political, economic, and social equality of the sexes.

G

Geneticist: A biologist who studies the genetic makeup of an organism.

Geophysicist: A scientist who studies the physical properties of the earth and its environment.

H

Hinduism: The dominant religion of India that emphasizes mystical reflection and self discipline as a way to reach inner peace.

I

Islam: The religious faith of Muslims based on the belief in Allah as the sole deity and in Muhammad as his prophet.

J

Judaism: A religion developed among the ancient Hebrews and based on the belief in one God who revealed himself to Abraham, Moses, and the Hebrew prophets. Judaism encourages leading a religious life in accordance with the Scriptures and rabbinical traditions.

M

Marine biologist: A scientist who studies living organisms in the oceans and seas.

Medieval: Pertaining to the Middle Ages, the period of European history from about A.D. 500 to about 1500.

Meteorologist: A scientist who studies the atmosphere and makes weather predictions.

Mysticism: The belief that direct knowledge of God, spiritual truth, or ultimate reality can be attained through personal experience.

N

Naturalist: A scientist who studies nature and the environment.

Neurobiologist: A scientist who studies the nervous system.

Neuroendocrinologist: A scientist who studies the interaction between the nervous system and the endocrine (or glandular) system.

Neuropsychologist: A scientist who studies the influence of the nervous system on behavior.

O

Ornithologist: A scientist who studies birds.

P

Patent: A document granting an inventor the right to make, use, or sell an invention.

Physicist: A scientist who studies the interaction between energy and matter.

Primatologist: A scientist who studies apes and monkeys, as well as smaller primates such as lemurs and tarsiers.

Prime minister: The chief minister of a country.

Psychologist: A scientist who studies the human mind and behavior.

R

Renaiassance: The transitional movement between medieval and modern times, beginning in Italy in the fourteenth century and lasting into the seventeenth century; a period marked by a revival of classical arts and literature and the beginnings of modern science.

Revolution: Major political, social, or cultural change.

Roman Catholicism: the faith, practice, and system of the ancient Christian church.

S

Saint: A person who has been officially recognized by a religious body (such as the Catholic Church) as being holy and therefore worthy of public veneration, or worship.

Suffrage: The right to vote; a suffragette is a woman who advocates the right to vote for women.

T

Temperance: The use of moderation or self-restraint in personal activities, such as eating or drinking; also the name given to the movement that advocated moderation in and abstinence (total avoidance) from alcohol compumption.

Z

Zoologist: A biologist who studies and classifies animal life.

Activism

Abolition
Community Service
Feminism
Labor Activism
Pacifism
Suffrage
Temperance

Abolition

1832 ▪ **Maria Weston Chapman** (1806-1885), an American abolitionist, was cofounder of the Boston Female Anti-Slavery Society in 1832. (An abolitionist is a person who favors doing away with a particular custom, law, or practice, such as slavery.) Chapman spoke and wrote in support of the abolition of slavery in Massachusetts and continued to fight for black civil rights after the Civil War (1861-1865). Chapman served as treasurer of the Massachusetts Anti-Slavery Society and edited the *Liberator,* a journal devoted to the anti-slavery cause.

Source: James, Edward T., and others, *Notable American Women, 1607-1950: A Biographical Dictionary.* Cambridge, Massachusetts: Harvard University Press, 1971, pp. 324-25.

1836 ▪ American abolitionists **Angelina Emily Grimké** (1805-1879) and **Sarah Moore Grimké** (1792-1873) were the first women to lecture for the American Anti-Slavery Society

American abolitionist Maria Weston Chapman cofounded the Boston Female Anti-Slavery Society. (See "Abolition" entry dated 1832.)

Sarah Grimké and her sister Angelina were the first women to lecture for the American Anti-Slavery Society.

in New York. (An abolitionist is a person who favors doing away with a particular custom, law, or practice, such as slavery.) The sisters' lectures, which began in 1836, elicited violent criticism—partly because of the controversial nature of their subject matter, and partly because the speakers were female. The Grimké sisters also spoke out on the issue of women's rights.

Source: James, Edward T., and others, *Notable American Women, 1607-1950: A Biographical Dictionary.* Cambridge, Massachusetts: Harvard University Press, 1971, pp. 592-95.

Community Service

First century ▪ Dorcas, a wealthy woman living in first-century Jerusalem, began the "Dorcas Sewing Societies." This organization took Dorcas's name because she was known for her charity, especially for making clothes for the poor.

Source: Chicago, Judy, *The Dinner Party.* New York: Anchor, 1979, p. 129.

1591 ▪ Veronica Franco (1546-1591), an Italian Renaissance poet, was the first person to open a refuge for homeless women, in Venice. Her poetry was neglected for centuries, but she is now considered an able writer with a concern for social issues of particular interest to women.

Source: Uglow, Jennifer S., ed., *The Continuum Dictionary of Women's Biography*. New York: Continuum, 1989, p. 211.

1776 ▪ **Suzanne Necker** (1739-1817), a Swiss author and philanthropist, founded the Necker Hospital in Paris, France. (A philanthropist is someone who donates their time and usually large sums of money for the promotion of humanitarian causes.) Necker converted a local convent into a 120-bed institution and maintained it as a particularly clean and efficiently run establishment. The hospital took Necker's name in 1820 and remained a significant center of pediatric medicine and research.

Source: Uglow, Jennifer S., *The Continuum Dictionary of Women's Biography*. New York: Continuum, 1989, p. 398.

1780 ▪ **Esther De Berdt Reed** (1746-1780) and **Sarah Franklin Bache** (1743-1808), whose father was Benjamin Franklin (1706-1790; American statesman, journalist, philosopher, and noted kite flyer), founded the first relief organization of the American Revolutionary War (1775-1783). Reed and Bache formed a committee of 35 women called the "Ladies Association of Philadelphia," which later became known as "George Washington's Sewing Circle." The group's sole purpose was to raise money to purchase clothing and supplies for soldiers serving in the Continental Army.

Source: Read, Phyllis J., and Bernard L. Witlieb, *The Book of Women's Firsts*. New York: Random House, 1992, p. 363.

1821 ▪ **Elizabeth Gurney Fry** (1780-1845), a Quaker, was the first woman in England to suggest that prisons be a place for rehabilitation rather than just punishment. (Quakers, also known as the "Society of Friends," are a religious group with no formal creed or holy offices. Quakers oppose violence in any form, especially warfare.) Appearing before the British House of Commons in 1821, Fry influenced the passage of an important prison reform bill later that year.

Source: Magnusson, Magnus, *Larousse Biographical Dictionary*. Edinburgh: Larousse Kingfisher Chambers, Inc., 1994, p. 553.

1835 ▪ **Mary Carpenter** (1807-1877), an English philanthropist, founded the Working and Visiting Society in England. (A philanthropist is someone who donates their time and usually large sums of money for the promotion of humanitarian causes.) The society devoted itself to the needs of poor children. Carpenter was a lifelong activist on behalf of a variety of causes, among them penal (prison) reform and the education of women. In 1829 she opened a girls' school in Bristol, England.

Source: Magnusson, Magnus, *Larousse Biographical Dictionary*. Edinburgh: Larousse Kingfisher Chambers, Inc., 1994, p. 265.

1849 ▪ **Caroline Jones Chisholm** (1808-1877), an English philanthropist, founded the Family Colonization Loan Society in Australia. (A philanthropist is someone who donates their time and usually large sums of money for the promotion of humanitarian causes.) Chisholm established a government office in Australia to help immigrant women that serviced over 11,000 people. Concerned throughout her life with the plight of immigrants to the Far East, Chisholm was also the founder of the Female School of Industry for the Daughters of European Soldiers in Madras, India, in 1832, and the Female Immigrants' Home in Sydney, Australia, in 1841.

Source: Magnusson, Magnus, *Larousse Biographical Dictionary*. Edinburgh: Larousse Kingfisher Chambers, 1994, pp. 304-05.

1868 ▪ **Jane Cunningham Croly** (1829-1901), an American journalist who wrote under the pen name "Jenny June," was the organizer of "Sorosis," the first professional organization for women in the United States. Sorosis was founded in response to women's exclusion from the New York Press Club's reception for famous British novelist Charles Dickens (1812-1870). Croly served as president of Sorosis in 1870, and again between 1875 and 1886. She was also the author of the *History of the Women's Club Movement in America,* published in 1898.

Source: James, Edward T., and others, *Notable American Women, 1607-1950: A Biographical Dictionary*. Cambridge, Massachusetts: Harvard University Press, 1971, pp. 409-11.

1876 ▪ **Josephine Shaw Lowell** (1843-1905), an American philanthropist, became the first female member of the New York State Board of Charities in New York City. (A philanthropist is someone who donates their time and usually large sums of money for the promotion of humanitarian causes.) Lowell's appointment caused much publicity and opposition because of her gender. Heartbroken by the death of her husband in the Civil War (1861- 1865), and later by the death of her young daughter, Lowell directed her energies into philanthropy and soon became an active social reformer. She became the first president of the first Consumer Council in 1890, a position she held until 1896, when she set up the Women's Municipal League as a political lobby group. Her book, *Public Relief and Private Charity,* provided guidelines for state-administered charity.

> ## YWCA Organized
> The **Young Women's Christian Association** (YWCA) was the first social service organization for Christian women. Two groups founded in England in 1855—the English Prayer Union and the General Female Training Institute (a home for nurses returning from the Crimean War of 1854-1856)—formed the foundation of the Young Women's Christian Association. In 1877 the two organizations expanded their activities and merged as the Young Women's Christian Association.

Source: James, Edward T., and others, *Notable American Women, 1607-1950: A Biographical Dictionary.* Cambridge, Massachusetts: Harvard University Press, 1971, pp. 437-39.

1886 ▪ **Julia Richman** (1855-1912), an American community activist, was the first president of the Young Women's Hebrew Association. Richman held the post for four years. Founded in New York City in 1886, the Young Women's Hebrew Association was the first national social service organization designed to meet the needs of Jewish women and girls.

Source: Read, Phyllis J., and Bernard L. Witlieb, *The Book of Women's Firsts.* New York: Random House, 1992, pp. 368, 501.

c. 1889 ▪ **Pandita Ramabai** (1858-1920), a pioneer in the women's rights movement in India, founded Sharada Sadan, an institutional home for Indian widows, many of whom were between the ages of nine and twelve. In 1897 Ramabai also founded an orphanage and a training institute for women and children.

Source: Uglow, Jennifer S., ed., *The Continuum Dictionary of Women's Biography.* New York: Continuum, 1989, p. 446.

1891 ▪ **Mary Smith Lockwood** (1831-?), Ellen Hardin Walworth (1832-1915), and Eugenia Washington founded the Daughters of the American Revolution (DAR) in Washington, D.C. The DAR was the first women's patriotic group based on heredity. To become a member, a woman had to be over age 18 and able to prove that she descended directly from persons who aided in establishing the independence of the United States from England. Chartered by the U.S. Congress in 1896, the DAR provides an annual report to Congress.

Source: James, Edward T., and others, *Notable American Women, 1607-1950: A Biographical Dictionary.* Cambridge, Massachusetts: Harvard University Press, 1971, pp. 150-52.

1895 ▪ **Octavia Hill** (1838-1912), an English social reformer, cofounded the National Trust for Places of Historic Interest or Natural Beauty. Commonly referred to as the National Trust, the organization began its work by preserving land in the Lake District of England. Hill also devoted her energies to housing and prison reform. In 1864, with financial resources provided by her art tutor John Ruskin, Hill began purchasing and improving run-down housing in slum neighborhoods. In 1869 she cofounded the Charity Organization Society with Frederick Denison Maurice. Hill also wrote *Homes of the London Poor* (1875) and *Our Common Land* (1878).

Source: Magnusson, Magnus, *Larousse Biographical Dictionary.* Edinburgh: Larousse Kingfisher Chambers, Inc., 1994, p. 711.

1896 ▪ **Maud Ballington Booth** (1865-1948), an American social activist, cofounded the Volunteers of America with her husband, Ballington Booth, in New York City. Before starting this organization, the Booths left the Salvation Army over a dispute concerning the authoritative rule of the Army's founder, General William Booth, Ballington Booth's father. The Volunteers of America was a social service organization that in many ways followed the structure and purposes of the Salvation Army. After her husband's death in 1940, Maud Booth was elected as general and commander in chief of the Volunteers of America, thus becoming the first woman to hold this position.

Source: James, Edward T., and others, *Notable American Women, 1607-1950: A Biographical Dictionary.* Cambridge, Massachusetts: Harvard University Press, 1971, pp. 208-10.

1896 ▪ **Margaret Murray Washington** (1865-1925), an American educator, founded the National Association of Colored Women in Washington, D.C. By doing so, Washington united two major organizations and hundreds of local groups for African-American women. Washington was also the first dean of women at the Tuskegee Institute in Alabama, which was founded by her husband, Booker T. Washington (1856-1915).

Source: Chicago, Judy, *The Dinner Party*. New York: Anchor, 1979, p. 183.

1907 ▪ **Grace Hoadley Dodge** (1856-1914), an American welfare worker, founded the New York Travelers Aid Society for the protection of young girls in New York City. After a career of unpaid work with needy people, Dodge left over $1.5 million to charity at the time of her death.

Source: James, Edward T., and others, *Notable American Women, 1607-1950: A Biographical Dictionary*. Cambridge, Massachusetts: Harvard University Press, 1971, pp. 489-92.

1907 ▪ **Margaret Olivia Slocum Sage** (1828-1918), an American philanthropist, established the Russell Sage Foundation. (A philanthropist is someone who donates their time and usually large sums of money for the promotion of humanitarian causes.) With an endowment of $10 million, the foundation provided funding for research devoted to the improvement of social and economic conditions in the United States.

Source: James, Edward T., and others, *Notable American Women, 1607-1950: A Biographical Dictionary*. Cambridge, Massachusetts: Harvard University Press, 1971, pp. 222-23.

1908 ▪ **Zaynab Anis** was an Egyptian community activist. Anis founded the first charity run by Muslim women in Egypt dedicated to the welfare of children called "Jam'iyyat al-Safaqa bi'l-Atfal" ("Society of Compassion for Children"). The group, made up of women from middle- and upper-class families, opened an orphanage with the support of other wealthy women.

Source: Baron, Beth, *The Women's Awakening in Egypt: Culture, Society, and the Press*. New Haven: Yale University Press, 1994, p. 172.

1910 ▪ Charlotte Vetter Gulick (1866-1928), an American community activist, cofounded the Camp Fire Girls in South Casco, Maine. This organization—the first non-sectarian (unlimited), interracial group of its kind for girls—stressed character development and good mental and physical health. Gulick cofounded the Camp Fire Girls with her husband, Luther Halsey Gulick, and William Chauncey Langdon, the

two men who had helped establish the Boy Scouts in the United States.

Source: Read, Phyllis J., and Bernard L. Witlieb, *The Book of Women's Firsts*. New York: Random House, 1992, pp. 186-87.

1912 ▪ Juliette Gordon Low (1860-1927), an American social activist, was the founder of the Girl Scouts of America. Low organized the first American group of Girl Guides in Savannah, Georgia, in 1912. Three years later the group's name was changed to the Girl Scouts. Low's niece, Margaret "Daisy" Gordon, became the first American Girl Scout when she joined the organization in 1912. Low served as the group's first president until 1920.

Source: McCullough, Joan, *First of All: Significant "Firsts" by American Women*. New York: Holt, 1980, p. 141.

1913 ▪ Winifred Holt (1870-1945), an American social activist, and her sister Edith founded the Lighthouses for the

In 1912 Juliette Low organized the first American group of Girl Guides—later called Girl Scouts—in Savannah, Georgia.

Blind (later The Lighthouse) in New York City. The organization was devoted to helping the blind become self-sufficient and to the prevention of blindness.

Source: Read, Phyllis J., and Bernard L. Witlieb, *The Book of Women's Firsts.* New York: Random House, 1992, p. 214.

1916 ▪ **Olave Baden-Powell** (1889-1977) and Agnes Baden-Powell (1858-1945), English community activists, cofounded the English Girl Guides in Sussex, England. The group was designed as a counterpart to the Boy Scouts, which was founded by Robert Baden-Powell. Olave Baden-Powell served as the first director of the English Girl Guides under the title of chief commissioner.

Source: Magnusson, Magnus, *Larousse Biographical Dictionary.* Edinburgh: Larousse Kingfisher Chambers, Inc., 1994, p. 89.

1919 ▪ **Eglantyne Jebb** (1876-1928), an English philanthropist, devoted her life to the cause of needy children throughout the world. (A philanthropist is someone who donates their time and usually large sums of money for the promotion of humanitarian causes.) Jebb's efforts to help poor children in Europe after World War I (1914-1918) resulted in her establishing the "Fight the Famine" council. In 1919 the council turned into the "Save the Children" fund. Save the Children provided direct aid to children as well as funding for the building of hospitals, homes, and schools. Jebb was also the sponsor of the Children's Charter, adopted by the League of Nations in Geneva, Switzerland, in 1924. She joined the League's "Council for the Protection of Children" in 1925.

Source: Parry, Melanie, ed., *Larousse Dictionary of Women.* New York: Larousse Kingfisher Chambers, Inc., 1995, p. 342.

1924 ▪ **Sophie Irene Loeb** (1876-1929) was cofounder and the first president of the Child Welfare Committee of America, located in New York City. A lifelong advocate of children's rights, Loeb campaigned in the United States and abroad (through the League of Nations) for children's care within their communities rather than in institutions. She was also active in the Zionist movement. (Zionism was an international movement started in the late nineteenth century that originally sought the establishment of a Jewish national and religious homeland in Palestine; later, the term came to be applied to support for modern Israel.)

Source: James, Edward T., and others, *Notable American Women, 1607-1950: A Biographical Dictionary.* Cambridge, Massachusetts: Harvard University Press, 1971, pp. 416-17.

1925 ▪ **Jessie Donaldson Hodder** (1867-1931), who made her career as a prison reformer within the Massachusetts state prison system, was the first American woman to serve as a delegate to the International Prison Congress held in London, England.

Source: James, Edward T., and others, *Notable American Women, 1607-1950: A Biographical Dictionary.* Cambridge, Massachusetts: Harvard University Press, 1971, pp. 197-99.

Dorothy Eustis founded "The Seeing Eye," an organization that trained dogs to serve as guides for the blind.

1926 ▪ **Gertrude Bonnin** (1876-1938), an American social activist, founded the National Council of American Indians. The council was a reform group and the successor to the Society of American Indians. Bonnin served as the first president of the organization until her death.

Source: Read, Phyllis J., and Bernard L. Witlieb, *The Book of Women's Firsts.* New York: Random House, 1992, p. 61.

1930 ▪ **Dorothy Harrison Wood Eustis** (1886-1946), an American social activist, founded "The Seeing Eye," an organization that trained dogs to serve as guides for the blind. Eustis based her school on a similar one in Potsdam, Germany, which trained guide dogs for World War I (1914-1918) veterans. Eustis was the first president of The Seeing Eye.

Source: James, Edward T., and others, *Notable American Women, 1607-1950: A Biographical Dictionary.* Cambridge, Massachusetts: Harvard University Press, 1971, pp. 585-86.

1935 ▪ **Mary McLeod Bethune** (1875-1955), an American educator and community activist, founded and was the first president of the National Council of Negro Women. Bethune began her career as a teacher, starting a school in 1904 that became, in 1929, Bethune-Cookman College. Bethune devoted her life to the needs of African Americans, especially girls and women. In 1936 she became the first black woman to serve as a presidential advisor, to Franklin Delano Roosevelt.

Source: Read, Phyllis J., and Bernard L. Witlieb, *The Book of Women's Firsts*. New York: Random House, 1992, pp. 50-51.

1953 ▪ **Sue Ryder** (1923-), Baroness of Warsaw and Cavendish, was an English philanthropist who founded the Mission for the Relief of Suffering. (A philanthropist is someone who donates their time and usually large sums of money for the promotion of humanitarian causes.) Under the Mission's auspices, Ryder opened a home for World War II (1939-1945) concentration camp victims in Suffolk, England, in 1953. Her organization soon extended its purpose to helping the physically and mentally ill and eventually became the Sue Ryder Foundation for the Sick and Disabled of All Age Groups. Ryder homes operated in Britain, Poland, Bosnia, and Italy.

Source: Parry, Melanie, ed., *Larousse Dictionary of Women*. New York: Larousse Kingfisher Chambers, Inc., 1995, p. 574.

1957 ▪ **Jacqueline Bernard** (1921-), an American journalist, cofounded Parents Without Partners with Jim Egleson. A self-help group for single parents, Parents Without Partners was one of the earliest such organizations; it now has a nationwide membership.

Source: O'Neill, Lois Decker, *The Women's Book of World Records and Achievements*. New York: Doubleday, 1979, pp. 722-23.

1957 ▪ **Eirlys Roberts** (1911-), a Welsh consumer activist, was founder of the British Consumers' Association. Roberts served the organization as the first head of the research and editorial division from 1958 through 1973 and as editor of its influential magazine *Which?* between 1961 and 1977. Roberts campaigned for safety standards and public accountability. She was also involved on behalf of consumers through various offices in the governance of the European Economic Community.

Source: Uglow, Jennifer S., ed., *The Continuum Dictionary of Women's Biography*. New York: Continuum, 1989, pp. 460-61.

1958 ▪ **Ethel Andrus** (1884-1967), an American community activist, founded and was the first president of the American Association of Retired Persons (AARP). In 1947 Andrus was the founder and first president of the National Retired Teachers Association (NRTA), work that led her to founding the AARP eleven years later.

Source: Read, Phyllis J., and Bernard L. Witlieb, *The Book of Women's Firsts.* New York: Random House, 1992, pp. 20-21.

c. 1970 ▪ **Franca Rame** (1929-), an Italian actress, director, and writer, was the founder of Soccorso Rosso, a movement for the rights of political prisoners. Rame is known for her work in the theater, which typically concerns political and radical feminist issues. Collaborating with her husband, the writer Dario Fo, she has been a leading force in political avant-garde drama (new or experimental drama) since 1956.

Source: Uglow, Jennifer S., ed., *The Continuum Dictionary of Women's Biography*. New York: Continuum, 1989, p. 447.

1970 ▪ **Margaret E. Kuhn** (1905-1995), an American community activist, was founder of the Gray Panthers. This organization, the first of its kind in the United States, devoted its energies to fighting ageism (discrimination against the elderly) and to bringing attention to the needs of the elderly in America.

Source: O'Neill, Lois Decker, *The Women's Book of World Records and Achievements.* New York: Doubleday, 1979, p. 722.

1973 ▪ **Marian Wright Edelman** (b. 1939), an American advocate for children's rights, was the founder and first president of the Children's Defense Fund. The Fund specialized in such issues as teenage pregnancy, early infant death, and child abuse.

Source: Read, Phyllis J., and Bernard L. Witlieb, *The Book of Women's Firsts.* New York: Random House, 1992, pp. 136-37.

1975 ▪ **Gloria D. Scott** (1938-), an American educator, became the first African-American president of the Girl Scouts. She joined the Girls Scouts' national board in 1969, after having received her doctorate in higher education.

Source: McCullough, Joan, *First of All: Significant "Firsts" by American Women.* New York: Holt, 1980, p. 142.

1977 ▪ **Nan Waterman** (b. 1920), a lifelong advocate of the rights of women, was the first woman to serve as chair of the board of Common Cause. A board member since 1971, Waterman supported Common Cause's concern for social and feminist issues.

Source: O'Neill, Lois Decker, ed., *The Women's Book of World Records and Achievements.* New York: Doubleday, 1979, p. 731.

1985 ▪ **Wilma P. Mankiller** (1945-), a Native American community activist, was the first woman to serve as tribal chief for the Cherokee Nation. Between 1985 and her retirement in 1994, she helped revitalize many aspects of Cherokee life. Mankiller increased the tribe's membership from 55,000 to 156,000 and added three health centers and nine children's programs to facilities on Cherokee land.

Source: Read, Phyllis J., and Bernard L. Witlieb, *The Book of Women's Firsts.* New York: Random House, 1992, p. 266.

1991 ▪ **Judith Daniels,** an American dog breeder and handler, was the first woman president of the American Kennel Club (AKC; the AKC is the nation's oldest dog care and dog registry organization). Daniels was a California breeder, owner, and handler of Staffordshire bull terriers. As the organization's eighteenth and first woman president, she said she did not view her appointment as a "woman's issue." Instead she called it an "opportunity to impact real and important change in a century-old, previously male-dominated organization."

Source: *The New York Times.* March 31, 1995.

1991 ▪ Sarah Williamson (1974-), an American student activist, was the first girl to serve as mayor of Boys Town. (Boys Town was founded in 1917 by Edward J. Flanagan, a Roman Catholic priest, as a community for homeless and orphaned boys. Maintained by voluntary contributions, the village is governed by the boys themselves. Girls were admitted to Boys Town for the first time in 1979.) Elected May 2, 1991, Williamson served as student council president at Boys Town High School, acted as a role model for Boys Town's underprivileged and troubled boys and girls, and presided over various ceremonies.

Source: Read, Phyllis J., and Bernard L. Witlieb, *The Book of Women's Firsts.* New York: Random House, 1992, p. 484.

Feminism

1789 ▪ Théroigne de Méricourt (1762-1817), an ardent feminist and revolutionary, was the first woman at the head of the Women's March to Versailles, France, during the French Revolution (1789-1799). de Méricourt was also probably the first woman, dressed as an Amazon (a member of a race of female warriors in Greek mythology), to storm the Bastille on July 14 of that year. (The Bastille was a prison where supporters of the French Revolution were held.)

Source: Uglow, Jennifer S., ed., *The Continuum Dictionary of Women's Biography.* New York: Continuum, 1989, p. 158.

1791 ▪ Etta Aelders Palm (1743-1793?) was the first Dutch woman to speak out for the rights of women during the French Revolution (1789-1799). Palm appeared before the legislative assembly in Paris, France, to plead for women's rights.

Source: Uglow, Jennifer S., ed., *The Continuum Dictionary of Women's Biography.* New York: Continuum, 1989, p. 416.

1793 ▪ Claire Lacombe (?-1795), a French actress, was the founder of the Republican Revolutionary Society, the first organization for working women in France. Inspired by the spirit of the French Revolution, Lacombe worked for women's rights

(including the right to vote and to participate in government) through this association. Lacombe was so ardent in her campaign that her club was suppressed by the Revolutionary government in November 1793, and in March 1794, Lacombe was arrested and imprisoned until 1795.

Source: Uglow, Jennifer S., ed., *The Continuum Dictionary of Women's Biography.* New York: Continuum, 1989, p. 309.

1840 ▪ Ernestine Rose (1810-1892) was the author of the first petition for a law granting married women the right to own property. The petition was reviewed by the New York State Legislature in Albany, New York, and in 1848 led to a law safeguarding the property of married women.

Source: Read, Phyllis J., and Bernard L. Witlieb, *The Book of Women's Firsts.* New York: Random House, 1992, p. 380.

Lucretia Mott helped organize the first Women's Rights Convention. The convention was held in Seneca Falls, New York.

1848 ▪ Lucretia Coffin Mott (1793-1880) and **Elizabeth Cady Stanton** (1815-1902) organized the first Women's Rights Convention in Seneca Falls, New York. Lucretia Coffin was born on the island of Nantucket (now part of the state of Massachusetts) on January 3, 1793. Her Quaker family was among those who sought refuge on Nantucket from religious persecution by the government of Massachusetts Bay Colony. (Quakers, also known as the "Society of Friends," are a religious group with no formal creed or holy offices. Quakers oppose violence in any form, especially warfare.) Lucretia was sent to boarding school in Duchess County, New York. Her future husband, James Mott, was a teacher there. In 1818, Lucretia was made assistant teacher, and three years later she and Mott married. The couple joined Lucretia's family in Philadelphia and established a profitable cotton business.

Troubled by the dependence of their cotton plantations on slave labor, the Motts gave up their business. Lucretia Mott established a private school to supplement the family's resources until her husband's business prospects improved. Mott then

devoted herself to Bible study and to the campaign against slavery. In June of 1840 she was a delegate to the world anti-slavery convention in London, England. Upon her arrival at the convention, Mott was denied access to the platform because no women were to be allowed to speak. This experience, in part, inspired her to add the cause of women's suffrage (right to vote) to her campaigns. In 1878, at the age of 86, Mott gave her last public speech at the suffrage convention held in New York.

Source: James, Edward T., and others, *Notable American Women, 1607-1950: A Biographical Dictionary.* Cambridge, Massachusetts: Harvard University Press, 1971, pp. 592-95.

1851 ▪ **Elizabeth Smith Miller** (1822-1911), an American feminist, was the first person to design "bloomers" (the costume to which Amelia Jenks Bloomer gave her name when she wrote about it in her reform newspaper, *The Lily*). Miller designed a short skirt covering Turkish-style, loose-fitting trousers as a gardening dress. She first wore the bloomers at her home in Gene-

Elizabeth Smith Miller was the first person to design "bloomers," an outfit consisting of a short skirt covering Turkish-style, loose-fitting trousers.

Hansteen Founded Movement

Hasta Hansteen (?-1824) was the founder of the women's rights movement in Norway. Through her writings, Hansteen advocated women's suffrage (the right to vote) and the overall improvement of women's social position.

va, New York, but the costume became well known to other women when she wore it while visiting her friend Elizabeth Cady Stanton (1815-1902) in Seneca Falls, New York. The attire was soon promoted as a more comfortable form of clothing for women.

Source: James, Edward T., and others, *Notable American Women, 1607-1950: A Biographical Dictionary.* Cambridge, Massachusetts: Harvard University Press, 1971, pp. 611-12.

1855 ▪ **Lucy Stone** (1818-1893) was the first woman on record to keep her own name after marriage. A lifelong crusader for women's rights, Stone graduated from Oberlin College in Ohio in 1847. She married Henry Blackwell in Boston, Massachusetts, in 1855 but, with his agreement, did not take his name. The couple wanted to omit the word "obey" from the marriage vows and had to send for a minister from over 30 miles away who would agree to their wishes. Lucy was known thereafter as "Mrs. Stone," and "doing a Lucy Stone" became a common phrase used to refer to an independent woman's action.

Source: James, Edward T., and others, *Notable American Women, 1607-1950: A Biographical Dictionary.* Cambridge, Massachusetts: Harvard University Press, 1971, pp. 387-90.

1859 ▪ **Jessie Boucherett** (1825-1905), an English feminist and writer, was the cofounder, with **Barbara Bodichon** (1827-1891) and **Adelaide Ann Procter** (1825-1864), of the Society for Promoting the Education of Women. This organization advocated numerous jobs for women such as farming, nursing, clerical work, engraving, teaching, and bookkeeping.

Source: Uglow, Jennifer S., ed., *The Continuum Dictionary of Women's Biography.* New York: Continuum, 1989, pp. 80-81.

c. 1860 ▪ **Caroline Dexter** (1819-1884), an Australian feminist, was the founder of the Institute of Hygiene in Melbourne in about 1860. In 1861 she was also the cofounder, with Harriet Clisby, of the radical journal *The Interpreter.*

Source: Uglow, Jennifer S., ed., *The Continuum Dictionary of Women's Biography.* New York: Continuum, 1989, p. 166.

1861 ▪ Maria Susan Rye (1829-1903) was the first woman in England to help other women emigrate to Australia, New Zealand, and Canada. In order to help women find work and gain economic independence, Rye cofounded the Female Middle Class Emigration Society in London, England. From 1861-1869 she used this organization to help large numbers of women leave England for better lives abroad.

Source: Uglow, Jennifer S., ed., *The Continuum Dictionary of Women's Biography.* New York: Continuum, 1989, pp. 470-71.

1866 ▪ Anna Nikitichna Shabanova (1848-1932), a Russian pediatrician (childran's doctor)and feminist activist, was the founder of the Ivanova Workshop, a dressmaking collective in Moscow. (A collective is a group of workers who share labor and management responsibilities.) In 1867 Shabanova became one of the first women to enroll at the new Women's Medical Academy. She later practiced medicine, wrote, taught, and continued to work for feminist causes.

Source: Uglow, Jennifer S., ed., *The Continuum Dictionary of Women's Biography.* New York: Continuum, 1989, pp. 492-93.

1867 ▪ Josephine Elizabeth Grey Butler (1828-1906) was an English activist for women's education who cofounded, with **Anne Jemima Clough** (1820-1892), the North of England Council for the Higher Education of Women. Butler also campaigned against the licensing of brothels (houses of prostitution) in England. Butler successfully worked for the repeal of the Contagious Diseases Act that required women in port cities to submit to compulsory examination for venereal (sexually transmitted) disease. Butler published her autobiography, *Personal Reminiscences of a Great Crusade,* in 1896.

Source: Magnusson, Magnus, *Larousse Biographical Dictionary.* Edinburgh: Larousse Kingfisher Chambers, Inc., 1994, p. 238.

1868 ▪ Marie Goegg (1826-1899), a Swiss feminist and pacifist, was the founder and first director of the Association International des Femmes (International Association of Women), begun in Geneva, Switzerland. In 1872 Goegg was also one of the leaders in the successful campaign to open the University of Geneva to women.

Source: Uglow, Jennifer S., ed., *The Continuum Dictionary of Women's Biography.* New York: Continuum, 1989, p. 228.

1869 ▪ **Mary Ashton Rice Livermore** (1820-1905), an American feminist, was the founder and first editor of *The Agitator,* a feminist publication that later merged into the *Woman's Journal.* Livermore was also the first president of the Association for the Advancement of Women (1873). She devoted her life to feminist causes and worked for both the temperance (the banning of alcoholic beverages) and suffragist (the fight for women's right to vote) movements .

Source: James, Edward T., and others, *Notable American Women, 1607-1950: A Biographical Dictionary.* Cambridge, Massachusetts: Harvard University Press, 1971, pp. 426-28.

1870 ▪ **Maria Desraismes** (1828-1894), a French feminist, founded the Association pour le Droit des Femmes ("The Association for Women's Rights") in 1870, one of the main moderate feminist organizations in France until the twentieth century. Desraismeswas a cofounder of the Société pour la Revendication des Droits de la Femme ("Society for the Claiming of Woman's Rights") in 1866, and in 1881 she founded the paper *Le Règublicain de Seine et Oise* ("The Republican of Seine and Oise").

Source: Uglow, Jennifer S., ed., *The Continuum Dictionary of Women's Biography.* New York: Continuum, 1989, p. 162.

1886 ▪ Danish feminist **Matilde Bajer** (1840-1934) founded the Danish Women's Progress Association, an early version of later suffrage groups (organizations seeking the right to vote for women). With the active support of her husband, Bajer worked for women's rights and founded a number of organizations that advocated women's education and suffrage.

Source: Uglow, Jennifer S., ed., *The Continuum Dictionary of Women's Biography.* New York: Continuum, 1989, pp. 42-43.

c. 1888 ▪ **Anna Maria Mozzoni** (1837-1920), an Italian feminist who used her wealth to campaign for women's rights, was the founder of a league in defense of women's interests in Milan, Italy. Mozzoni fought for women's right to vote and argued for social equality throughout her life.

Source: Uglow, Jennifer S., ed., *The Continuum Dictionary of Women's Biography.* New York: Continuum, 1989, pp. 390-91.

The Bremer League

Baroness of Adlersparre, a Swedish feminist who promoted her ideas in her journal *For the Home,* was the founder of the Frederika Bremer League, an organization named for the early Scandinavian women's rights leader.

1889 ▪ **Louisa Lawson** (1848-1920), an Australian feminist, founded the Dawn Club, in Sydney, Australia. The Dawn Club was a discussion group that focused on feminist issues. The club published a journal, called *The Dawn,* with an entirely female editorial staff. Lawson served as editor of the publication for seventeen years. She also founded the Darlinghurst Hostel for Working Girls.

Source: Uglow, Jennifer S. ed., *The Continuum Dictionary of Women's Biography.* New York: Continuum, 1989, pp. 315-16.

1892 ▪ **Eugénie Potonie-Pierre** (1844-1898), a French feminist, founded the Federation Française des Societées Feministes ("French Federation of Feminist Societies"), a combination of eight Parisian feminist groups. Among the groups was the Union des Femmes (cofounded by Potonie-Pierre with Léonie Rouzade and Marguerite Tinyre in 1880), La Ligue Socialiste des Femmes (founded by Potonie Pierre in 1889), and Le Groupe de la Solidarité des Femmes (cofounded by Potonie-Pierre and Maria Martin in 1891). By 1896 Potonie-Pierre was the undisputed leader of the Socialist Feminist movement. In 1897 she became the first woman to lead a French delegation to a feminist congress, in Brussels, Belgium.

Source: Uglow, Jennifer S., ed., *The Continuum Dictionary of Women's Biography.* New York: Continuum, 1989, pp. 438-39.

c. 1895 ▪ **Minna Cauer** (1841-1922) founded the German feminist journal called *The Women's Movement.* Influenced by American suffragist Susan B. Anthony (1820-1906), Cauer challenged the Prussian law forbidding women from holding or attending political meetings.

Source: Chicago, Judy, *The Dinner Party*. New York: Anchor, 1979, p. 187.

1896 ▪ Kallirhoe Parren (1861-1940) was the organizer of the Federation of Greek Women, a group formed in 1896 to work for the social and political equality of women in Greece. The group belonged to the International Council of Women.

Source: Uglow, Jennifer S., ed., *The Continuum Dictionary of Women's Biography*. New York: Continuum, 1989, pp. 420-21.

1899 ▪ Marianne Hainisch (1839-1936), an Austrian feminist and pacifist, was the first president of the General Austrian Women's Association, which she founded in Vienna. The organization fought for the reform of marriage laws, the rights of illegitimate children, and the abolition of legalized prostitution.

Source: Uglow, Jennifer S., ed., *The Continuum Dictionary of Women's Biography*. New York: Continuum, 1989, p. 243.

1900 ▪ Maud Gonne (1866-1953), an Irish actress and revolutionary, was the founder of the radical women's group Inghinidhe Na Eireann ("Daughters of Ireland"), in Dublin, Ireland. Devoted throughout her life to the Irish Republican cause, Gonne supported the Easter Rebellion of 1916. (Gonne's husband, John MacBride, was executed for his part in the uprising.) Maud Gonne was an active relief worker during the troubles that followed.

Source: Magnusson, Magnus *Larousse Biographical Dictionary*. Edinburgh: Larousse Kingfisher Chambers, Inc., 1994, p. 933.

1901 ▪ Hannah Sheehy-Skeffington (1877-1946), an Irish feminist and patriot, was a founding member of the Irish Association of Women Graduates, in Dublin. In 1908 Sheehy-Skeffington was also the cofounder, with **Constance Markiewicz** (1868-1927), of the Irish Women's Franchise League.

Source: Parry, Melanie, ed., *Larousse Dictionary of Women*. New York: Larousse Kingfisher Chambers, Inc., 1995, p. 595.

1901 ▪ **Franciska Plamnikova** (1875-1942) was the first Czech woman to organize a large feminist group, the Women's Club of Prague. Plamnikova went on to found the Committee for Women's Suffrage in 1905 and to work politically for the rights of women. She was also concerned about labor conditions and nationalist issues. Arrested for her activism, she died in a concentration camp (a wartime prison, usually characterized by inhumane living conditions) during World War II (1939-1945).

Source: Uglow, Jennifer S., ed., *The Continuum Dictionary of Women's Biography.* New York: Continuum, 1989, p. 434.

1904 ▪ **Helene Stöcker** (1869-1943), a German feminist and advocate of free (unrestricted by law or morality) love, was the founder of the Bund für Mutterschutz und Sexualreform ("League for the Protection of Motherhood and Sexual Reform"). This organization, perceived as strikingly radical by more numerous conservative feminists, later became known as the "Mutterschutz League."

Source: Uglow, Jennifer S., ed., *The Continuum Dictionary of Women's Biography.* New York: Continuum, 1989, pp. 518-19.

1907 ▪ **Teresa Billington-Greig** (1877-1964) was cofounder, with suffragettes **Charlotte Despard** (1844-1939) and **Edith How-Martyn** (1875?-1954), of the Women's Freedom League, a women's rights group in London, England. (Suffragists fought to get women the right to vote.) Billington-Greig was also active in the suffrage movement between 1902 and 1913. After their marriage in 1907, both Billington-Greig and her husband took the same combined surname.

Source: Uglow, Jennifer S., ed., *The Continuum Dictionary of Women's Biography.* New York: Continuum, 1989, p. 66.

1907 ▪ **Harriet Eaton Stanton Blatch** (1856-1940), daughter of activist and suffragist Elizabeth Cady Stanton (1815-1902), founded the Equality League of Self-Supporting Women. Campaigning tirelessly for women's rights, Blatch founded the Women's Political Union the following year.

Source: Magnusson, Magnus, *Larousse Biographical Dictionary.* Edinburgh: Larousse Kingfisher Chambers, Inc., 1994, p. 164.

1908 ▪ **Anna Pavlovna Filosova** (1837-1912), a Russian feminist concerned with the education of women, was the first chair of the first All-Russian Women's Congress.

Source: Uglow, Jennifer S., ed., *The Continuum Dictionary of Women's Biography.* New York: Continuum, 1989, p. 203.

1914 ▪ **Raicho Hiratsuka** (1886-1971) was the founder of the Japanese feminist group Seitosha ("Bluestocking Society"); she was also the founder and first editor of its journal *Seito* ("Blue Stocking"), in Tokyo. With other Japanese feminists, Hiratsuka later founded the New Women's Association. The New Women's Association achieved the first political success for the Japanese women's movement—the amendment of the Public Order and Police Law—making possible women's limited participation in Japanese politics.

Source: Uglow, Jennifer S., ed., *The Continuum Dictionary of Women's Biography.* New York: Continuum, 1989, pp. 260-61.

c. 1920 ▪ **Hsiang-ning Ho** (1879-1972), a Chinese feminist raised in Hong Kong, was one of the first women in China to bob (cut short) her hair as a sign of independence. This was one of many feminist acts Ho engaged in while living in Kuomintang in the early 1920s. From 1949 to 1960, Ho was head of the Overseas Chinese Affairs Commission in Peking; in 1960 she was made honorary chairwoman of the China Women's Federation.

Source: Uglow, Jennifer S., ed., *The Continuum Dictionary of Women's Biography.* New York: Continuum, 1989, p. 262.

1920 ▪ **Huda Sh'arawi** (1882-1947), an Egyptian feminist and pacifist (a person who opposes war), was the founder and first head of her country's first women's rights association, located in Cairo. In 1924 Sh'arawi established the Women's Union, which advocated education for girls and women. That same year she founded the Union's journal, *Egyptian Woman,* which was published in both Arabic and French in order to reach a wider audience. Sh'arawi was instrumental in founding her country's first secondary school for girls (in 1927) and in establishing the first coeducational university classes (in 1929). In 1944 she helped to set up the All Arab Federation of Women.

Source: Uglow, Jennifer S., ed., *The Continuum Dictionary of Women's Biography.* New York: Continuum, 1989, p. 494.

1920 ▪ **Avra Theodoropoulou** (1880-1963), a Greek feminist, was the founder of the League for Women's Rights. Trained as a musician, Theodoropoulou was a committed feminist who did much in her country to further equal rights for women. In 1911 she founded the School for Working Women in Athens, and in 1918 she started an organization called "The Soldier's Sister." Theodoropoulou served as the first president of the League for Women's Rights for 37 years.

Source: Uglow, Jennifer S., ed., *The Continuum Dictionary of Women's Biography.* New York: Continuum, 1989, p. 539.

1922 ▪ **Bertha Lutz** (1899-1976) was the organizer of the Brazilian Association for the Advancement of Women, a group dedicated to child welfare, women's suffrage (the right to vote), and education. Lutz served as the organization's first president, beginning in 1922. A graduate of the Sorbonne in Paris, France, she joined the staff of the National Museum in Rio de Janeiro in the 1920s, thus becoming the first woman in Brazilian government service. A delegate in 1923 to the Pan-American Association for the Advancement of Women, Lutz also organized and led the fight for women's suffrage in her country. While remaining active on behalf of women, she taught biology for many years at the University of Rio de Janiero.

Source: Uglow, Jennifer S., ed., *The Continuum Dictionary of Women's Biography.* New York: Continuum, 1989, p. 338.

1922 ▪ **Margaret Llewelyn Davies** (1861-1944), an English feminist who worked for women's suffrage (the right to vote) and workers' rights, was the first female president of the Co-operative Congress. Davies supported the Russian Revolution (the violent overthrow of the czarist government in 1917) and was one of the founders of the International Women's Co-operative Guild in 1921.

Source: Uglow, Jennifer S., ed., *The Continuum Dictionary of Women's Biography.* New York: Continuum, 1989, pp. 149-50.

Alice Paul introduced the original draft of the Equal Rights Amendment to the U.S. Constitution.

1923 ▪ **Alice Paul** (1885-1977) organized a celebration in July of 1923 to honor the seventy-fifth anniversary of the First Women's Rights Convention at Seneca Falls, New York. At the celebration, Paul introduced the original draft of the Equal Rights Amendment to the U.S. Constitution (a draft she wrote). The Equal Rights Amendment was first introduced in the U.S. Congress in November the same year (but the amendment did not pass). In 1928 Paul also founded the World Party for Equal Rights for Women.

Source: Magnusson, Magnus, *Larousse Biographical Dictionary.* Edinburgh: Larousse Kingfisher Chambers, Inc., 1994, p. 1134.

1924 ▪ **Dora Russell** (1894-1986), an English feminist, was the founder of the Workers' Birth Control Group, in London. A lifelong advocate of birth control, women's rights, and international peace, Russell demonstrated for her beliefs and publicized her activism through speeches and books.

Source: Uglow, Jennifer S., ed., *The Continuum Dictionary of Women's Biography.* New York: Continuum, 1989, p. 469.

1929 ▪ **Ona Masiotene** (1883-1949), a Lithuanian feminist, was the founder and first president of the Council of Lithuanian Women, in Vilnius. Masiotene was active on behalf of women throughout her life. Educated as a teacher, she founded the Alliance of Lithuanian Women in 1905 in Vilnius. In 1917 Masiotene organized the Lithuanian Women's Freedom Association, through which she campaigned for Lithuanian independence from Russia.

Source: Uglow, Jennifer S., ed., *The Continuum Dictionary of Women's Biography.* New York: Continuum, 1989, pp. 364-65.

1933 ▪ **Dorothy Day** (1897-1980), an American social activist, was the cofounder (with Peter Maurin) of the Catholic

Worker movement. This movement established shelters and farm communities where people struggling during the Great Depression (1929-1939) could seek refuge. Day wrote about the movement in *House of Hospitality,* published in 1939. Using her life savings, she launched the newspaper called the *Catholic Worker* in 1933. A lifelong activist, Day was arrested in 1973 for challenging limits on United Farm Workers Union pickets in California.

Source: Parry, Melanie, ed., *Larousse Dictionary of Women.* New York: Larousse Kingfisher Chambers, Inc., 1995, p. 180.

c. 1940 ▪ **Dori'a Shafiq** (1910-1975), an Egyptian feminist educated at the Sorbonne in Paris, France, was the founder of Bint-E-Nil, ("The Daughters of the Nile"), a women's rights organization, in Cairo. Through this group Shafiq was instrumental in gaining the vote for women in her country in 1956.

Source: Uglow, Jennifer S., ed., *The Continuum Dictionary of Women's Biography.* New York: Continuum, 1989, p. 494.

1960 ▪ **Vilma Espin** (1930-), a Cuban feminist, was the first head of the Federation of Cuban Women, an organization she helped to found in Havana. The group was designed to fight illiteracy (the inability to read) to increase women's political involvement. Espin later became a member of the Central Committee of the Cuban Communist Party and worked in Fidel Castro's government in the Ministry of Food.

Source: Uglow, Jennifer S., ed., *The Continuum Dictionary of Women's Biography.* New York: Continuum, 1989, p. 192.

1961 ▪ **Bella Savitzky Abzug** (b. 1920), an American politician, lawyer, and feminist, was the founder of Woman Strike for Peace in the 1961 and cofounder of the National Women's Political Caucus in 1971. These organizations, each of which Abzug directed for a period, reflect her dual concerns with peace and women's activism. In 1971 Abzug won a seat in U.S. Congress, where she earned the nickname, "Battling Belle."

Source: Magnusson, Magnus, *Larousse Biographical Dictionary.* Edinburgh: Larousse Kingfisher Chambers, Inc., 1994, p. 7.

Betty Friedan (foreground) signs a telegram asking President Jimmy Carter to support the Equal Rights Amendment.

1966 ▪ Betty Goldstein Friedan (1921-) cofounded (with Dorothy Haener, Aileen Hernandez, and others) the National Organization of Women (NOW) and served as its first president until 1970. Friedan dedicated her life to working for and writing about feminist causes. She is perhaps best known for her groundbreaking book about contemporary attitudes toward women, *The Feminine Mystique,* published in 1963. In 1970 Friedan led the National Women's Strike for Equality. Her later publications include *It Changed My Life* (1977) and *The Second Stage* (1981).

Source: Magnusson, Magnus, *Larousse Biographical Dictionary.* Edinburgh: Larousse Kingfisher Chambers, Inc., 1994, p. 550.

1969 ▪ Shulamith Firestone (1945-), a Canadian feminist, was the cofounder and first editor of two radical journals: *Redstockings* (1969) and *Notes from the Second Year* (1970). Firestone was best known for her book *The Dialectic of Sex: The Case for Feminist Revolution,* published in 1970.

Source: Uglow, Jennifer S., ed., *The Continuum Dictionary of Women's Biography*. New York: Continuum, 1989, p. 204.

1970 ▪ **Monique Wittig** (1935-), a radical French lesbian feminist and writer, founded and was the first spokeswoman for Feministes Révolutionaires (Feminist Revolutionaries), in Paris, France. Eventually disillusioned with the organized protest for which she became notorious in the late 1960s, Wittig was later known for her feminist fiction and for her lesbian and philosophical tracts. Wittig was a frequent contributor to the French journal *Questions Feministes* ("Feminist Questions").

Thurman Won Suit

Tracey Thurman was the first woman to win a civil suit for being a battered wife. She won her case against the police department in Torrington, Connecticut, in June of 1985. The judge in the case decided that the police had violated Thurman's civil rights by ignoring her repeated complaints against her husband.

Source: Uglow, Jennifer S., ed., *The Continuum Dictionary of Women's Biography*. New York: Continuum, 1989, pp. 585-96.

1971 ▪ **Erin Pizzey** (1939-), an English leader in the feminist campaign against domestic violence, was the founder of the Chiswick Women's Aid Society in Chiswick, London. In 1979 she became director of Chiswick Family Rescue. Pizzey has written both fiction and nonfiction on the subject of family violence.

Source: Uglow, Jennifer S., ed., *The Continuum Dictionary of Women's Biography*. New York: Continuum, 1989, p. 434.

c. 1972 ▪ **Natalia Malakhovskaya** (1947-), a Russian teacher, was the founder of the feminist group "Club Maria" in St. Petersburg. This illegal organization campaigned against domestic oppression and inadequate state provision for maternity and child care. In 1980, Malakhovskaya and other group leaders were exiled to Vienna, Austria.

Source: Uglow, Jennifer S., ed., *The Continuum Dictionary of Women's Biography*. New York: Continuum, 1989, p. 350.

1972 ▪ **Phyllis Schlafly** (1924-), a right-wing political activist, was the first woman to lead the so-called "Silent

Class-Action Suit Settled

In 1991 a federal judge in Minneapolis, Minnesota, issued a ruling that allowed the first-ever class-action sexual harassment lawsuit. (A class-action suit usually involves a large group of people suing for the same thing.) A group of approximately 100 women miners alleged that the Eveleth Taconite Company engaged in hiring, compensation, and promotion practices that discriminated against women, and that male employees verbally abused them.

Majority" of conservative Americans in an anti-feminist backlash beginning in 1972. In the 1970s Schlafly led the campaign against the Equal Rights Amendment (a proposed amendment to the U.S. Constitution that would give women equal legal status). She published her anti-feminist book, *The Power of the Positive Woman*, in 1977.

Source: Uglow, Jennifer S., ed., *The Continuum Dictionary of Women's Biography.* New York: Continuum, 1989, pp. 483-84.

Labor Activism

1824 ▪ **Lavinia Waight** and **Louise Mitchell** founded the United Tailoresses Society of New York, the first women's labor organization. Approximately 600 female members of the union struck for better working conditions in 1831.

Source: Read, Phyllis J., and Bernard L. Witlieb, *The Book of Women's Firsts.* New York: Random House, 1992, p. 436.

1844 ▪ **Sarah G. Bagley** (1806-c. 1847), an American mill worker and early labor organizer, was the founder and first president of the Lowell Female Labor Reform Association, in Lowell, Massachusetts. Bagley was one of the first people to campaign for a ten-hour working day.

Source: James, Edward T., and others, *Notable American Women, 1607-1950: A Biographical Dictionary.* Cambridge, Massachusetts: Harvard University Press, 1971, pp. 81-82.

1860 ▪ **Emily Faithfull** (1835-1895), an English feminist, founded Victoria Press in London, England, the first printing house to employ only women compositors (type-setters). In 1862 Faithfull was the first woman to earn the title of Printer and Publisher in Ordinary to the Queen. Between 1860 and 1883 she founded and published *The Victoria Magazine* and the *English Woman's Journal*, periodicals dedicated to matters of interest to the working woman. In 1876 Faithful founded the Women's Printing Society.

Source: Magnusson, Magnus, *Larousse Biographical Dictionary.* Edinburgh: Larousse Kingfisher Chambers, Inc., 1994, p. 498.

1875 ▪ **Emma Paterson** (1848-1886), an English labor leader, was the founder of the Women's Provident and Protective League and the first female delegate to the Trade Union Congress held at Glasgow, Scotland. Paterson was also the first female inspector of working conditions for women's trades and the founder of the Women's Trade Union League.

Source: Uglow, Jennifer S., ed., *The Continuum Dictionary of Women's Biography.* New York: Continuum, 1989, pp. 424-25.

1880 ▪ **Elizaveta Kovalskaya** (1850-1933), a Russian socialist and historian of the Russian Revolution of 1917, was the cofounder (with Saltykov Shchedrin) of the Union of Russian Workers of the South. Kovalskaya's protests against factory owners resulted in her exile to Siberia (a harsh region where "undesirables" were sent as punishment) beginning in 1881. After her release in 1903, she went to Geneva and joined the Socialist Revolutionary Party. Kovalskaya returned to Russia in 1917 and worked in the state archives.

Source: Uglow, Jennifer, S., ed., *The Continuum Dictionary of Women's Biography.* New York: Continuum, 1989, p. 305.

1885 ▪ **Leonora Barry** (1849-1930), a hosiery (pantyhose or stockings) worker, was the first organizer and investigator for a department of women's work in an American labor union. Barry organized the Women's Work Union of the Knights of Labor in Amsterdam, New York.

Source: Read, Phyllis J., and Bernard L. Witlieb, *The Book of Women's Firsts.* New York: Random House, 1992, pp. 491-92.

1888 ▪ **Clementina Black** (1853-1922), an English labor activist, was the first woman to propose the Equal Pay resolu-

DOSC Founded

In 1869 the Daughters of St. Crispin (DOSC), the first national labor organization for women, was founded in Lynn, Massachusetts. The DOSC elected Carrie Wilson as its first president, and thirty delegates from six states attended the first DOSC convention. The organization disbanded in 1876.

tion. Black introduced her resolution at the Trade Union Congress held in England in 1888. A union organizer throughout her life, Black wrote three tracts (long articles) about the needs of women workers, as well as five novels about the oppression of women. Black was also an active campaigner for women's suffrage (the right to vote).

Source: Uglow, Jennifer S., ed., *The Continuum Dictionary of Women's Biography.* New York: Continuum, 1989, pp. 67-68.

1889 ▪ Harriet Morison (1862-1925) was the founder of the first women's union in New Zealand, an association called the "Tailoresses' Union." An ardent Unitarian and leader in the labor movement, Morison was also one of the first women to preach in New Zealand. (Unitarians reject the doctrine of a Holy Trinity in favor emphasizing freedom of religion and tolerance for other faiths.)

Source: Uglow, Jennifer S., ed., *The Continuum Dictionary of Women's Biography.* New York: Continuum, 1989, p. 389.

1893 ▪ Adelheid Popp (1869-1939), an Austrian trade unionist who also worked for feminist causes, led the first women's strike in Austria in 1893. Popp led 600 female textile workers in a protest near Vienna. That same year, Popp founded Libertas, a discussion group that offered women experience in political debate. Popp became increasingly interested in women's suffrage (the right to vote). After women gained the vote in Austria, she served briefly in Austria's government before the Nazi occupation (begun in 1938; the Nazi invasion of Austria was called the "Anschluss").

Source: Uglow, Jennifer S., ed., *The Continuum Dictionary of Women's Biography.* New York: Continuum, 1989, p. 437.

1894 ▪ Kate Richards O'Hare Cunningham (1877-1948) was the first woman to join the International Order of Machinists. Apprenticed to her father, Cunningham became a member of the order in 1894. (Apprentices work for an employer for a specific amount of time in order to learn a skill or trade.) She went on to a career as an ardent socialist and reformer, publishing a socialist novel, *What Happened to Dan,* in 1904.

Source: Read, Phyllis J., and Bernard L. Witlieb, *The Book of Women's Firsts.* New York: Random House, 1992, pp. 109-10.

1899 ▪ **Helen Blackburn** (1842-1903) and **Jessi Boucherett,** English labor activists, cofounded the Freedom of Labour Defense League. This group opposed protective legislation on the grounds that it diminished the earning capacity and personal liberty of women. A lifelong advocate of women's suffrage, Blackburn worked to improve the conditions of women workers in industry.

Source: Magnusson, Magnus, *Larousse Biographical Dictionary.* Edinburgh: Larousse Kingfisher Chambers, Inc., 1994, p. 160.

1903 ▪ **Agnes Nestor** (1880-1948), an American labor activist, was the first woman elected president of an international labor union. Nestor headed the Chicago branch of the International Glove Workers Union, a group she founded in 1902.

Source: Read, Phyllis J., and Bernard L. Witlieb, *The Book of Women's Firsts.* New York: Random House, 1992, p. 308.

1906 ▪ **Mary Reid MacArthur** (1880-1921), a Scottish trade unionist, founded the National Federation of Women Workers in London, England. In 1907 MacArthur began publishing the organization's magazine, a popular publication called *Woman Worker.*

Source: Uglow, Jennifer S., ed., *The Continuum Dictionary of Women's Biography.* New York: Continuum, 1989, p. 342.

c. 1910 ▪ **Marie Juhacz** (1880-1956), a German socialist and feminist, was the founder of the Workers' Welfare Organization in Berlin, Germany. Juhacz went on to become a member of the National Assembly in 1919 and a member of the Reichstag (imperial parliament) from 1923 to 1933. While the Nazis were in power (1933 to 1945), Juhacz lived in France. She returned to Germany in 1949 and resumed her work with the organization she founded.

Source: Uglow, Jennifer S., ed., *The Continuum Dictionary of Women's Biography.* New York: Continuum, 1989, p. 288.

1910 ▪ **Adele Schreiber** (1872?-1957), an Austrian feminist, founded the German Association for the Rights of Mothers and Children. Representing the Social Democratic Party, Schreiber became one of the members of the first Reichstag (imperial parliament) of the Weimar Republic in 1919.

Source: Uglow, Jennifer S., ed., *The Continuum Dictionary of Women's Biography.* New York: Continuum, 1989, p. 485.

1910 ▪ **Alexandra van Grippenberg** (1856-1911), a leading Finnish feminist, was the founder and first president of the Finnish National Council of Women, in Helsinki, Finland. (She had earlier served as the first vice president of the International Council of Women in 1889.) Van Grippenberg campaigned for women's suffrage (the right to vote) in her country and throughout the world. When Finnish women were granted the right to vote in 1909, Van Grippenberg was one of the first women elected to the Finnish Diet (national legislature), where she directed her energies to increasing women's opportunities. van Grippenberg was also active in the temperance movement (an organized effort to ban the sale and consumption of alcoholic beverages).

Source: Chicago, Judy, *The Dinner Party.* New York: Anchor, 1979, p. 130.

c. 1914 ▪ **Gertrude Baumer** (1873-1954), a German feminist, founded the Nationaler Fraudienst ("National Women's Service") during World War I (1914-1918). Baumer worked for women's rights and peace throughout her life, but advocated a national liberalism (a liberal political philosophy) as opposed to the individual pacifism (opposition to violence) of other feminists. From 1910 to 1919, she was president of the League of German Women's Associations. In 1917 Baumer founded a socialist school for women in Germany, and in 1920 she was elected to the Reichstag (imperial parliament).

Source: Magnusson, Magnus, *Larousse Biographical Dictionary.* Edinburgh: Larousse Kingfisher Chambers, 1994, p. 117.

1917 ▪ **Anusyabehn Sarabhai** (1885-1972), an Indian woman educated at the London School of Economics, was the first woman to chair a meeting in India at which a labor strike was called. Sarabhai chaired a meeting of mill workers where there was a call for the first labor strike in India. She supported Indian independence leader Mohandas K. Gandhi (1869-1948) in his strike at Ahmedabad the following year and continued to work throughout her life for workers' rights.

Source: Uglow, Jennifer S., ed., *The Continuum Dictionary of Women's Biography*. New York: Continuum, 1989, p. 479.

1917 ▪ Dorothy Jacobs Bellanca (1894-1946), a U.S. union organizer born in Latvia, was the first woman to serve full time as an organizer for the Amalgamated Clothing Workers of America, a position to which she was appointed in New York City. A tireless worker for the cause of unionism and for the Labor Party in New York politics, Bellanca was one of the few immigrant women who rose to prominence in the U.S. trade union movement.

Source: James, Edward T., and others, *Notable American Women, 1607-1950: A Biographical Dictionary*. Cambridge, Massachusetts: Harvard University Press, 1971, pp. 124-26.

1918 ▪ Frances Perkins (1882-1965) was appointed by New York governor Alfred E. Smith as the first woman member of the New York State Industrial Commission. In 1926 Perkins became chair of the commission and, in 1929, commissioner. Her annual salary of $8,000 was the highest amount paid to any woman in state government at that time. Perkins served as the U.S. Secretary of Labor from 1933 to 1945, where she supervised New Deal labor regulations such as the Social Security Act (1935) and the Wages and Hours Act (1938).

Source: Magnusson, Magnus, *Larousse Biographical Dictionary*. Edinburgh: Larousse Kingfisher Chambers, Inc., 1994, pp. 1145-46.

c. 1920 ▪ Rachel Katznelson (1888-19?) was the cofounder of the Women Workers Council in Israel. Instrumental in the formation of Israel's governmental policies toward women, Katznelson also established and edited the weekly paper *Savor Hapocht.*

Source: Chicago, Judy, *The Dinner Party*. New York: Anchor, 1979, p. 201.

1920 ▪ **Mary Anderson** (1872-1964) was the first woman to head the U.S. Women's Bureau, the only federal agency concerned solely with women's issues. Anderson, who immigrated to the United States from Sweden at the age of 16, joined her first labor union—the International Boot and Shoe Workers' union—at age 22. Anderson served as president of Local 94 of her union for 15 years and was the only woman on the union's executive board for 11 years. She headed the Women's Bureau until her retirement in 1944.

Source: O'Neill, Lois Decker, ed., *The Women's Book of World Records and Achievements.* Garden City, New York: Doubleday, 1979, p. 330.

1922 ▪ **Anna Weinstock** was appointed to the U.S. Conciliation Service, becoming the first woman qualified to serve as a federal mediator (or negotiator) in labor disputes. In 1947 Weinstock was appointed commissioner for New England under the then-new independent federal agency known as the Federal Mediation and Conciliation Service (FMCS). In 1957 Weinstock received the FMCS Distinguished Service Award.

Source: O'Neill, Lois Decker, ed., *The Women's Book of World Records and Achievements.* Garden City, New York: Doubleday, 1979, p. 331.

1926 ▪ **Marion Phillips** (1881-1932), an English socialist with a particular concern for women's rights, was the first person to organize relief for miners' families during the General Strike of 1926. In London she organized the Women's Committee for the Relief of Miners' Wives and Children.

Source: Uglow, Jennifer S., ed., *The Continuum Dictionary of Women's Biography.* New York: Continuum, 1989, pp. 431-32.

1931 ▪ **Louise Bennett** (1870-1956) was the first woman to serve as president of the Irish Trades Union Congress. Bennett worked throughout her life for women's suffrage (the right to vote) and for the rights of women workers.

Source: Uglow, Jennifer S., ed., *The Continuum Dictionary of Women's Biography.* New York: Continuum, 1989, p. 61.

1934 ▪ **Elizabeth Hoeppel** (1900-), an American opera singer, organized and became the first president of the Grand Opera

Artists Association. In 1936 Hoeppel helped found the American Guild of Musical Artists.

Source: O'Neill, Lois Decker, ed., *The Women's Book of World Records and Achievements.* Garden City, New York: Doubleday, 1979, p. 298.

1943 ▪ Anne Loughlin (1894-1979) was an English union organizer who went to work in a clothing factory at the age of 12. In 1943 Loughlin was the first woman to serve as president of the General Council of the Trades Union Congress (the same year she was made a Dame of the British Empire). In 1948, when Loughlin was elected general secretary of the Tailors and Garment Workers Union, she was the first woman in England to head a mixed union.

Source: Uglow, Jennifer S., ed., *The Continuum Dictionary of Women's Biography.* New York: Continuum, 1989, p. 334.

1944 ▪ Ruth Weyand (1912-1989), an American lawyer, was the first female attorney to argue before the U.S. Supreme Court for the National Labor Relations Board (NLRB). Weyland's argument stated that it was unethical for an employer to offer a pay increase to an employee if he or she quit the union. Weyand won the case.

Source: O'Neill, Lois Decker, ed., *The Women's Book of World Records and Achievements.* Garden City, New York: Doubleday, 1979, p. 334.

1948 ▪ Shirley Vivien Teresa Brittain Williams (b. 1930), an English labor advocate, was the first woman to serve as chair of the Labour Club, an organization concerned with issues of interest to British workers. Williams was the daughter of English writer Vera Brittain. Educated like her mother at Somerville College, Oxford, Williams worked as a journalist before becoming a politician.

Source: Magnusson, Magnus, *Larousse Biographical Dictionary.* Edinburgh: Larousse Kingfisher Chambers, Inc., 1994, p. 1565.

1960 ▪ Ana Figueroa (1908-1970) of Chile became the first woman to hold the position of assistant director-general of the

Women Joined Union

As a result of the pressing need for shipbuilders in the United States during World War II (1939-1945), the International Brotherhood of Boilermakers, Iron Shipbuilders, and Helpers opened the union to women for the first time. Women were allowed to join the Brotherhood beginning in 1942.

International Labor Organization (ILO). In 1951 Figueroa was also the first woman to serve as head of a main committee of the United Nations General Assembly.

Source: O'Neill, Lois Decker, ed., *The Women's Book of World Records and Achievements.* Garden City, New York: Doubleday, 1979, p. 346.

1962 ▪ Margaret L. Plunkett was appointed a U.S. labor attaché (diplomat), the first woman to hold the post. She served in The Hague, the Netherlands (1962-1967), and in Israel (1967-1971).

Source: O'Neill, Lois Decker, ed., *The Women's Book of World Records and Achievements.* Garden City, New York: Doubleday, 1979, p. 337.

1963 ▪ Ella Jensen (1907-), chair of the Tobacco Worker Union, was the first woman to head a union in Denmark with both male and female members. Jensen held the post until 1975.

Source: O'Neill, Lois Decker, ed., *The Women's Book of World Records and Achievements.* Garden City, New York: Doubleday, 1979, p. 320.

1970 ▪ Olga Madar (1915-1996), a union organizer once called "the first lady of labor," was the first woman named international vice president of the United Auto Workers (UAW) union, in Detroit, Michigan. Madar was hired at the Chrysler Corporation's Kercheval plant at the height of the Great Depression (1929-1933) simply because she could play softball. When she found out the circumstances of her employment, Madar became angry and began her work for the union. She joined the staff of the union in 1944 and in 1974 was elected the first national president of the Coalition of Labor Union Women.

Source: Read, Phyllis J., and Bernard L. Witlieb, *The Book of Women's Firsts.* New York: Random House, 1992, p. 265.

1970 ▪ Della Lowe, a Native-American activist, started the union called "Realistic Professional Indian Performers of America." An affiliate of the American Federation of Labor and Congress of Industrial Organizations (AFL-CIO), the union represented Native American ceremonial dance performers at the Wisconsin Dells resort.

Source: O'Neill, Lois Decker, ed., *The Women's Book of World Records and Achievements.* Garden City, New York: Doubleday, 1979, p. 297.

1972 ▪ **Margo St. James** (1937-) founded COYOTE ("**C**all **O**ff **Y**our **O**ld **T**ired **E**thics"), a prostitutes' union. A former prostitute, St. James started the union to help protect prostitutes and to work for the legalization of the profession.

Source: McCullough, Joan, *First of All: Significant "Firsts" by American Women.* New York: Holt, pp. 66-67.

1975 ▪ **Kathleen Nolan** (1933-) was the first woman elected president of the Screen Actors Guild. An actor, she appeared as Wendy in *Peter Pan* and made more than 800 guest appearances on television programs.

Source: O'Neill, Lois Decker, ed., *The Women's Book of World Records and Achievements.* Garden City, New York: Doubleday, 1979, p. 297.

1975 ▪ **Grace Hartman** (1919?-) was the first woman to head a major union in North America when she was elected president of Canada's largest union, the Canadian Union of Public Employees.

Source: O'Neill, Lois Decker, ed., *The Women's Book of World Records and Achievements.* Garden City, New York: Doubleday, 1979, p. 319.

1977 ▪ **Carin A. Clauss** became the first woman to hold the post of solicitor (chief law officer) in the U.S. Department of Labor—the agency's top legal post—when she was appointed by President Jimmy Carter (served in office 1977-1981).

Source: O'Neill, Lois Decker, ed., *The Women's Book of World Records and Achievements.* Garden City, New York: Doubleday, 1979, p. 340.

1977 ▪ **Eula Bingham** (1929-) was the first woman to head the Occupational Safety and Health Administration (OSHA) division of the U.S. Department of Labor.

Source: O'Neill, Lois Decker, ed., *The Women's Book of World Records and Achievements.* Garden City, New York: Doubleday, 1979, p. 340.

1977 ▪ Mary Maynard (1938-) was the first woman to serve as president of a local branch of the United Mine Workers of America. Maynard was elected to head Local 1971, a 98-member, all-male union in Run Creek, West Virginia.

Source: Read, Phyllis J., and Bernard L. Witlieb, *The Book of Women's Firsts.* New York: Random House, 1992, p. 274.

1980 ▪ Joyce D. Miller (1928-) was the first woman elected to the American Federation of Labor and Congress of Industrial Organizations (AFL-CIO) executive council. A lifelong union leader, Miller has devoted her attention particularly to social services and to women's concerns.

Source: Read, Phyllis J., and Bernard L. Witlieb, *The Book of Women's Firsts.* New York: Random House, 1992, pp. 292-93.

Pacifism

The First Female Pacifist

Abigail, the wife of Nabal in the Hebrew Bible, has been called the first female pacifist (or person who opposes violence, especially warfare) because she persuaded David not to kill her husband. She later married David after Nabal died. Abigail was considered the wisest woman in the Old Testament.

Sarah Winnemucca, the daughter of a Piute chief, helped persuade Native Americans to make peace with the United States government.

c. 800 B.C. ▪ **Hersilia** was the first Sabine woman to plead with an enemy for peace. (The Sabines were members of an ancient tribe living outside of Rome.) According to legend, no women lived in Rome when Romulus founded the city. When neighboring cities refused to allow Roman men to choose wives from among their women, Romulus staged a great festival to which all citizens from the surrounding areas were invited, and Roman men took Sabine women by force to be their wives. Known as the "Rape of the Sabine Women," the event became an important Roman legend. By the time the Sabine men came to Rome to retrieve them, the abducted women had established families with their Roman husbands, and Hersilia became a heroine when she argued for peace. The Roman festival of the Matronalia commemorates her success.

Source: Chicago, Judy, *The Dinner Party*. New York: Anchor, 1979, p. 114.

1880 ▪ **Sarah Winnemucca** (1844-1891), the daughter of a Piute (sometimes spelled Paiute) chief and a leader of Native Americans in the United States, was the first woman to persuade Native Americans to make peace with the United States government. Winnemucca went on to lecture throughout the country about the ill-treatment of the Piutes and other Native Americans

Folksinger and political activist Joan Baez founded the Institute for the Study of Non-Violence.

and was an ardent campaigner in Washington for Native American rights. Called Thos-me-tony, or "Shell Flower," by the Piutes, Winnemucca met in 1880 with U.S. President Rutherford B. Hayes (served in office 1877-1881). She established two schools for Native-American children, one in Washington Territory and the other near Lovelock, Nevada.

Source: Malinowski, Sharon, ed., *Notable Native Americans.* Detroit: Gale, 1995, pp. 460-62.

1908 ▪ Fannie Fern Phillips Andrews (1867-1950), an American pacifist born in Canada, was the founder of the American School Peace League, in Boston, Massachusetts. (A pacifist strongly opposes violence, especially warfare.) In 1918 the League was renamed the American School Citizenship League. The organization promoted international justice and understanding.

Source: James, Edward T., and others, *Notable American Women, 1607-1950: A Biographical Dictionary.* Cambridge, Massachusetts: Harvard University Press, 1971, pp. 46-48.

1915 ▪ Emily Greene Balch (1867-1961), an American feminist, was cofounder of the Women's International Commission for Permanent Peace (later the Women's International Committee for Peace and Freedom) in The Hague, the Netherlands. In 1906 Balch became a socialist and openly opposed World War I (1914-1918). Although Balch had been a member of the Wellesley College faculty since 1896, her appointment was not renewed in 1919 (in part due to her pacifist activities. A pacifist is a person who opposes violence, especially warfare.) For her lifelong work on behalf of peace and justice, Balch received the Nobel Peace Prize—which she shared with John R. Mott—in 1946.

Source: Magnusson, Magnus, *Larousse Biographical Dictionary.* Edinburgh: Larousse Kingfisher Chambers, Inc., 1994, p. 95.

1965 ▪ Joan Baez (b. 1941), American folksinger and political activist, founded the Institute for the Study of Non-Violence in

Carmel, California. Baez was also the cofounder of Humanitas, part of the International Human Rights Commission, in 1979.

Source: *Who's Who of American Women.* Chicago: Marquis, 1993, p. 39.

1973 ▪ Amalia Fleming (1909-1986), a Greek physician and political activist, was the first woman to head the Greek Committee of Amnesty International. (Amnesty International defends the human rights of political prisoners and oppressed people around the world.) Fleming assumed her post upon returning to Athens from political exile in 1973.

Source: Uglow, Jennifer S., ed., *The Continuum Dictionary of Women's Biography.* New York: Continuum, 1989, p. 206.

1976 ▪ Betty Williams (1943-), an Irish housewife, founded the Northern Ireland Peace Movement in Belfast, Northern Ireland. In response to the violent death of three children in her neighborhood, Williams began a grass-roots organization to work for peace. (A grass-roots organization is one founded and managed by individual citizens who act on behalf of the general population.) Soon joined by **Mairéad Corrigan** (1944-), Williams remained a leader in the organization until 1980. In 1976 Williams and Corrigan were recognized for their work and awarded the Nobel Peace Prize, the first Irish women to receive such acclaim.

Source: Magnusson, Magnus, *Larousse Biographical Dictionary.* Edinburgh: Larousse Kingfisher Chambers, Inc., 1994, p. 348.

1983 ▪ Helen Broinowski Caldicott (1938-), an Australian-born physician, was the leading founder of Women's Action for Nuclear Disarmament. Caldicott has devoted her life to working against nuclear power and weapons.

Source: Uglow, Jennifer S., ed., *The Continuum Dictionary of Women's Biography.* New York: Continuum, 1989, pp. 102-03.

Dr. Helen Caldicott, an activist for peace and nuclear disarmament, cofounded Women's Action for Nuclear Disarmament.

Susan B. Anthony spent most of her life working for women's voting rights and equality for women and African Americans.

Suffrage

1648 ▪ **Margaret Brent** (1601?-1671?) was the first woman in America to demand suffrage (the right to vote). A landowner and businesswoman, Brent petitioned the Maryland Assembly in 1647 for the right to vote, but her request was denied.

Source: Chicago, Judy, *The Dinner Party*. New York: Anchor, 1979, p. 167.

1655 ▪ **Deborah Moody** (1580?-1659?) was the first woman in America legally entitled to vote. As a landowner in Kings County, New York, Moody was authorized to cast a vote.

Source: Read, Phyllis J., and Bernard L. Witlieb, *The Book of Women's Firsts*. New York: Random House, pp. 297-98.

1866 ▪ **Lucretia Coffin Mott** (1793-1880) was the first president of the American Equal Rights Association (AERA), founded in Seneca Falls, New York. AERA was the first organization in the United States to advocate national women's suffrage (the right to vote), adopting its constitution on May 10, 1866, in New York City. A lifelong advocate of women's rights, Mott devoted her energies to the issues of women's suffrage, the abolition of slavery, and suffrage for African Americans.

Source: James, Edward T., and others, *Notable American Women, 1607-1950: A Biographical Dictionary*. Cambridge, Massachusetts: Harvard University Press, 1971, pp. 592-95.

1868 ▪ **Lydia Ernestine Becker** (1827-1890) became the first English woman to speak publicly on women's suffrage when she addressed a meeting at the Free Trade Hall in Manchester, England. Becker was also a founding member of the Manchester Women's Suffrage Committee and, in 1870, she founded the *Women's Suffrage Journal*.

Source: Uglow, Jennifer S., ed., *The Continuum Dictionary of Women's Biography*. New York: Continuum, 1989, pp. 56-57.

1869 ▪ **Elizabeth Cady Stanton** (1815-1902) was the cofounder, with **Susan B. Anthony** (1820-1906), of the National Women's Suffrage Association (NWSA), an organization dedicated to winning the right to vote for women through an amendment to the U.S. Constitution. A lifelong feminist activist, Stanton worked for women's right to vote and for equality for women and African Americans. Stanton and Anthony also collaborated on the multi-volume *History of American Suffrage*.

Source: James, Edward T., and others, *Notable American Women, 1607-1950: A Biographical Dictionary.* Cambridge, Massachusetts: Harvard University Press, 1971, pp. 342-47.

1870 ▪ **Marilla Marks Young Ricker** (1840-1920), an American lawyer and life-long feminist and freethinker, was the first woman in America to insist on casting a ballot. She based her position on the Fourteenth Amendment to the U.S. Constitution and claimed that, as a taxpayer, she was thus qualified as an "elector" under the terms of the amendment. Ricker voted in New Durham, New Hampshire, but her ballot was refused. She did vote successfully the following year, thus becoming the first woman in the United States to cast a ballot.

Source: James, Edward T., and others, *Notable American Women, 1607-1950: A Biographical Dictionary.* Cambridge, Massachusetts: Harvard University Press, 1971, pp. 154-56.

c. 1875 ▪ **Mary Lee** was the founder and leader of the women's suffrage movement in the state of South Australia. Due in large measure to Lee's efforts, women won the right to vote in South Australia in 1895, seven years before Parliament granted them voting rights in federal elections.

Source: Chicago, Judy, *The Dinner Party.* New York: Anchor, 1979, p. 188.

1878 ▪ **Hubertine Auclert** (1848-1914), a French feminist, was the founder of the women's rights group Le Droit des

Elizabeth Cady Stanton cofounded the NWSA, an organization dedicated to winning the right to vote for women through an amendment to the U.S. Constitution.

Femmes ("The Right of Women"). The organization was renamed the Societé de Suffrage des Femmes ("Society for Women's Suffrage") in 1883.

Source: Uglow, Jennifer S., ed., *The Continuum Dictionary of Women's Biography*. New York: Continuum, 1989, p. 34.

1884 ▪ Henrietta Dugdale (1826-1918), an Australian feminist, was the first president of the first Women's Suffrage Society in Victoria. A freethinker and a forceful writer, Dugdale campaigned for women's rights, including social and economic equality and educational opportunity.

Source: Uglow, Jennifer S., ed., *The Continuum Dictionary of Women's Biography*. New York: Continuum, 1989, p. 176.

1888 ▪ Katherine Sheppard (1848-1934) was the author of the first petition for women's suffrage (the right to vote) submitted to the New Zealand House of Representatives. Sheppard also submitted petitions in 1891, 1892, and 1893, the year in which one-third of the country's adult women signed the petition and in which the House of Representatives finally granted women the right to vote. Sheppard was also elected the first president of the National Council of Women in 1893.

Source: Parry, Melanie, ed., *Larousse Dictionary of Women*. New York: Larousse Kingfisher Chambers, Inc., 1995, p. 596.

1891 ▪ Rose Scott (1847-1925), an Australian feminist and pacifist, was the founder and first secretary of the Womanhood Suffrage League in Sydney, Australia. (A pacifist is a person who opposes violence, especially warfare.) Scott also organized the League for Political Education in Australia in 1910 and served as its first president.

Source: Uglow, Jennifer S., ed., *The Continuum Dictionary of Women's Biography*. New York: Continuum, 1989, p. 489.

1893 ▪ Mary Muller (1820-1902), leader of the women's suffrage movement in New Zealand, was instrumental in helping New Zealand become the first country in the world to grant women the right to vote.

Source: Chicago, Judy, *The Dinner Party*. New York: Anchor, 1979, p. 188.

1897 ▪ **Millicent Garrett Fawcett** (1847-1929) was the first president of the National Union of Women's Suffrage Societies in England. A lifelong advocate of women's rights to education and the vote, Fawcett was also a founder of the first Women's Suffrage Committee, the group that first petitioned Parliament to grant women the vote.

Source: Chicago, Judy, *The Dinner Party,* New York: Anchor, 1979, p. 186.

Blatch Led Parade

In 1907 Harriet Eaton Stanton Blatch (1856-1940) led the first parade for women's suffrage (the right to vote) in New York City. Over the next few years, suffrage parades were held in many cities across the United States.

1899 ▪ **Margarete Forchhammer** founded the Danish National Council of Women, an organization that fought for suffrage and women's rights.

Source: Chicago, Judy, *The Dinner Party.* New York: Anchor, 1979, p. 188.

1903 ▪ **Emmeline Goulden Pankhurst** (1858-1928) and her daughter **Christabel Harriette Pankhurst** (1880-1958) founded the National Women's Social and Political Union (WSPU) in England with the slogan "Votes for Women." The Pankhursts were known for their extreme militancy and vocal opposition to the oppression of women.

Source: Magnusson, Magnus, *Larousse Biographical Dictionary.* Edinburgh: Larousse Kingfisher Chambers, 1994, p. 1122.

1905 ▪ **Annie Kenney** (1879-1953), a militant (aggressively active) feminist, and her friend, **Christabel Harriette Pankhurst** (1880-1958), were the first women arrested and imprisoned for suffrage protest. When reporting on the women's arrest, newspapers used the label "suffragette" for the first time in print. Kenney had gone to work in a mill at the age of 10 and soon involved herself in labor union activity. She was the first woman in the textile unions elected to the District Committee and used her salary to enroll as a correspondence student at Ruskin College, Oxford. Kenney published her autobiography, *Memories of a Millhand,* in 1924.

Source: Parry, Melanie, ed., *Larousse Dictionary of Women.* New York: Larousse Kingfisher Chambers, Inc., 1995, p. 366.

1908 ▪ **Mary Augusta Ward** (1851-1920), an English anti-suffrage leader (a person who opposes women's right to vote) and writer who published fiction under the pen name "Mrs. Humphrey Ward," was the first person to serve as president of the Anti-Suffrage League. While sympathetic to women's plight, Ward was wary of radical solutions and preferred to stress women's fulfillment in traditional roles and through higher education and voluntary social work. With these goals in mind, Ward founded the Local Government Advancement Committee in London, England, in 1911.

Source: Magnusson, Magnus, *Larousse Biographical Dictionary*. Edinburgh: Larousse Kingfisher Chambers, 1994, p. 1532.

1908 ▪ **Elizabeth Robins** (1862-1952), an American actress and author who settled in England in 1889, was the cofounder and first president of the Women Writers Suffrage League. Robins is remembered for her influential play, *Votes for Women!*, first performed in London in 1907, and for her struggle to bring drama with substantial and unusual roles for women to the London stage.

Source: Uglow, Jennifer S., ed., *The Continuum Dictionary of Women's Biography*. New York: Continuum, 1989, p. 461.

1908 ▪ **Chrystal Macmillan** (1871-1937), a college graduate in mathematics and natural sciences and a lifelong feminist and pacifist, was the first woman to address the House of Lords, in London, England. (A pacifist is a person who opposes violence, especially warfare.) Macmillan appealed for her right as a graduate to vote for the parliamentary candidates for the Scottish Universities seat. Her case was defeated after seven days of heated argument. Macmillan went on to campaign for suffrage (the right to vote), and in 1923 she founded the Open Door International for Economic Emancipation of Women Workers, an association which fought for the removal of legal restraints on women.

Source: Parry, Melanie, ed., *Larousse Dictionary of Women*. New York: Larousse Kingfisher Chambers, 1995, p. 425.

c. 1909 ▪ **Alva Erskine Belmont** (1853-1933) was the founder and first president of the Political Equality League, a women's suffrage (right to vote) group based in New York City that flourished in the early 1900s. A woman of tremendous wealth, Belmont devoted her time and resources to militant (aggressively active) feminism after her husband's death in 1908.

Source: Magnusson, Magnus, *Larousse Biographical Dictionary*. Edinburgh: Larousse Kingfisher Chambers, 1994, p. 134.

1912 ▪ **Alice Paul** (1885-1977) broke away from the National American Women's Suffrage Association to found and serve as first chair of the Congressional Union for Woman Suffrage (later the National Woman's Party). Later that year, Paul began publishing *The Suffragist*.

Source: Read, Phyllis J., and Bernard L. Witlieb, *The Book of Women's Firsts*. New York: Random House, 1992, pp. 332-34.

1913 ▪ **Estelle Sylvia Pankhurst** (1882-1960) was expelled by her mother, Emmeline Goulden Pankhurst (1857-1928), and sister, Christabel Harriette Pankhurst (1880-1958), from the organization the women founded, Women's Social and Political Union. Known as Sylvia, Estelle was expelled from the organization because her focus was not only on women's suffrage, but also on socialist solutions to women's oppression and working class poverty. Estelle Pankhurst was arrested thirteen times during her life while working for women's rights.

Source: Chicago, Judy, *The Dinner Party*. New York: Anchor, 1979, p. 187.

1913 ▪ **Emily Wilding Davidson** (1872-1913), a militant (aggressively active) English feminist, was the first woman to kill herself for the cause of women's suffrage. Davidson wrapped herself in the flag of the Women's Suffrage and Political Union and threw herself under the king's horse during the Derby (a famous horse race) at Epsom, England. She was trampled and died of her injuries four days later.

Source: Uglow, Jennifer S., ed., *The Continuum Dictionary of Women's Biography*. New York: Continuum, 1989, p. 151.

Carrie Chapman Catt was the first woman to call for the establishment of the League of Women Voters.

c. 1915 ▪ **Emilie Gourd** (1879-1946), a Swiss feminist, was the founder and first editor of the suffragist periodical *Le Mouvement Féministe* ("The Feminist Movement"), a periodical she continued to oversee until her death.

Source: Uglow, Jennifer S., ed., *The Continuum Dictionary of Women's Biography.* New York: Continuum, 1989, p. 232.

1919 ▪ **Carrie Clinton Lane Chapman Catt** (1859-1947), an American suffrage (right to vote) activist, was the first woman to call for the establishment of the League of Women Voters in 1919, a year before the vote was granted to women in the United States. Catt devoted her life to the cause of women's suffrage, not only in the United States, but throughout the world. She was also a vocal activist in the cause of world peace.

Source: Chicago, Judy, *The Dinner Party.* New York: Anchor, 1979, p. 184.

1919 ▪ **Maud Wood Park** (1871-1955), a lifelong advocate for women's suffrage (the right to vote) and women's rights, became the first national president of the League of Women Voters in 1919, just before the Nineteenth Amendment to the U.S. Constitution became law in 1920.

Source: Read, Phyllis J., and Bernard L. Witlieb, *The Book of Women's Firsts.* New York: Random House, 1992, pp. 330-31.

Temperance

1873 ▪ **Eliza Daniel Stewart** (1816-1908) was the founder of the first American women's temperance league. (The temperance movement sought to ban the sale and consumption of alcohol.) Stewart's Ohio-based organization was an early version of the Women's Christian Temperance Union (WCTU), organized by Stewart and others in Cleveland, Ohio, in 1874.

Source: Read, Phyllis J., and Bernard L. Witlieb, *The Book of Women's Firsts*. New York: Random House, 1992, p. 424.

Wittenmyer and the WCTU

Annie Turner Wittenmyer (1827-1900), an American activist, was the first president of the Woman's Christian Temperance Union (WCTU). A conservative Methodist church leader, Wittenmyer soon won wide support for her organization and was instrumental in establishing the WCTU's first official journal, *Our Union,* in 1875. Wittenmyer lost the presidency to a more liberal challenger in 1879. During her five-year tenure, Wittenmyer established more than one thousand local WCTU unions with nearly 26,000 members.

The Arts

Dance
Film
Theater
Music
Literature
Fashion Design
Painting and Sculpture

Rita Dove was the first African American named poet laureate of the United States. (See "Literature" entry dated 1993.)

Dance

c. 1730 ▪ **Marie-Anne Cupis de Camargo** (1710-1770), a French dancer, was considered the first ballerina whose performance dominated specific dance productions. De Camargo was also noted for her ability to perform complicated steps and routines. Among her admirers were Giovanni Giacomo Casanova (1725-1798) and the writer Voltaire (1694-1778).

Source: Uglow, Jennifer, S., ed., *The Continuum Dictionary of Women's Biography.* New York: Continuum, 1989, p. 142.

1832 ▪ **Marie Taglioni** (1804-1884), an Italian ballerina born in Sweden, was the first woman to go "on pointe" on stage. (When a dancer goes "on pointe," he or she is balancing on the hard wooden toe of a ballet shoe.) Taglioni impressed audiences in Paris, France, when she went up on her toes in the Romantic ballet *La Sylphide*. This ballet was written by Taglioni's father—a dancer and choreographer (a person who arranges dance steps and movements)—in 1832. Taglioni toured throughout Europe and was known for her graceful and seemingly effortless movements.

Source: Uglow, Jennifer, S., ed., *The Continuum Dictionary of Women's Biography*. New York: Continuum, 1989, p. 528.

c. 1841 ▪ Augusta Maywood (1825-1876), a ballerina trained in Philadelphia, Pennsylvania, and Paris, France, was the first American woman to form her own traveling ballet company and win international fame. Maywood performed at the Paris Opera beginning in 1838, and she toured Europe in the 1840s with her own managers, partners, decors, and costumes. Maywood was particularly popular in Italy, where she performed to wide acclaim in the 1840s and 1850s. A colorful personality, she made a fortune before retiring to a villa near Lake Como in northern Italy.

Source: Uglow, Jennifer, S., ed., *The Continuum Dictionary of Women's Biography*. New York: Continuum, 1989, pp. 367-68.

1895 ▪ Mathilde Maria-Felixovna Kschessinskaya (1872-1971) was the first Russian ballerina to dance the 32 *fouettés,* a series of difficult, whipping leg movements first introduced by the Italian ballerina Pierina Legnani. The dancer's performance took place in 1895 in St. Petersburg, where Kschessinskaya was trained at the Imperial Ballet School. In the same year she also became the first Russian ballerina to dance Aurora in *Sleeping Beauty;* she later received the title of "prima ballerina assoluta" ("absolute first ballerina"). She fled her homeland during the Russian Revolution of 1917 and settled in Paris, France, where she opened her own ballet school in 1929. Kschessinskaya continued as an influential teacher until her retirement at the age of 91 in 1963.

Source: Uglow, Jennifer, S., ed., *The Continuum Dictionary of Women's Biography*. New York: Continuum, 1989, p. 306.

c. 1902 ▪ Isadora Duncan (1878-1927) was an American dancer known as much for her unconventional life as for her art. Duncan was widely considered the founder of modern dance. Trained in classical ballet, Duncan rejected traditional

Isadora Duncan is widely considered the founder of modern dance. Duncan rejected traditional dance forms and costumes for movements that emphasized the body's natural motions.

dance forms and costumes for movement that emphasized the body's natural motion. She opened a dance school for children in Berlin, Germany, in 1905 and a school for dance in Moscow at the invitation of the Soviet government in 1921.

Source: James, Edward T., and others, *Notable American Women, 1607-1950: A Biographical Dictionary.* Cambridge, Massachusetts: Harvard University Press, 1971, pp. 529-31.

1903 ▪ Loie Fuller (1862-1928), an influential American dancer, was the first person to use luminous phosphorescent materials (materials that glow) on a darkened stage. Fuller produced stunning lighting effects in this way for her "Fire Dance" in Paris, France. She also helped to launch the careers of Isadora Duncan (1878-1927; she joined Fuller's troop in 1903) and Maud Allan, other pioneers of modern dance.

Source: James, Edward T., and others, *Notable American Women, 1607-1950: A Biographical Dictionary.* Cambridge, Massachusetts: Harvard University Press, 1971, pp. 675-77.

1913 ▪ Anna Pavlova (1885-1931), the famous Russian ballerina, was the first woman to introduce western dance to countries such as Egypt, Japan, China, and India. Pavlova went on international tours beginning in 1913, and performed in the provinces as well as in capital cities in order to encourage the reputation and appreciation of classical ballet.

Source: Uglow, Jennifer S., ed., *The Continuum Dictionary of Women's Biography.* New York: Continuum, 1989, pp. 425-26.

1916 ▪ Flora Elizabeth Burchenal (1876-1959) founded the American Folk Dance Society in 1916 and served as its first president. When the society became a division of the National Committee of Folk Arts in 1929, Burchenal became head of the new National Committee, a position she held until 1959.

Source: Read, Phyllis J., and Bernard L. Witlieb, *The Book of Women's Firsts.* New York: Random House, 1992, pp. 75-76.

1920 ▪ **Mary Wigman** (1886-1973), a German dancer, choreographer, and teacher, founded her own school in Dresden, Germany, in 1920. With Wigman as its first director and principal teacher, the school became the center of Central European dance style, emphasizing angular movements and psychological truth. Wigman's work has been called the most significant influence on European modern dance.

Source: O'Neill, Lois Decker, ed., *The Women's Book of World Records and Achievements.* Garden City, New York: Doubleday, 1979, pp. 646-47.

1920 ▪ **Ruth St. Denis** (1879-1968), an American dancer and choreographer (a person who designs dances and dance movement), cofounded, with her husband Ted Shawn, the Denishawn School in Los Angeles, California. Many prominent twentieth-century choreographers, including Martha Graham (1894-1991), were trained at Denishawn. St. Denis later founded the Society of Spiritual Arts in Los Angeles, as well as the Church of the Divine Dance in Hollywood, California.

Source: O'Neill, Lois Decker, ed., *The Women's Book of World Records and Achievements.* Garden City, New York: Doubleday, 1979, p. 647.

1921 ▪ **Lydia Lopokova** (1892-1981) was a Russian ballerina with an international reputation who was married to British economist John Maynard Keynes (1883-1946). In 1921 the couple founded the Arts Theatre in Cambridge, England. This theatre fostered both touring drama and local productions featuring Cambridge students.

Source: Uglow, Jennifer S., ed., *The Continuum Dictionary of Women's Biography.* New York: Continuum, 1989, p. 333.

1926 ▪ **Marie Rambert** (1888-1982), an English choreographer (a person who designs dances and dance movements), dancer, and teacher, was the founder and first director of the Ballet Rambert, in Hammersmith, London. Rambert continued to direct this innovative company until 1966. The Ballet Rambert, which was known for its emphasis on classical dance as well as its encouragement of new ideas, put on a regular London season in addition to provincial and continental

Lopez Founded Ballet

Encarncion Lopez (1895-1945) was the cofounder, with Spanish poet and dramatist Federico Garcia Lorca (1898-1936), of the Ballet de Madrid. Lopez was known throughout her career as "La Argentenita" because she was born in Buenos Aires, Argentina.

tours. The company reflected the personality of its founder, for Rambert was known for her inspirational ability and energy. Until her late seventies, she was known to turn cartwheels in unexpected places.

Source: Uglow, Jennifer S., ed., *The Continuum Dictionary of Women's Biography*. New York: Continuum, 1989, p. 446.

1926 ▪ **Carlotta Zambelli** (1875-1968), an Italian ballerina who became principal dancer at the Paris Opera in 1898, was the first person to enter the French Légion d'Honneur for dance. Zambelli was recognized for her brilliant technique and interpretations. She retired as a dancer in 1930 and went on to serve as director of the Paris Opera ballet school, a position she held until 1950.

Source: Uglow, Jennifer S., ed., *The Continuum Dictionary of Women's Biography*. New York: Continuum, 1989, p. 598.

1930 ▪ **Hanya Holm** (1893-1992), a German dancer and choreographer (a person who arranges dances and dance movements), was the first person to introduce the "Dalcroze Central European" style of dance in the United States. In 1930 Holm performed in New York City, where she founded her own school the following year. She also lectured about her art and created dances for Broadway shows, among them *My Fair Lady* and *Camelot*.

Source: Uglow, Jennifer S., ed., *The Continuum Dictionary of Women's Biography*. New York: Continuum, 1989, pp. 263-64.

1931 ▪ **Ninette de Valois** (b. 1898), an Irish dancer, was the founder and first director of the Vic-Wells Ballet (which later became Sadler's Wells Ballet, then the Royal Ballet) in London, England. De Valois continued to head the company until her retirement in 1963. A dancer of great energy and charm, de Valois was also the founder of the National School of Ballet in Turkey, in 1947, and in 1974, the first woman to receive the Erasmus Prize Foundation Award.

Source: Parry, Melanie, ed., *Larousse Dictionary of Women*. New York: Larousse Kingfisher Chambers, Inc., 1995, p. 662.

1933 ▪ Alicia Markova (1910-), a distinguished English dancer of international reputation, was the first "prima ballerina" (the equivalent of music's "first chair"; the best in the company) of the Vic-Wells Ballet Company, in London, England. Markova held this position for two years, partnered by dancer and choreographer (a person who designs dances and dance movements) Anton Dolin. With Dolin she founded the Markova-Dolin Ballet, with which she toured between 1935 and 1938, becoming the first great ballerina to undertake tours to provincial areas. In 1950 Markova was a cofounder of the London Festival Ballet. She went on to become director of the Metropolitan Opera Ballet in 1963, governor of the Royal Ballet in 1973, and president of the London Festival Ballet in 1986.

Source: Uglow, Jennifer S., ed., *The Continuum Dictionary of Women's Biography*. New York: Continuum, 1989, p. 359.

1941 ▪ Pearl Primus (1919-1994) was the first woman to study and perform African dance as a scholarly subject. A native of Trinidad, Primus studied anthropology at Columbia University in New York City before turning to dance as a full-time career. Primus's first solo performance occurred in New York in 1941. She took up racial issues in her choreography (the composition and arrangement of dance), studied in Africa as well as the Caribbean, and established a reputation in Africa as well as the United States.

Source: Uglow, Jennifer S. ed., *The Continuum Dictionary of Women's Biography*. New York: Continuum, 1989, p. 440.

c. 1946 ▪ Margot Fonteyn (1919-1991) was the first ballerina of international stature trained and developed in England. Fonteyn joined the Vic-Wells Ballet School in London, England in 1934 and went on to a distinguished career in dance. In 1962 she began her acclaimed ten-year partnership with Russian dancer Rudolf Nureyev.

Source: Magnusson, Magnus, *Larousse Biographical Dictionary*. Edinburgh: Larousse Kingfisher Chambers, Inc., 1994, p. 527.

Margot Fonteyn was
the first ballerina of
international stature
trained in England.

1957 ▪ **Agrippina Vaganova** (1879-1951), a Russian ballerina known as a particularly gifted teacher, was the first
woman to have a ballet school in St. Petersburg renamed
after her. In 1957 the Leningrad Choreographic School,
where Vaganova taught from 1921 until her death, was
renamed the Vaganova School in her honor. She was also the

first woman to write a book that became the basis for ballet training not only in Russia, but in many dance schools in the West.

Source: Uglow, Jennifer S., ed., *The Continuum Dictionary of Women's Biography*. New York: Continuum, 1989, p. 553.

1961 ▪ Barbara Karinska (1886-1983), a Russian costume designer, was the first designer to win the prestigious Capezio Dance Award. Karinska was best known for her work with the Russian-born American choreographer George Balanchine and the New York City Ballet. Karinska was honored for her imaginative and colorful costuming in Paris, Hollywood, and New York, and for a long and distinguished career. Karinska continued to work productively until 1977.

Source: Uglow, Jennifer S., ed., *The Continuum Dictionary of Women's Biography*. New York: Continuum, 1989, p. 292.

1965 ▪ Twyla Tharp (1941-), an American choreographer who studied at Pomona College, the American Ballet Theatre School, and Barnard College, was the founder of the Twyla Tharp Dance Company in New York City. Tharp created dances not only for her own troupe, but for other companies and was known as one of the most original contemporary choreographers (people who design dances and dance movements).

Source: Uglow, Jennifer S., ed., *The Continuum Dictionary of Women's Biography*. New York: Continuum, 1989, p. 537.

1967 ▪ Brigit Ragnhild Cullberg (1908-) was the first director of the Cullberg Ballet, a company she founded in 1967. She was also a cofounder of the Svenska Dansteater in 1946. Cullberg has worked as a dancer and choreographer (a dance director) throughout Europe and the United States.

Source: Uglow, Jennifer S., ed., *The Continuum Dictionary of Women's Biography*. New York: Continuum, 1989, pp. 141-42.

1972 ▪ Judith Jamison (1943-), an American dancer, was the first dancer elected to the board of the National Endowment for the Arts. Jamison was also the first African-American

Judith Jamison (performing here in 1977) was the first dancer elected to the board of the National Endowment for the Arts.

woman and the first African-American artist to serve in this capacity. In being named to the post, she was recognized for her wide experience in dance in the United States, Europe, and Africa. She was especially admired for her statuesque performances characterized by passionate intensity.

Source: Uglow, Jennifer S., ed., *The Continuum Dictionary of Women's Biography.* New York: Continuum, 1989, p. 281.

In 1932 Martha Graham became the first dancer to receive a Guggenheim Fellowship.

1981 ▪ **Martha Graham** (1894-1991) was the first woman to receive the Samuel H. Scripps American Dance Festival Award. She was honored in Durham, North Carolina, in 1981 for her lifelong dedication to modern American dance. Graham is regarded as one of the most influential figures in modern dance. Born in Pittsburgh, Pennsylvania, she spent her childhood in California. After studying with Ted Shawn at the Denishawn School (which he cofounded with his wife, Ruth St. Denis) in Los Angeles, Graham performed, choreographed (directed), and taught through the 1920s. In 1932, she became the first dancer to receive a Guggenheim Fellowship.

Among Graham's best-known works are dances based on the lives of famous women, such as Joan of Arc, Mary Queen of Scots, Emily Dickinson, and Charlotte and Emily Brontë. After 1938 Graham created dances for music written expressly for her by composers Aaron Copeland (*Appalachian Spring*), Gian-Carlo Menotti, and Samuel Barber. Graham choreographed over 180 works before her retirement in 1969. Over the course of her career, she received numerous awards, including the Presidential Medal of Freedom in 1976.

Source: Read, Phyllis J., and Bernard L. Witlieb, *The Book of Women's Firsts.* New York: Random House, 1992, pp. 182-83.

Film

1896 ▪ Alice Guy-Blaché (1873-1968), a French filmmaker, was the world's first producer-director of films; she may also have been the first person to bring a fictional film story to the screen. At the International Exhibition in Paris in 1896, Guy-Blaché's movie *La Fée aux Choux* ("The Cabbage Fairy") was shown for the first time by the Gaumont film company. Guy-Blaché went on to make numerous one-reelers for Gaumont, even experimenting with sound as early as 1905. In 1910 she founded Solax, her own studio and production company, in Paris, and served as its first president and director-in-chief. The French government awarded Guy-Blaché the Legion d'Honneur in 1953.

Source: Uglow, Jennifer S., ed., *The Continuum Dictionary of Women's Biography.* New York: Continuum, 1989, p. 240.

c. 1900 ▪ Elvira Notari (1875-1946) was the first female filmmaker in Italy. Notari began her prolific career early in the twentieth century and is remembered for her documentary-style work on the street life of Naples, Italy. Her popular movies were forerunners of the style known as neorealism (a movement in Italian fiction filmmaking characterized by documentary techniques and concerns for social issues and the lives of the lower-classes). Notari's work was suppressed by Italy's Fascist regime (led by Benito Mussolini, 1883-1945) in the late 1930s. (Fascism is a system of government marked by strong central control of social and economic structures.)

Source: Bruno, Giuliana, *Streetwalking on a Ruined Map: Cultural Theory and the City Films of Elvira Notari.* Princeton, New Jersey: Princeton University Press, 1993.

1913 ▪ Mabel Ethelreid Normand (1893?-1930), an American actress, was the first film star to throw a custard pie, thus starting a classic movie comedy routine. Normand starred in a string of Mack Sennett (1880-1960) comedies and often appeared opposite Charlie Chaplin (1889-1977) early in the comic actor's career. Normand first flung a pie at actor Ben Turpin (1874-1940) in an early Sennett movie made in Edendale, California.

Source: James, Edward T., and others, *Notable American Women, 1607-1950: A Biographical Dictionary.* Cambridge, Massachusetts: Harvard University Press, 1971, pp. 635-37.

1915 ▪ Natalie Kalmus (1892-1965), an American filmmaker, co-invented—with her husband, Herbert T. Kalmus— Technicolor, a film-colorizing and processing technique the couple first developed in 1915. As the leading consultant for Technicolor, Natalie Kalmus persuaded Hollywood to use her process on a wide scale. Until 1948 her name appeared as "Color Consultant" on every motion picture using Technicolor.

Source: Acker, Ally, *Reel Women: Pioneers of the Cinema, 1896 to the Present.* New York: Continuum, 1991, pp. 277-79.

1915 ▪ Musidora (Jeanne Roques) (1884-1957), a French filmmaker who took the stage name "Musidora," was the first woman to portray a vampire in a motion picture. Musidora starred in *Les Vampires* ("The Vampires") in Paris, France, wearing a single-piece black leotard. Musidora went on to a distinguished career in film, collaborating with French author Sidonie-Gabrielle Colette (1873-1954) and founding her own

company, La Société des Films Musidora, in Paris in 1918. She starred in, produced, and directed films until 1950. Musidora was also a fiction writer and journalist.

Source: Katz, Ephraim, *The Film Encyclopedia.* New York: Crowell, 1979, p. 990.

1916 ▪ **Nell Shipman** (1892-1970), an American actress, film director, and producer, was one of the first filmmakers to make films entirely on location (not in a studio) and may have been the first woman to direct a feature-length wildlife adventure film, *God's Country and the Woman* (1916). Also a novelist, Shipman's autobiography is entitled *The Talking Screen and My Silent Heart* (1987).

Source: Foster, Gwendolyn, *Women Film Directors: An International Bio-Critical Dictionary.* Connecticut: Greenwood Press, 1995, pp. 340-41.

Actress Mary Pickford was the first movie star to form and own a film company.

1916 ▪ **Mary Pickford** (1893-1979), an Canadian-born American actress, was the first movie star to form and own a film company when she created the Mary Pickford Film Corporation in Hollywood, California. In 1919 she helped establish United Artists (which absorbed her company) with her friends, director D. W. Griffith, and actors Charlie Chaplin and Douglas Fairbanks (Pickford's husband from 1920-1935).

Source: Parry, Melanie, ed., *Larousse Dictionary of Women.* New York: Larousse Kingfisher Chambers, Inc., 1995, p. 527.

1917 ▪ **Marion E. Wong,** an American actress, was the first president of the Mandarin Film Company, in Oakland, California. The first film production company to be staffed entirely by Chinese Americans, Mandarin had its own studio and starred Wong and her sister in its first movie, *The Curse of Quon Qwan,* released in 1917.

Source: Weiser, Marjorie P. K., and Jean S. Arbeiter, *Womanlist.* New York: Atheneum, 1981, p. 185.

1918 ▪ **Anne Bauchens** (1881-1967), a pioneering American film editor, was the first film editor to be written into a director's contract. When Cecil B. De Mille (1881-1959) began making films in Hollywood, California, in 1918, he was so impressed with Bauchens's editing that he refused to work with any other editor. Every one of De Mille's films from 1919 until 1956 was cut (edited) by Bauchens.

Source: Read, Phyllis J., and Bernard L. Witlieb, *The Book of Women's Firsts.* New York: Random House, 1992, p. 42.

Rin Tin Tin's Screenwriter

Jane Murfin (1893-1955), an American playwright and screenwriter, was the first person to write a series of film scripts starring a dog. In 1922 in Hollywood, California, Murfin began writing screenplays featuring her own German shepherd, Rin Tin Tin. The films starring her canine protagonist debuted in 1924.

1927 ▪ **Esther Shub** (1894-1959) was the first woman to become a creative editor of Soviet compilation films. In 1927 she wrote and edited a compilation film for the ten-year anniversary of the Russian Revolution called *The Fall of the Romanov Dynasty.* Filmmaker Sergei Eisenstein (1898-1948) consulted Shub when he made his famous film *October.* Shub is also remembered for her outstanding work on such films as *Spain* (1939), *Twenty Years of Soviet Cinema* (1940), and *Across the Araks* (1947).

Source: Uglow, Jennifer S., ed., *The Continuum Dictionary of Women's Biography.* New York: Continuum, 1989, p. 497.

1920 ▪ **Maria Nikolaijevna Yermolova** (1853-1928), a Russian actress known for her portrayal of active and independent women, was the first woman to receive the title of People's Artist of the Republic, in Moscow in 1920. Yermolova supported the Russian Revolution of 1917, and in 1922 a studio of the famous Maly Theatre in Moscow was named after her, later becoming the well-known Yermolova Theatre.

Source: Uglow, Jennifer S., ed., *The Continuum Dictionary of Women's Biography.* New York: Continuum, 1989, p. 596.

1922 ▪ **Pola Negri** (1894-1987), a Polish actress, was the first European actress invited to make films in Hollywood, California. Negri had a popular career in silent films, but her heavy

accent prevented her from playing parts after the coming of sound. In 1934 she returned to Europe; the onset of World War II (1939-1945) forced her back to the United States.

Source: Uglow, Jennifer S., ed., *The Continuum Dictionary of Women's Biography*. New York: Continuum, 1989, p. 398.

1926 ▪ **Lotte Reiniger** (1899-1981), a German filmmaker, was the first woman to make a full-length animated film. Collaborating with her husband, Carl Koch, she developed animation techniques using silhouette figures made out of cardboard, tin, and paper. The film, made in Germany, was called *The Adventures of Prince Achmed* (1926).

Source: Parry, Melanie, ed., *Larousse Dictionary of Women*. New York: Larousse Kingfisher Chambers, Inc., 1995, p. 552.

In 1928 actress Janet Gaynor was the first woman to win an Academy Award.

1927 ▪ **Germaine Dulac** (1882-1942), a French journalist and filmmaker, was the first person to make a Surrealist film (a film characterized by dreamlike imagery and hallucinatory logic). *The Seashell and the Clergyman,* written by French dramatist, actor, and poet Antonin Artaud (1896-1948), was released in 1927.

Source: Uglow, Jennifer S., ed., *The Continuum Dictionary of Women's Biography*. New York: Continuum, 1989, p. 289-92.

1928 ▪ **Janet Gaynor** (1906-1984) became the first woman to win an Academy Award when she was named best actress in 1928. The first Oscars were awarded for cumulative work for the year. Gaynor's award included three films: *Sunrise, Seventh Heaven* (both 1927), and *Street Angel* (1928). Gaynor received a second Academy Award for her best-known film, *A Star Is Born,* in 1937.

Source: Read, Phyllis J., and Bernard L. Witlieb, *The Book of Women's Firsts*. New York: Random House, 1992, pp. 174-75.

1929 ▪ **Dorothy Arzner** (1900-1979) was the first woman to direct a sound film. An experienced editor and director, she was chosen by Paramount to direct its first sound film, *The Wild Party,* in 1929. Arzner was also the first woman to become a major Hollywood director. She began her film career as a typist at Paramount, but moved on to movie editing and in 1925 wrote, helped shoot, and edited *Old Ironsides.* Arzner directed 17 feature films and worked with many female stars.

Source: Read, Phyllis J., and Bernard L. Witlieb, *The Book of Women's Firsts.* New York: Random House, 1992, pp. 25-26.

1931 ▪ **Frances Marion** (1888-1973) was the first woman to win an Academy Award for writing. She was honored in Hollywood, California, for her work on *The Big House* (1930), one of the first "talkies" (sound films).

Source: Read, Phyllis J., and Bernard L. Witlieb, *The Book of Women's Firsts.* New York: Random House, 1992, pp. 268-69.

1931 ▪ **Kinuyo Tanaka** (1910-1971) was the first Japanese film actress to star in a "talkie" (a motion picture with a dialogue soundtrack synchronized with the film images) when she played the female protagonist in *Madame and Wife.* One of Japan's most famous film stars, Tanaka had a career that spanned over 50 years.

Source: Uglow, Jennifer S., ed., *The Continuum Dictionary of Women's Biography.* New York: Continuum, 1989, p. 530.

1932 ▪ **Claire Parker** (1906-1981), a pioneering American film animator, was the co-inventor of the "pinboard" animation technique. Working with Russian filmmaker Alexander Alexeieff (1901-1982) in Paris, France, she developed the process which utilizes an upright board through which hundreds of thousands of pins are pushed; images of remarkable detail are achieved by manipulating the heights of the pins and the lighting from the sides of the board. Parker and Alexeieff first used this technique in their now-classic film *Night on Bald Mountain* (1933)—the pinboard used in this film contained 500,000 pins; later films were made with a million-pin board.

Source: Acker, Ally, *Reel Women: Pioneers of the Cinema, 1896 to the Present.* New York: Continuum, 1991, p. 243.

Actress Bette Davis was the first woman to serve as head of the Academy of Motion Picture Arts and Sciences.

c. 1935 ▪ **Marlene Dietrich** (1901-1992), the German film actress who moved to the United States in 1930, was the first woman to refuse to make films in Nazi Germany. In the 1930s she refused Adolf Hitler's (1889-1945) personal (and lucrative) offer to return to act in German films.

Source: Uglow, Jennifer S., ed., *The Continuum Dictionary of Women's Biography.* New York: Continuum, 1989, p. 168.

c. 1940-1960 ▪ **Ida Lupino** (1918-1995), an English-born American actress, was the first woman to make her career in four areas of American film: as an actress, a director, a producer, and a writer. After working with Paramount and Warner Bros., Lupino founded her own production company, called Film Makers, with Collier Young. She wrote the script for its first production, and when the director died while on the film, she took over. Lupino directed, produced, and co-wrote each subsequent film. The company was innovative in covering controversial subjects, such as unmarried mothers and career women, and in fostering new talent.

Source: Parry, Melanie, ed., *Larousse Dictionary of Women.* New York: Larousse Kingfisher Chambers, Inc., 1995, pp. 412-13.

1941 ▪ **Joy Batchelor** (1914-1991), an English film animator, cofounded Halas and Batchelor Cartoon Films in England with her husband, Hungarian animator John Halas. An innovator in the production of animated cinema, the company produced and directed cartoons for cinema, television, and commercials as well as for promotional, scientific, and instructional films.

Source: Parry, Melanie, ed., *Larousse Dictionary of Women.* New York: Larousse Kingfisher Chambers, Inc., 1995, p. 58.

1941 ▪ **Bette Davis** (1908-1989), an American screen actress, was the first woman to serve as head of the Academy of Motion Picture Arts and Sciences. Davis was also the first

woman to receive the American Film Insti-
tute's highest honor, the Life Achievement
Award, in 1977. During her long career
Davis made more than eighty films.

Source: Read, Phyllis J., and Bernard L. Witlieb, *The Book of Women's Firsts.* New York: Random House, 1992, p. 115.

1942 ▪ **Lena Horne** (1917-), an American
singer and actress, was the first African-
American artist given a long-term contract
with Metro-Goldwyn-Mayer (MGM), in Hollywood, California, after World War I (1914-
1918). Horne went on to a distinguished
career in film, refusing to play stereotyped
roles. In the 1960s she was active in the civil
rights movement and continued to be outspo-
ken about politics and discrimination.

Source: Parry, Melanie, ed., *Larousse Dictionary of Women.* New York: Larousse Kingfisher Chambers, Inc., 1995, p. 325.

Lena Horne was the first African-American artist given a long-term contract with Metro-Goldwyn-Mayer (MGM).

1946 ▪ **Maya Deren** (1922?-1961), an
American avant-garde (cutting edge) filmmaker and the first
woman to succeed in making independent films, was the first
person to receive an award from the John Simon Guggenheim
Memorial Foundation. Deren's major works include *Meshes of
the Afternoon* (1943) and *Ritual in Transfigured Time* (1946).

Source: Read, Phyllis J., and Bernard L. Witlieb, *The Book of Women's Firsts.* New York: Random House, 1992, p. 119.

1953 ▪ **Dorothy Jean Dandridge** (1923-1965), an African-
American film star, was the first African-American woman
whose picture appeared on the cover of *Life* magazine. The
first African-American actress to be acclaimed as a star in
American cinema, Dandridge was featured in the magazine for
her role in the all-African-American film *Bright Road* (1953).
In 1955 Dandridge was nominated for an Oscar for her performance in *Carmen Jones* (1954).

Source: Parry, Melanie, ed., *Larousse Dictionary of Women.* New York: Larousse Kingfisher Chambers, Inc., 1995, p. 173.

1952 ▪ **Nancy Littlefield** (1929-), an American film director, was the first woman granted membership in the Directors Guild of America. Littlefield made her film career in New York City, teaching and working in the television industry.

Source: Read, Phyllis J., and Bernard L. Witlieb, *The Book of Women's Firsts.* New York: Random House, 1992, pp. 255-56.

1962 ▪ **Shirley Clarke** (1925-), an American filmmaker, was the cofounder—with Jonas Mekas—of the New York Film Makers Cooperative. Clarke was also the first person to shoot a film in Harlem, called *The Cool World* (1963).

Source: O'Neill, Lois Decker, *The Women's Book of World Records and Achievements.* Garden City, New York: Doubleday, 1979, p. 669.

1963 ▪ **Brianne Murphy** (1937-), an American camerawoman born in England, was the first female director of photography admitted into the Hollywood feature-film union. Murphy made her career both in Hollywood films and in television.

Source: Acker, Ally, *Reel Women: Pioneers of the Cinema, 1896 to the Present.* New York: Continuum, 1991, pp. 280-82.

1967 ▪ **Dede Allen** (1923-), an American film editor who first started working in Hollywood in 1943, was the first woman in her field to receive a solo credit among the screen titles. Allen was recognized for her skill and creativity in editing *Bonnie and Clyde* (1967). She was also praised for her imaginative work on such films as *The Hustler* (1961), *Serpico* (1974), and *The Milagro Beanfield War* (1988).

Source: Parry, Melanie, ed., *Larousse Dictionary of Women.* New York: Larousse Kingfisher Chambers, Inc., 1995, p. 15.

1968 ▪ **Katharine Hepburn** (1909-), an American film star, became the first woman to win an Oscar for best actress three times: in 1933, for *Morning Glory;* in 1967, for *Guess Who's Coming to Dinner;* and in 1968, for *The Lion in Winter.* In 1981 Hepburn was the first actress to win the Oscar for best actress four times when she won for *On Golden Pond.*

Source: Uglow, Jennifer S., ed., *The Continuum Dictionary of Women's Biography.* New York: Continuum, 1989, p. 255.

c. 1970s ▪ **Christine Choy** (1954-), an American filmmaker born in China to a Korean father and a Chinese mother, was the first Asian-American woman to have a successful career in documentary filmmaking. Choy worked as an editor, director, and producer beginning in 1971, completing nearly 40 films. Her works include *Who is Vincent Chin?,* which was nominated for an Academy Award, and *Fortune Cookie,* a film for the Public Broadcasting Service (PBS). Choy founded Third World Newsreel and has served as chair of the New York University School of Film.

Christine Choy was the first Asian-American woman to have a successful career in documentary filmmaking.

Source: Acker, Ally, *Reel Women: Pioneers of the Cinema, 1896 to the Present.* New York: Continuum, 1991, pp. 123-25.

c. 1970s ▪ **Chantal Anne Akerman** (1950-), a Belgian filmmaker who directed in both Europe and America, was the first to filmmaker to work with an all-female staff of technicians. Akerman began her career in the early 1970s and focused both on relationships among women and female sexuality.

Source: Uglow, Jennifer S., ed., *The Continuum Dictionary of Women's Biography.* New York: Continuum, 1989, p. 11.

1970 ▪ **Barbara Loden** (1934-1980), a film actress and director who grew up in poverty in Asheville, North Carolina, was the first American feminist film director. She made her reputation by directing *Wanda,* a documentary study of a poor woman from the coalfields of her childhood. The film won the International Critic's Prize in Venice in 1970 and has come to be seen as a plea not only for more opportunities for women, but for female directors as well.

Source: Uglow, Jennifer S., ed., *The Continuum Dictionary of Women's Biography.* New York: Continuum, 1989, pp. 331-32.

1971 ▪ Hannah Weinstein (1911-1984), an American film producer and civil rights and peace activist, was the founder of Third World Cinema, in New York City. This association, with 40 percent of its stock owned by the East Harlem Community Organization, encouraged films that involved blacks and women in all aspects of production. Among the motion pictures Weinstein made with this group were *Claudine* (1972), *Greased Lightning* (1977), and *Stir Crazy* (1980).

Source: Uglow, Jennifer S., ed., *The Continuum Dictionary of Women's Biography.* New York: Continuum, 1989, p. 573.

1974 ▪ Julia Miller Phillips (1944-) was the first woman to win an Academy Award as a producer. She was honored in 1974 for *The Sting,* which won an Oscar for best movie. Phillips wrote a popular book on life in Hollywood entitled *You'll Never Eat Lunch in This Town Again* (1990).

Source: Read, Phyllis J., and Bernard L. Witlieb, *The Book of Women's Firsts.* New York: Random House, 1992, p. 345.

1975 ▪ Kathleen Nolan (1933-) became the first woman elected president of the Screen Actors' Guild in Hollywood, California. While the nominating committee favored a man for the job, Nolan ran successfully by petitioning to be slated as an independent candidate.

Source: O'Neill, Lois Decker, *The Women's Book of World Records and Achievements.* Garden City, New York: Doubleday, 1979, pp. 309-12.

1982 ▪ Susan Seidelman (1952-), an American filmmaker, was the first American to direct an independent film shown in competition at the Cannes Film Festival in France. Although *Smithereens,* her first film, won no awards when shown at

Cannes in 1982, Seidelman went on to a promising career when she directed the successful *Desperately Seeking Susan* in 1985.

Source: Acker, Ally, *Reel Women: Pioneers of the Cinema, 1896 to the Present.* New York: Continuum, 1991, pp. 40-42.

1983 ▪ Barbra Streisand (1942-), an American singer and actress, was the first woman to produce, direct, co-author, star, and sing in a major motion picture, performing these multiple roles in her film *Yentl.* Streisand is known for her concert performances, Broadway musicals, numerous popular recordings, and a film career in which she is assertive about maintaining a high degree of creative control.

Source: Uglow, Jennifer S., ed., *The Continuum Dictionary of Women's Biography.* New York: Continuum, 1989, p. 522.

1985 ▪ Donna Deitch (1945?-) was the first female filmmaker to make a hit movie about a so-called taboo sexual topic. Her *Desert Hearts* (1985), based on Jane Rule's 1964 novel *Desert of the Heart,* was the first lesbian love (romance between two women) story to obtain mainstream distribution.

Source: Acker, Ally, *Reel Women: Pioneers of the Cinema, 1896 to the Present.* New York: Continuum, 1991, pp. 42-44.

1989 ▪ Euzhan Palcy (1957-), an American filmmaker born in Martinique, was the first black woman to direct a feature-length Hollywood film. *A Dry White Season,* based on a novel by André Brink, concerns apartheid in South Africa and was released, with Marlon Brando as its star, in 1989. (Apartheid was the government sanctioned system of segregation, or separation by race, in South Africa.)

Source: Smith, Jessie Carney, *Black Firsts: 2,000 Years of Extraordinary Achievement.* Detroit: Gale Research, 1994, p. 9.

1990 ▪ Ruby Oliver (1942-) was the first African- American woman to direct, write, produce, and sing in a 35 mil-

Adato Won Guild Award

In 1977 Perry Miller Adato was the first woman to win an award from the Directors Guild of America. She was honored for her television documentary *Georgia O'Keeffe.*

limeter film. Oliver created the film *Love Your Mama* while earning a degree from Columbia College in Chicago, Illinois, in 1990. This autobiographical film focuses on a mother-daughter relationship.

Source: Acker, Ally, *Reel Women: Pioneers of the Cinema, 1896 to the Present.* New York: Continuum, 1991, pp. 121-22.

1993 ▪ Linda Woolverton, an American writer, was the first female writer employed by Walt Disney Pictures on an animated feature film. Woolverton was one of the writers who created the script for the Disney movie *Beauty and the Beast.*

Source: *Working Woman.* November/December, 1996.

Theater

c. 1580 ▪ Isabella Andreini (1562-1604) was the first actress to establish a reputation throughout Europe. Born in Padua, Italy, she made her debut in Florence in 1578, then toured northern Italy and France for many years before dying in childbirth in Lyons. Andreini is also known for her poetry.

Source: Uglow, Jennifer S., ed., *The Continuum Dictionary of Women's Biography.* New York: Continuum, 1989, p. 18.

1670 ▪ Marie Desmares Champmeslé (1642-1698) was the first woman to play the title role of Bérénice in the play written for her by French playwright Jean Racine (1639-1699). Champmeslé is remembered as the actress responsible for initiating the traditional declamatory chant (a speech delivered with dramatic flourish) of French classical acting.

Source: Uglow, Jennifer S., ed., *The Continuum Dictionary of Women's Biography.* New York: Continuum, 1989, p. 117.

c. 1821 ▪ Rallou Karatza (1778-1830), a freedom fighter in the Greek War of Independence (1821-1829), was the first Greek woman to form a theatre group. Karatza's productions of sophisticated revolutionary plays and ethnic dramas transformed Greek theatre from simple entertainment to didactic art

(art that is designed to teach), rallying the Greek people to the cause of independence against the Turks.

Source: Uglow, Jennifer S., ed., *The Continuum Dictionary of Women's Biography.* New York: Continuum, 1989, p. 292.

1899 ▪ **(Isabella) Augusta Gregory** (1852-1932) was the cofounder, along with William Butler Yeats (1865-1939) and Edward Martyn (1859-1923), of the Irish Literary Theatre in Dublin, Ireland. This important center for the literary and artistic movement known as the "Irish Renaissance" later attained international fame as the Abbey Theatre. Lady Gregory dedicated her energies to the restoration of Irish culture and to Irish political independence.

Source: Parry, Melanie, ed., *Larousse Dictionary of Women.* New York: Larousse Kingfisher Chambers, Inc., 1995, p. 285.

1899 ▪ **Sarah Bernhardt** (1844-1923), the celebrated French actress known as "The Divine Sarah," founded the "Théatre Sarah Bernhardt." Remembered as one of the greatest stage actresses of all time, Bernhardt also appeared in several early silent films, including *La Reine Elizabeth ("Queen Elizabeth")* and *La Dame aux Camélias ("The Lady of the Camelias")*. In addition to her acting, Bernhardt was also an accomplished painter, poet, and playwright. Although one of her legs was amputated in 1915, Bernhardt continued her acting career.

Source: Parry, Melanie, ed., *Larousse Dictionary of Women.* New York: Larousse Kingfisher Chambers, Inc., 1995, p. 73.

1910 ▪ **Alla Nazimova** (1879-1945), a Russian actress who settled in the United States in 1906, was the founder of the Nazimova Theatre in New York City. Nazimova specialized in dramas by acclaimed playwrights Henrik Ibsen (1828-1906), Anton Chekhov (1860-1904), Ivan Turgenev (1818-1883), and Eugene O'Neill (1888-1953).

Source: Parry, Melanie, ed., *Larousse Dictionary of Women.* New York: Larousse Kingfisher Chambers, Inc., 1995, p. 490.

Vestris Introduced Boxes

Lucia Elisabetta Vestris (1797-1856), an English actress and theatre manager, was the first person to introduce box, or private, seating. She developed her innovation at the Olympic Theatre in London, England, in 1832. After 1838 Vestris managed Covent Garden and the Lyceum Theatre (both in London).

1912 ▪ **Lilian Baylis** (1874-1937), an English theatre manager, was the founder of both the Old Vic (established 1912) and Sadler's Wells (established 1931) theatre companies in London, England. Baylis made the Old Vic Theatre a principal center for the performance of Shakespeare's plays, while Sadler's Wells specialized in opera and ballet.

Source: Parry, Melanie, ed., *Larousse Dictionary of Women*. New York: Larousse Kingfisher Chambers, Inc., 1995, p. 61.

1914 ▪ **Beatrice Stella Tanner Campbell** (1865-1940), the English actress known as Mrs. Patrick Campbell, was the first woman to play the part of Eliza Doolittle in the famous drama *Pygmalion* by George Bernard Shaw (1856-1950). Campbell debuted in this work, written specifically for her, in London, England, in 1914.

Source: Uglow, Jennifer S., ed., *The Continuum Dictionary of Women's Biography*. New York: Continuum, 1989, pp. 104-05.

1923 ▪ **Ida Kaminska** (1899-1980) was a Polish actress and a driving force in the establishment of Yiddish (Jewish language) theatre. Kaminska founded the Warsaw Jewish Art Theatre in 1923 and the Ida Kaminska Theatre in Warsaw, Poland, in 1932. Forced to leave Europe because of anti-Semitism (discrimination against Jews), Kaminska went to New York City where she continued her work on behalf of Yiddish drama. In 1965 Kaminska starred in the highly regarded Czech film *Obchod na korze* ("The Shop on Main Street"), directed by Ján Kadár and Elmar Klos.

Source: Chicago, Judy, *The Dinner Party*. New York: Anchor, 1979, p. 215.

1931 ▪ **Cheryl Crawford** (1902-1986), an American theatre director, was cofounder—with Harold Clurman (1901-1980) and Lee Strasberg (1901-1982)—of the "Group Theater," an organization which developed "method" acting (a technique by which an actor develops an intimate understanding of the mind of the character he or she is portraying). In 1946 Crawford cofounded the American Repertory Theater with Eva Le Gallienne (1899-1991) and Margaret Webster (1905-1972); in 1947 she joined Elia Kazan (b. 1909) and Robert Lewis in opening the Actors' Studio.

Source: Parry, Melanie, ed., *Larousse Dictionary of Women*. New York: Larousse Kingfisher Chambers, Inc., 1995, p. 165.

1935 ▪ **Joan Maud Littlewood** (1914-), an English director, cofounded the Theatre Union in Manchester, England, with her husband, singer and writer Ewan McColl. In 1945 the company was reorganized as Theatre Workshop and opened with a performance of Shakespeare's *Twelfth Night* in London, England, in 1953. A supporter of experimental drama, Littlewood influenced both British and continental directors.

Source: Parry, Melanie, ed., *Larousse Dictionary of Women*. New York: Larousse Kingfisher Chambers, Inc., 1995, p. 404.

1947 ▪ **Judith Malina** (1926-), an American actress and director, cofounded the Living Theater with her husband, Julian Beck. (The Living Theater specialized in intellectual and avant-garde, or cutting edge, drama.) Malina toured Europe with her theater in 1961 and settled with the troupe in Bordeaux, France, in 1975.

Source: O'Neill, Lois Decker, ed., *The Women's Book of World Records and Achievements*. Garden City, New York: Doubleday, 1979, p. 665.

1963 ▪ **Hazel Bryant** (1939-1983) was the founder and first president of the Afro-American Total Theater Arts Foundation (established in 1963) and the Richard Allen Center of Culture and Art (established in 1968), both in New York City. Bryant's lifelong efforts on behalf of African-American theatre were cut short by her early death.

Source: Uglow, Jennifer S., ed., *The Continuum Dictionary of Women's Biography*. New York: Continuum, 1989, pp. 93-94.

1963 ▪ **Ariane Mnouchkine** (1939-), a French theater director, founded the Théâtre du Soleil, an innovative collective (a group in which members share responsibilities), in Paris,

The Federal Theater Project

Playwright Hallie Flanagan (1890-1969) organized and acted as first director of the Federal Theater Project. An offshoot of the Works Progress Administration (WPA; a federal jobs program instituted during the Great Depression of the 1930s), this federal venture sponsored a national network of regional theatres throughout the United States. The Federal Theater Project sponsored stage productions ranging from Shakespeare to vaudeville. In 1925 Flanagan founded the Vassar Experimental Theater at Vassar College, where she was a professor from 1925 to 1942.

France. The group explored mime (dramatic presentation using gestures without words) as well as other theatrical traditions, including Chinese and Greek drama and commedia dell'arte (a form of comedy developed in Italy in the sixteenth century).

Source: Parry, Melanie, ed., *Larousse Dictionary of Women.* New York: Larousse Kingfisher Chambers, Inc., 1995, p. 468.

1973 ▪ **Buzz (Mary Ann) Goodbody** (1946-1975) was the first person to serve as artistic director of "The Other Place," an alternative theatre in Stratford, England. Goodbody assumed her directorship in 1973. Before her death two years later, she established the theatre as both a popular success and a site for artistic innovation.

Source: Uglow, Jennifer S., ed., *The Continuum Dictionary of Women's Biography.* New York: Continuum, 1989, p. 231.

1983 ▪ **Glenda Jackson** (1936-), a versatile English actress known internationally for her film roles, was one of the cofounders of the Women's Playhouse Trust (a support group for women in the performing arts). Jackson made her film debut in 1963 in *This Sporting Life;* that same year she joined the Royal Shakespeare Company in London, England. Jackson won two Academy Awards for best actress, one in 1969 for *Women in Love,* and one in 1973 for the comedy *A Touch of Class.* In 1971 Jackson won an Emmy Award for the title role in the television drama "Elizabeth R," broadcast in the United States as a presentation of PBS's *Masterpiece Theatre.*

Source: Parry, Melanie, ed., *Larousse Dictionary of Women.* New York: Larousse Kingfisher Chambers, Inc., 1995, pp. 337-38.

1984 ▪ **Judith Anderson** (1898-1992) was the first Australian-born woman to have a Broadway theatre in New York City named after her. Anderson was honored for her lifetime achievement in playing strong female roles on stage. In addition to her theatrical awards, Anderson was named Dame of the British Empire (an honorary British title) in 1960.

Source: Uglow, Jennifer S., ed., *The Continuum Dictionary of Women's Biography.* New York: Continuum, 1989, p. 16.

Music

c. 1620 ▪ **Francesca Caccini** (1587-1640) was the first female opera composer. A talented musician in the court of the Medicis, Caccini was commissioned (contracted) to compose an opera during the 1620s.

Source: Uglow, Jennifer S., ed., *The Continuum Dictionary of Women's Biography*. New York: Continuum, 1989, p. 102.

1723 ▪ **Marguerite-Louise Couperin** (1705-1778), member of a noted French family of musicians and organists and a musician at the court of the French king, was the first woman to receive the honor of being appointed a member of the Ordinaire de la Musique.

Source: Chicago, Judy, *The Dinner Party*. New York: Anchor, 1979, p. 198.

c. 1791 ▪ **Josepha Weber** (1759-1819), a German soprano, was the first woman to sing the role of the "Queen of the Night" in Wolfgang Amadeus Mozart's opera *The Magic Flute*, in Vienna, Austria. Mozart (1756-1791) composed the part for Weber, whom he knew well, for he was married to her sister Constanze. Mozart also composed music for a third Weber sister, Aloysia.

Source: Uglow, Jennifer S., ed., *The Continuum Dictionary of Women's Biography*. New York: Continuum, 1989, p. 571.

c. 1820-1835 ▪ **Giuditta Maria Costanza Pasta** (1797-1865), an Italian soprano, was the first woman to inspire operas by three of the great composers of her day: Vincenzo Bellini (1801-1835), Gaetano Donizetti (1797-1848), and Giovanni Pacini (1796-1867). The title roles of Donizetti's *Norma* (1831) and *Anna Bolena* (1830) were written for her, as was the part of Amina in Bellini's *La Sonnambula* (1831). Pasta is also associated with the title role of Pacini's *Niobe* (1826).

Source: Uglow, Jennifer S., ed., *The Continuum Dictionary of Women's Biography*. New York: Continuum, 1989, p. 423.

1824 ▪ **Karoline Unger** (1803-1877), an Austrian contralto (a singer with a voice in a range between tenor and mezzo-soprano), was the first person to involve the by-then deaf composer Ludwig van Beethoven (1770-1872) in the late performances of his work. During the premiére of his *Missa solemnis* and Ninth Symphony in Vienna in 1824, Unger turned the composer around to face the audience so that he could at least see the applause. Unger is also remembered due to the large number of operas written for her (and in which she was the first woman to sing the central female roles) by such composers as Gaetano Donizetti, Vincenzo Bellini, Mercadante, and Pacini—at least six operas in all.

Source: Uglow, Jennifer S., ed., *The Continuum Dictionary of Women's Biography.* New York: Continuum, 1989, p. 552.

1843 ▪ **Pauline Viardot-Garcia** (1821-1910), a mezzo-soprano (a singer with a voice in a range between that of a soprano and a contralto) whose father was the famous Spanish tenor Manuel Garcia, was the first woman to introduce Russian music to the West. After a visit to St. Petersburg in 1843, Viardot sang Russian songs in the original language in Paris. She is also remembered as the first woman to sing the central female parts in works composed for her, among them the role of Fidès in Giacomo Meyerbeer's *Le Prophète* and of Dalila in Charles-Camille Saint-Säens's *Samson et Dalila.*

Source: Parry, Melanie, ed., *Larousse Dictionary of Women.* New York: Larousse Kingfisher Chambers, Inc., 1995, p. 666.

1867 ▪ **Clara Louise Kellogg** (1842-1916), a dramatic soprano from South Carolina, was the first American female singer to achieve a considerable reputation in Europe. She made her European debut in London in 1867, then toured regularly both in the United States and on the continent, even singing to acclaim in St. Petersburg, Russia, during the 1880-1881 season.

Source: James, Edward T., and others, *Notable American Women, 1607-1950: A Biographical Dictionary.* Cambridge, Massachusetts: Harvard University Press, 1971, pp. 319-21.

1878 ▪ **Amy Fay** (1844-1928), an American musician, was the first pianist to play a full-length concerto (a piece for one or more soloists and orchestra with three contrasting movements), at the Cambridge, Massachusetts, music festival. For several years prior to World War I (1914-1918), Fay also served as the first president of the Women's Philharmonic Society in New York City.

Source: James, Edward T., and others, *Notable American Women, 1607-1950: A Biographical Dictionary*. Cambridge, Massachusetts: Harvard University Press, 1971, pp. 602-03.

1869 ▪ **Vesta Tilley** (1864-1952), an English music hall star, was the first female to make her career on the English stage by wearing male attire consisting of a top hat and tails. This outfit, later popularized in the twentieth century by such famous film stars as Marlene Dietrich and Judy Garland, came to signify complex gender relations both from the point of view of the performer and the spectator. Tilley first dressed as a man in 1869 at the age of five, and went on to make her name as a male impersonator.

Source: Parry, Melanie, ed., *Larousse Dictionary of Women*. New York: Larousse Kingfisher Chambers, Inc., 1995, p. 647.

1876 ▪ **Adelina Patti** (1843-1919), the famous Italian soprano, was the first woman to sing the title role in Guiseppi Verdi's opera *Aida* when it was initially performed in London, England. Patti's career spanned 45 years and earned her a worldwide reputation as well as a financial fortune.

Source: Uglow, Jennifer S., ed., *The Continuum Dictionary of Women's Biography*. New York: Continuum, 1989, pp. 424-25.

1878 ▪ **Emma Abbott** (1850-1891), an English opera director, was the first woman to form her own opera company. In 1878 she organized The Emma Abbott English Opera Company, which presented shortened versions of contemporary operas.

Source: Read, Phyllis J., and Bernard L. Witlieb, *The Book of Women's Firsts*. New York: Random House, 1992, p. 3.

1879 ▪ **Maude Valérie White** (1855-1937), an English composer and writer, was the first woman to win the Mendelssohn Scholarship, in London. White had to give up the prize in 1881

because of ill health, but went on to a distinguished career in music, writing over 200 songs and translating many of her texts as well as poems by Victor-Marie Hugo and Heinrich Heine.

Source: Uglow, Jennifer S., ed., *The Continuum Dictionary of Women's Biography.* New York: Continuum, 1989, p. 579.

1881 ▪ Emma Cecilia Thursby (1845-1931), a concert singer and teacher trained in Pennsylvania and New York, was the first American to receive the commemorative medal of the Société des Concerts of the Paris Conservatory, in Paris, France. Thursby was well known for her tours throughout both the United States and Europe.

Source: James, Edward T., and others, *Notable American Women, 1607-1950: A Biographical Dictionary.* Cambridge, Massachusetts: Harvard University Press, 1971, pp. 459-61.

Cosima Wagner was the first woman to serve as music director of the Bayreuth Festival in Bayreuth, Germany.

1883 ▪ Cosima Wagner (1837-1930), the daughter of composer Franz Liszt (1811-1886) and the wife of composer Richard Wagner (1813-1883), was the first woman to serve as director of the Bayreuth Festival in Bayreuth, Germany. She assumed this position after the death of her husband, to whom she had devoted her life, in 1883. Rigidly adhering to what she felt were Wagner's intentions, Cosima controlled all aspects of the opera productions until she handed over direction to the couple's son Siegfried in 1906.

Source: Uglow, Jennifer S., ed., *The Continuum Dictionary of Women's Biography.* New York: Continuum, 1989, p. 563.

1888 ▪ Matilda Sissieretta Joyner Jones (1869-1933) was the first African-American woman to sing opera and art songs in the United States. Trained in Boston and New York City, she made her debut in New York in 1888. A dramatic soprano, she toured in the United States and Europe, even performing at the White House in 1892, and was hailed in the press at the time as the greatest singer her race had produced. By 1916 she had stopped performing.

Source: James, Edward T., and others, *Notable American Women, 1607-1950: A Biographical Dictionary.* Cambridge, Massachusetts: Harvard University Press, 1971, pp. 288-90.

1893 ▪ Ethel Mary Smyth (1858-1944) was England's first significant female composer. Her stature was first recognized with the performance of her *Mass in D* at Albert Hall in London in 1893. Educated in Leipzig and Berlin, she was remembered for her orchestral works and especially for her operas. She is also known for her active role in the women's suffrage movement (the campaign for the right to vote), for which in 1911 she wrote the *March of the Women.* Smyth also wrote several autobiographical books.

Source: Parry, Melanie, ed., *Larousse Dictionary of Women.* New York: Larousse Kingfisher Chambers, Inc., 1995, pp. 607-08.

1897 ▪ Olga Samaroff (1882-1948), a pianist and teacher, was the first American woman to win a scholarship at the Paris Conservatory in France. Educated in Texas, Paris, and Berlin, she made her debut in 1905 at Carnegie Hall in New York City. Samaroff went on to an illustrious career as a performer, writer, and teacher. She is also remembered as the wife of conductor Leopold Stokowski, whom she married in 1911 and divorced in 1923.

Source: James, Edward T., and others, *Notable American Women, 1607-1950: A Biographical Dictionary.* Cambridge, Massachusetts: Harvard University Press, 1971, pp. 225-27.

c. 1874 ▪ Maggie Cline (1857-1934), a vaudeville performer, was the first female Irish comedy singer in America. Cline established her career in Boston, Massachusetts, but by the end of the century she was well known in Cincinnati, Ohio, and New York City as well.

Source: James, Edward T., and others, *Notable American Women, 1607-1950: A Biographical Dictionary.* Cambridge, Massachusetts: Harvard University Press, 1971, pp. 352-53.

c. 1887 ▪ **Jenny Lind** (1820-1887), a Swedish operatic soprano of international fame, was the first woman to be represented in Poets' Corner at Westminster Abbey in London, England. Lind was honored after her death for her performances in works by Giacomo Meyerbeer, Vincenzo Bellini, Gaetano Donizetti, and Guiseppe Verdi and for a career dedicated to singing and teaching. She was the cofounder with her husband, the pianist Otto Goldschmidt, of the Bach Choir in London, England. Lind became professor of singing at the Royal College of Music in London in 1883.

Source: Uglow, Jennifer S., ed., *The Continuum Dictionary of Women's Biography.* New York: Continuum, 1989, pp. 326-27.

c. 1927 ▪ **Wanda Landowska** (1879-1959), a Polish musician, was one of the first people to revive the harpsichord (a piano-like instrument), on which she continued to play and record throughout her life. Landowska studied in Berlin, and beginning in 1903, she toured Europe and America. She founded the Ecole de Musique Ancienne at St-Leu-la-Fôret near Paris in 1925. After the German occupation of France in 1940, she moved to the United States. Harpsichord concertos were composed for her by Manuel de Falla and Francis Poulenc, but she is primarily associated with seventeenth- and eighteenth-century music, especially works composed by Johann Sebastian Bach (1685-1750).

Source: Uglow, Jennifer S., ed., *The Continuum Dictionary of Women's Biography.* New York: Continuum, 1989, p. 311.

1906 ▪ **Maud Powell** (1868-1920), an American violinist educated in Europe, was the first person to perform the *Jean Sibelius violin concerto in D minor* in the United States. Powell played this piece with the New York Philharmonic in New York City. Committed to the music of her time, Powell was a pioneering performer, and her career included a number of such firsts, among them the first American performances of violin concerti by Charles-Camille Saint-Saëns, Harry Rowe Shelley, and Antonín Dvorák.

Source: James, Edward T., and others, *Notable American Women, 1607-1950: A Biographical Dictionary.* Cambridge, Massachusetts: Harvard University Press, 1971, pp. 90-92.

1908 ▪ **Corinne Rider-Kelsey** (1877-1947), a concert and oratorio soprano, was the first singer trained in the United States to perform a major role with the Royal Opera at Covent Garden in London, England. She made her London debut in the part of Micaela in the opera *Carmen* by the French composer Georges Bizet (1838-1875) in 1908.

Source: James, Edward T., and others, *Notable American Women, 1607-1950: A Biographical Dictionary*. Cambridge, Massachusetts: Harvard University Press, 1971, pp. 157-58.

England's Second Anthem

Clara Butt (1872-1936), an English contralto (a singer with a voice having a range between tenor and mezzo-soprano), was the first woman to sing Edward Elgar's "Land of Hope and Glory." The song has become England's unofficial second national anthem.

1914 ▪ **Lotte Lehmann** (1888-1976) was a German opera singer who settled in the United States near the end of her career. Beginning in 1914, she was the first woman to appear successively in all three soprano roles (Sophie, the Marschallin, and Octavian) in the opera *Rosenkavalier* by Richard Strauss (1864-1949). She was also the first woman to sing the starring roles in the premiéres of Strauss's *Die Frau ohne Shatten* (in Vienna in 1919) and *Intermezzo* (in Dresden in 1924).

Source: Uglow, Jennifer S., ed., *The Continuum Dictionary of Women's Biography*. New York: Continuum, 1989, p. 320.

1912 ▪ **Margarethe Dessoff** (1874-1944) was the first woman to conduct a women's chorus in public, in New York City. From 1925 through 1935, Dessoff directed the female Adesor Choir in New York City, a chorus that performed only music specifically composed for female voices.

Source: Chicago, Judy, *The Dinner Party*. New York: Anchor, 1979, p. 198.

1913 ▪ **Lili Boulanger** (1893-1918), a French composer, was the first woman to be awarded the Prix de Rome for her cantata *Faust et Hélène*. Boulanger composed prolifically and was known primarily for her choral work.

Source: Uglow, Jennifer S., ed., *The Continuum Dictionary of Women's Biography*. New York: Continuum, 1989, p. 81.

1917 ▪ Marguerite Canal (1890-1978) was the first woman to conduct orchestral concerts in France. She conducted a series of performances at the Palais de Glace in Paris in 1917 and 1918. Canal had a distinguished career as a conductor, composer, and teacher at the Paris Conservatory.

Source: Uglow, Jennifer S., ed., *The Continuum Dictionary of Women's Biography.* New York: Continuum, 1989, p. 105.

1918 ▪ Adella Prentiss Hughes (1869-1950) became the first woman to serve as manager of a major symphony orchestra when she assumed this position in the newly formed Cleveland Symphony Orchestra, conducted by Nikolai Sokoloff. Hughes made several innovations, including children's concerts, orchestra radio broadcasts, summer "pops" concerts, and music appreciation courses in public schools.

Source: Read, Phyllis J., and Bernard L. Witlieb, *The Book of Women's Firsts.* New York: Random House, 1992, pp. 220-21.

1918 ▪ Rosa Ponselle (1897-1981), an American soprano, was the first person to sing the role of Leonora in *La Forza del Destino* at the Metropolitan Opera House in New York City. At the suggestion of Italian tenor Enrico Caruso (1873-1921), this was Ponselle's first operatic appearance. Ponselle went on to a distinguished career both as a performer and as a teacher.

Source: Uglow, Jennifer S., ed., *The Continuum Dictionary of Women's Biography.* New York: Continuum, 1989, pp. 436-37.

1919 ▪ Alma Gluck (1884-1938), an American singer who was famous for her performances at the Metropolitan Opera, was the first female recording artist to sell a million copies. In 1911-1912 she recorded James Bland's "Carry Me Back to Old Virginny," which was released as a single-sided disk. The song was re-released as a double-faced disk (paired with "Old Black Joe") in 1915. This second version is reputed to have sold over a million copies by 1919.

Source: James, Edward T., and others, *Notable American Women, 1607-1950: A Biographical Dictionary.* Cambridge, Massachusetts: Harvard University Press, 1971, pp. 53- 55.

1919 ▪ **Marguerite Marie Charlotte Long** (1874-1966), a French pianist and teacher at the Paris Conservatory from 1906 until 1940, was the first person to perform Maurice Ravel's *Tombeau de Couperin,* in Paris. She was also the first person to record Ravel's *Piano Concerto in G* and the first to play this work (with the composer conducting), also in Paris, in 1932. Long was the first pianist to record this concerto (a piece for one or more soloists and orchestra with three contrasting movements). In 1943 she founded, with Jacques Thibaud, the international piano and violin competition that bears their names.

Source: Uglow, Jennifer S., ed., *The Continuum Dictionary of Women's Biography.* New York: Continuum, 1989, p. 332.

c. 1922 ▪ **"Ma" (Gertrude Pridgett) Rainey** (1886-1939), an American singer known for her performances of the blues (a form of music that originated in the United States that is frequently characterized by a 12-bar structure of phrases and lamenting or mournful lyrics). Rainey toured the eastern United States with the group during the 1920s. Rainey made 90 recordings between 1923 and 1928, but retired during the Great Depression (1929-1939) in 1933.

Source: Uglow, Jennifer S., ed., *The Continuum Dictionary of Women's Biography.* New York: Continuum, 1989, p. 445.

1921 ▪ **Mary Garden** (1874-1967), a Scottish singer, became the first woman to serve as director of a major opera company. She assumed this position at the Chicago Lyric Opera during the 1921-1922 season. Known primarily as a singer, Garden was particularly accomplished in performing soprano roles in works by French composers.

Source: Parry, Melanie, ed., *Larousse Dictionary of Women.* New York: Larousse Kingfisher Chambers, Inc., 1995, p. 258.

1925 ▪ **Ethel Leginska** (1886-1970), an American musician and composer, was the first woman to conduct a major American orchestra when she led the New York Symphony Orchestra in a concert in New York City. Trained as a pianist, Leginska founded the Boston Philharmonic in 1926, and she composed works for both orchestra and opera. In 1932 she became the first American woman to compose an opera when she wrote *The Rose and the Ring,* which is based on a story by the British novelist William Makepeace Thackeray (1811-1863).

Source: Read, Phyllis J., and Bernard L. Witlieb, *The Book of Women's Firsts.* New York: Random House, 1992, pp. 250-51.

1926 ▪ **Amy Marcy Cheney Beach** (1867-1944) was the first president of the Association of American Women Composers, a society she helped to found. Beach was a concert pianist and symphonic composer who played her own compositions in Europe and the United States. Her *Mass in E-flat Major* was the first work by a woman performed by the Boston Symphony Orchestra, in 1892. Her aria *Eilende Wolken* was the first work by a woman to be performed by the New York Symphony Orchestra, in 1892.

Source: Uglow, Jennifer S., ed., *The Continuum Dictionary of Women's Biography.* New York: Continuum, 1989, p. 54.

1928 ▪ **Lotte Lenya** (1898-1981), an Austrian singer of international reputation, was the first woman to play the part of Jenny, a major character in her husband Kurt Weill's *The Three-Penny Opera,* in Berlin, Germany. She later starred in George Wilhelm Pabst's film version of this work. Lenya and Weill left Germany in 1933 as the Nazis were taking power and settled in New York City. Lenya's voice, familiar through her numerous recordings, recalled the atmosphere of Berlin in the 1920s and 1930s.

Source: Uglow, Jennifer S., ed., *The Continuum Dictionary of Women's Biography.* New York: Continuum, 1989, p. 322.

1931 ▪ **Anne Catherine Macnaghten** (1908-), an English musician, was the cofounder (with Iris Lemare and Elisabeth Lutyens) of the Macnaghten-Lemare Concerts, an ongoing series of performances of contemporary music, in London, England. The concerts featured work by modern composers, mostly British, including Lutyens, Benjamin Britten, and Nicola Lefanu. Today the series is known as the "New Macnaghten

Concerts," and many musicians have dedicated their work to its founder.

Source: Uglow, Jennifer S., ed., *The Continuum Dictionary of Women's Biography.* New York: Continuum, 1989, p. 347.

1935 ▪ Grazyna Bacewicz (1909-1962), a Polish composer and violinist, was the first woman to win a prize at the Wieniawski

Dorothy Fields won an Oscar for writing the lyrics to the Jerome Kern tune "The Way You Look Tonight."

Competition in Poland. She taught in Lodz and in Warsaw, and in 1950 retired from performance to devote her musical skills to composition.

Source: Uglow, Jennifer S., ed., *The Continuum Dictionary of Women's Biography.* New York: Continuum, 1989, p. 40.

1937 ▪ **Nadia Boulanger** (1887-1979) was the first woman to conduct a symphony orchestra, in London, England. A French composer, teacher, and conductor, she was the first woman to conduct regular subscription concerts with the Boston Symphony Orchestra (in 1938) and with the New York Philharmonic (in 1939). Boulanger was also the first woman to conduct the Hallé Orchestra (in 1963).

Source: Uglow, Jennifer S., ed., *The Continuum Dictionary of Women's Biography.* New York: Continuum, 1989, pp. 81-82.

1937 ▪ **Dorothy Fields** (1905-1974), an American songwriter, was the first woman to win an Oscar for songwriting. She was honored for the lyrics she wrote for Jerome Kern's tune "The Way You Look Tonight." The song was featured in the film *Swing Time,* starring Ginger Rogers and Fred Astaire, the previous year. In 1971 Fields became the first woman to be elected to the Songwriters' Hall of Fame.

Source: Read, Phyllis J., and Bernard L. Witlieb, *The Book of Women's Firsts.* New York: Random House, 1992, p. 156.

1939 ▪ **Elisabeth Lutyens** (1906-1983) was the first British woman to use serialism (the theory or practice of composing a series of related pieces) in her musical compositions. This technique appeared in her *Chamber Concerto No. 1* in 1939. A prolific composer, Lutyens was also the cofounder of Macnaughten-Lemare Concerts (in London in 1931), which fostered the work of young musicians such as Benjamin Britten.

Source: Uglow, Jennifer S., ed., *The Continuum Dictionary of Women's Biography.* New York: Continuum, 1989, pp. 337-38.

c. 1940 ▪ **Myra Hess** (1890-1965), a English pianist, was the first person to organize alternative music performances when London concert halls were closed down during World War II (1939-1945). Hess herself performed at many of the concerts, and in 1941 she was named Dame of the British Empire in recognition of her services as a public benefactor.

Source: Parry, Melanie, ed., *Larousse Dictionary of Women.* New York: Larousse Kingfisher Chambers, Inc., 1995, p. 315.

1940 ▪ **Peggy Glanville-Hicks** (1912-1990), an Australian composer, was the cofounder (with her husband Stanley Bate) of Les Trois Arts, a ballet company, in London, England. In the 1940s she was also the cofounder of the International Music Fund. Glanville-Hicks later founded The Artists' Company to promote American opera.

Source: Uglow, Jennifer S., ed., *The Continuum Dictionary of Women's Biography.* New York: Continuum, 1989, p. 226.

c. 1942 ▪ **Mary Lou Williams** (1910-1981), a jazz pianist and composer, became the first successful woman jazz musician

Vera Lynn Scored Hit

Vera Lynn (1917-) was the first British singer to reach the top of the American hit parade (a list of the most popular songs of the day). She was so popular during World War II (1939-1945) that she was the first woman to be named "Forces' Sweetheart." Lynn sang in London revues and for the troops in England and in Burma as well as on the radio. After the war, she appeared on television and in cabaret and variety shows throughout the world.

and arranger. She founded the Bel Canto Foundation, an organization to aid down-and-out musicians. Largely self-educated, Williams taught music at Duke University for many years.

Source: O'Neill, Lois Decker, ed., *The Women's Book of World Records and Achievements.* Garden City, New York: Doubleday, 1979, pp. 631-32.

1945 ▪ **Camilla Williams** (1925-) was the first African-American woman to sing with the New York City Opera. In 1945 she performed the title role in *Madame Butterfly,* an opera by Italian composer Giacomo Puccini (1858-1924). In 1954 Williams went on to become the first African-American singer to appear on the stage of the Vienna State Opera. She was also the first African-American woman to become a regular member of an opera company in the United States. A soprano, she sang the role of Cio-Cio-San in Puccini's *Madame Butterfly* in 1946 and performed at the White House for President John F. Kennedy in 1960.

Source: Smith, Jessie Carney, *Black Firsts: 2,000 Years of Extraordinary Achievement.* Detroit: Gale Research, 1994, p. 21.

1946 ▪ **Billie Holiday** (1915-1959), an American performer of international renown, was the first female jazz singer to give a solo performance at New York Town Hall. Holiday also recorded hits with Benny Goodman, Count Basie, and Lester Young, and died as a result of her addiction to heroin in a New York City hospital in 1959.

Source: Uglow, Jennifer S., ed., *The Continuum Dictionary of Women's Biography.* New York: Continuum, 1989, p. 263.

1948 ▪ **Joan Cross** (1900-), English soprano and opera producer, was the founder and first director (until 1964) of the Opera School in London. (The school was renamed the National School of Opera in 1955.) Cross was also known as the first woman to sing the central female roles in a number of Benjamin Britten's works, including Ellen in *Peter Grimes* (1945), Mrs. Billows in *Albert Herring* (1947), Elizabeth in *Gloriana* (1953), and Mrs. Grose in *Turn of the Screw* (1954). Cross was a founding member of the English Opera Group.

Source: Uglow, Jennifer S., ed., *The Continuum Dictionary of Women's Biography.* New York: Continuum, 1989, p. 141.

1949 ▪ Edna White Chandler (1892-1992) was the first person to give a solo trumpet recital at Carnegie Hall in New York City. During her pioneering career as a female trumpeter and composer for that instrument, Chandler achieved a number of firsts: she was the first female cornetist to play a solo at Carnegie Hall (on May 3, 1902, at the age of nine); she played for the first transcontinental telephone transmission (in March 1915); she was the first person to perform George Antheil's "Trumpet Sonata," at Columbia University in 1954; and she was the first woman to write a treatise on trumpet playing, *On Taming the Devil's Tongue,* published in 1982.

Source: *Women of Note Quarterly: The Magazine of Historical and Contemporary Women Composers.* November, 1994, pp. 7-12.

c. 1950 ▪ Florence Kathleen Stobart (1925-), a British saxophonist, was the first female modern jazz musician to achieve international acclaim. Born in South Shields, Stobart played in town bands before going to London in 1942. For the next 40 years she played with leading British and American jazz musicians, and in 1974, she formed her own group called the "Kathy Stobart Quintet."

Source: Uglow, Jennifer S., ed., *The Continuum Dictionary of Women's Biography.* New York: Continuum, 1989, p. 518.

1952 ▪ Doriot Anthony Dwyer, an American musician, was the first woman to be first chair in a major orchestra. (First

Rothwell's Music

Evelyn Rothwell (1911-), an English oboist, was the first person to perform oboe works written specifically for her by such composers as Elizabeth Maconchy, Edmund Rubbra, and Gordon Jacob. Rothwell has written several books on oboe technique, and in 1971 was appointed a Professor at the Royal Academy of Music in London.

chair generally refers to the best musician of a particular instrument.) Dwyer was hired as first-chair flutist by the Boston Symphony Orchestra in 1952.

Source: O'Neil, Lois Decker, *The Women's Book of World Records and Achievements.* Garden City, New York: Doubleday, 1979, pp. 633-34.

1955 ▪ **Joan Sutherland** (1926-), the famous Australian coloratura soprano (a soprano with a light agile voice specializing in the elaborate embellishment of vocal lines), was the first person to sing the part of Jenifer in Michael Tippett's opera *The Midsummer Marriage,* at Covent Garden in London, England. Trained in Australia and at the Royal College of Music and Opera School in London, Sutherland quickly established an international reputation. She was known particularly for her interpretations of Gaetano Donizetti's *Lucia* and Vincenzo Bellini's *Norma.* Sutherland was named a Dame of the British Empire in 1979.

Source: Parry, Melanie, ed., *Larousse Dictionary of Women.* New York: Larousse Kingfisher Chambers, Inc., 1995, p. 630.

1955 ▪ **Marian Anderson** (1902-1993), an American singer, became the first African-American woman soloist to sing on the stage of the Metropolitan Opera House in New York City. Her debut role at the Met was as Ulrica in *Un Ballo in Maschera (The Masked Ball).* Born in 1902 in Philadelphia, Pennsylvania, Anderson began singing at age six in her church choir. Her solo career was launched when she was selected over 300 other singers in a contest, giving her the opportunity to sing with the New York Philharmonic Orchestra. Although praised by the famous conductor Arturo Toscanini as having a voice "heard once in a hundred years," Anderson was forced— because of racial bigotry—to perform in segregated concert halls. In 1939, the Daughters of the American Revolution (DAR) refused to allow Anderson to perform a concert in Philadelphia's Constitution Hall, claiming that the date had been previously booked. This action caused first lady Eleanor Roosevelt to resign her membership in the DAR, and to assist Anderson in performing an open-air concert on Easter Sunday at the Lincoln Memorial in Washington, D.C. More than

75,000 people attended the concert, where Anderson performed the United States National Anthem and *Ave Maria,* among other works.

Anderson's repertoire included both spirituals (religious songs) and opera. President Franklin Roosevelt later invited Anderson to perform for King George VI of England at the White House, making Anderson the first African-American artist to sing there. In 1961 Anderson sang at the inauguration of President John F. Kennedy, and in 1963, she won the Presidential Medal of Freedom.

Source: O'Neill, Lois Decker, ed., *The Women's Book of World Records and Achievements.* Garden City, New York: Doubleday, 1979, p. 620.

1958 ▪ Kirsten Malfrid Flagstad (1895-1962), a Norwegian soprano known primarily for her Wagnerian roles (opera roles written by composer Richard Wagner, 1813-1883), was the first person to serve as director of the Norwegian State Opera in Oslo, from 1958 until 1960. In 1935-1936 (the year of her New York City debut) Flagstad was also the first woman to sing the demanding roles of Sieglinde, Isolde, and Brunnhilde at the Metropolitan Opera.

Source: Uglow, Jennifer S., ed., *The Continuum Dictionary of Women's Biography.* New York: Continuum, 1989, pp. 206-07.

1958 ▪ Miriam Makeba (1932-) was the first black woman from South Africa to gain an international reputation as a singer. Makeba performed in her native country as a girl, but gained international attention with her performance in the anti-apartheid film *Come Back Africa* in 1958. In the 1960s, encouraged by American singer Harry Belafonte, she made several hit records in the United States. Makeba took an active role in the American civil rights movement, then settled in African Guinea in the 1970s.

Source: Uglow, Jennifer S., ed., *The Continuum Dictionary of Women's Biography.* New York: Continuum, 1989, pp. 349-50.

1959 ▪ Elizabeth Maconchy (1907-1994), an English composer, became the first woman to chair the Composers Guild of

Great Britain. She was remembered particularly for her chamber music and for her many stage works for children.

Source: Parry, Melanie, ed., *Larousse Dictionary of Women.* New York: Larousse Kingfisher Chambers, Inc., 1995, p. 426.

1960 ▪ **Liza Redfield** (1930-) became the first woman to conduct an orchestra on Broadway when she took over the podium of the stage musical *The Music Man.* After Herb Greene, the show's co-producer and conductor, decided to step down, Redfield led the 24-piece orchestra at the Majestic Theater in New York.

Source: McCullough, Joan, *First of All: Significant "Firsts" by American Women.* New York: Holt, 1980, p. 27.

1961 ▪ **Ruth Gipps** (1921-), an English composer and conductor, founded the Chanticleer Orchestra, in London, England. Gipps had a distinguished career in music, becoming musical director of the London Repertoire Orchestra in 1955 and a professor at the Royal College of Music in 1967.

Source: Uglow, Jennifer S., ed., *The Continuum Dictionary of Women's Biography.* New York: Continuum, 1989, p. 225.

1964 ▪ **Dorothy (Dottie) March West** (1932-1991) was the first female vocalist to win a country music Grammy award. She was honored in Nashville, Tennessee, in 1964 for her hit song "Here Comes My Baby."

Source: Read, Phyllis J., and Bernard L. Witlieb, *The Book of Women's Firsts.* New York: Random House, 1992, pp. 475-76.

1965 ▪ **Maria Callas** (1923-1977), the American-born Greek opera diva, was the first woman to sing the title role in Peggy Glanville-Hicks's *Sappho,* in San Francisco, California. Callas was widely considered one of the greatest dramatic sopranos of the twentieth century, known for both her voice and ability to act. Her retirement teaching career is chronicled in the play *Master Class.*

Source: Uglow, Jennifer S., ed., *The Continuum Dictionary of Women's Biography.* New York: Continuum, 1989, p. 103.

1966 ▪ **Leontyne Price** (1927-) was the first African-American singer to open a season at the Metropolitan Opera House in New York City. Her rich soprano voice is primarily associated with Guiseppe Verdi's work, but she was also the first woman to sing the leading role in Samuel Barber's *Antony and Cleopatra,* which had its debut as the first opera performed at the new Metropolitan Opera House at Lincoln Center in New York City in 1966. Price retired from the stage in 1985.

Source: Uglow, Jennifer S., ed., *The Continuum Dictionary of Women's Biography.* New York: Continuum, 1989, p. 440.

1967 ▪ **Jeanne Demessieux** (1921-1968), a French organist and composer, was the first woman to play the organ in Westminster Cathedral and Westminster Abbey, in 1967. Trained at the Paris Conservatory, she gave concerts throughout Europe and America.

Source: Uglow, Jennifer S., ed., *The Continuum Dictionary of Women's Biography.* New York: Continuum, 1989, p. 158.

1968 ▪ **Jacqueline du Pré** (1945-1987), an English cellist of international reputation, was the first person to perform Alexander Goehr's *Romanze.* A composition for cello and orchestra, the work was written for du Pré by Goehr. Du Pré's career was cut short by multiple sclerosis (a long-term, degenerative disease of the central nervous system).

Source: Parry, Melanie, ed., *Larousse Dictionary of Women.* New York: Larousse Kingfisher Chambers, Inc., 1995, p. 426.

1971 ▪ **Eve Queler** (1936-), an American conductor, was the first woman to conduct at Philharmonic Hall in New York City. Queler's career includes a number of firsts for women: she was the first woman to conduct at a major European opera house (in Barcelona, Spain, in 1974) and the first woman to serve as associate conductor of the U. S. Metropolitan Orchestra (in New York City in 1965). In 1967 she founded the Opera Orchestra of New York and served as its first director.

Source: Read, Phyllis J., and Bernard L. Witlieb, *The Book of Women's Firsts.* New York: Random House, 1992, pp. 352-53.

Sarah Caldwell was the first woman to conduct the Metropolitan Opera in New York City.

1976 ▪ **Sarah Caldwell** (1928-) was the first woman to conduct the Metropolitan Opera in New York City when she led the orchestra through a performance of Guiseppe Verdi's *La Traviata* with soprano Beverly Sills in the lead singing role. Known as an innovative and independent conductor, Caldwell founded the Opera Company of Boston in 1957. She also taught at the Berkshire Music Center from 1948 to 1952, headed the Opera Workshop Department at Boston University from 1952 to 1960, and, in 1983, became artistic director of the New Opera Company of Israel.

Source: Uglow, Jennifer S., ed., *The Continuum Dictionary of Women's Biography.* New York: Continuum, 1989, p. 103.

1977 ▪ **Xiaoying Zeng** (1929-) was the first woman to become a conductor in China. She first performed at the age of 14, then she received further training both in China and in Moscow, Russia, in the 1950s. On her return to China, Zeng soon established a national reputation, and in 1977 she became principal conductor at the Central Opera Theatre in Beijing.

Source: Uglow, Jennifer S., ed., *The Continuum Dictionary of Women's Biography.* New York: Continuum, 1989, pp. 599-600.

1979 ▪ **Beverly Sills** (1929-), an American soprano, was the first female opera singer appointed director of the New York City Opera. Sills joined the company as a performer in 1955 and created an international reputation. She did not make her debut at the rival Metropolitan Opera, however, until 1975. Sills was particularly noted for her performance as Manon in Jules Émile Frédéric Massenet's *Manon.*

Source: Parry, Melanie, ed., *Larousse Dictionary of Women.* New York: Larousse Kingfisher Chambers, Inc., 1995, p. 599.

1980 ▪ **Jane Alison Glover** (1949-), an English pianist and conductor, was the first woman to serve as director of the Glyndebourne Festival Opera. Glover joined the musical staff the previous year and, in 1984, became the first woman to serve as Festival Conductor.

Source: Parry, Melanie, ed., *Larousse Dictionary of Women.* Larousse Kingfisher Chambers, Inc., 1995, p. 599.

Women's Orchestra

In 1980 the San Francisco Women's Orchestra, conducted by Joanne Flecta, became the first women's orchestra to consist entirely of women and to perform only works composed by women.

1983 ▪ **Ellen Taaffe Zwilich** (1939-) was the first woman to win a Pulitzer Prize for music. Zwilich was honored for her *Symphony No. 1,* originally titled *Three Movements for Orchestra.* The composition was commissioned by the American Composers Orchestra. In 1975 Zwilich was also the first woman to earn a doctorate in music composition from the Julliard School.

Source: Read, Phyllis J., and Bernard L. Witlieb, *The Book of Women's Firsts.* New York: Random House, 1992, pp. 503-04.

1989 ▪ **Deborah Borda** (1949-) became the first woman to serve as executive director of a major U. S. symphony orchestra. Borda was appointed to this position with the Detroit Symphony Orchestra in Detroit, Michigan. Previously she had been with the San Francisco Symphony Orchestra for eight years; in 1990 she was named president of the Minnesota Orchestra. In 1991 Borda became managing director of the New York Philharmonic.

Source: Read, Phyllis J., and Bernard L. Witlieb, *The Book of Women's Firsts.* New York: Random House, 1992, p. 62.

1991 ▪ **Shulamit Ran** (1949-) was the first woman appointed composer-in-residence by a major U. S. orchestra. Ran took the position at the Chicago Symphony Orchestra, for which she composed full-length works and directed contemporary-music programming.

Source: Read, Phyllis J., and Bernard L. Witlieb, *The Book of Women's Firsts.* New York: Random House, 1992, pp. 357-58.

Woman Created Poetry Form

Marie de France (c. 1150-c. 1190) was the first poet to write in a European vernacular (a spoken native dialect or language). De France is credited with originating the *Lais*, which became a standard form of French poetry. Known for emphasizing the feminine perspective in her work, Marie also wrote short narratives and collected folktales, legends, and songs.

Literature

Early eleventh century ▪ Lady Shikibu

Murasaki (978-1030), a Japanese novelist and poet, wrote *Genji monogatari* ("The Tale of Genji"), the world's earliest surviving long novel. The work consists of 54 volumes, which Murasaki probably wrote over a period of several years for reading aloud at the emperor's court. The story of the romances and adventures of a royal family, *The Tale of Genji* is regarded by many critics as the finest work of Japanese literature and one of the greatest novels of the world.

Source: Uglow, Jennifer S., ed., *The Continuum Dictionary of Women's Biography.* New York: Continuum, 1989, p. 392.

Twelfth century ▪ Frau Ava (?-1127) was the first woman to compose biblical stories in German. Since the Bible was at that time written in Latin, Frau Ava's writings helped make Christian ideas available to the common people of Germany. Among her works are *The Life of Christ,* and *The Anti-Christ and The Last Judgment.* Frau Ava was also the first woman poet to write in the German language.

Source: Chicago, Judy, *The Dinner Party.* New York: Anchor, 1979, p. 136.

1436 ▪ Margery Kempe (c. 1373-?) was the author of *The Book of Margery Kempe,* one of the first autobiographies in English. An uneducated woman, Kempe dictated the story of her life to scribes (people who write things down) between 1432 and 1436. Kempe describes her experience with religious persecution as a Lolard (a follower of the English religious reformer John Wycliffe) as well as her travels to Jerusalem and Germany. After *The Book of Margery Kempe* was discovered in an English library in 1934, it was published in English (1936) and Middle English (1940). The book is now considered a classic in women's literature.

Source: Parry, Melanie, ed., *Larousse Dictionary of Women.* New York: Larousse Kingfisher Chambers, Inc., 1995, p. 364.

Early 1600s ▪ **Madeleine de Sable** (1598-1678), French writer, introduced and popularized the literary form known as the maxim. A maxim is the written condensation of life experiences in the form of an epigram (a brief poem or saying), and has become a characteristically French form. De Sable also presided over a literary salon in Paris.

Source: Chicago, Judy, *The Dinner Party*, New York: Anchor, 1979, p. 207.

1611 ▪ **Catherine de Vivonne, Marquise de Rambouillet** (1588-1665), a French noblewoman, founded an influential literary salon (gathering of notable persons) in Paris, France. For over 50 years she entertained important writers and intellectuals at her fashionable home, the Hôtel Rambouillet, where she presided over cultural conversations. Encouraging her guests to share ideas in a sophisticated and refined manner, de Rambouillet insisted on the equality of the sexes in her home. De Rambouillet's salon had a significant influence on the revival of classical literature in France during the seventeenth century.

Source: Magnusson, Magnus, *Larousse Biographical Dictionary*. Edinburgh: Larousse Kingfisher Chambers, Inc., 1994, p. 1213.

Katherine Fowler Philips's poems were printed secretly in 1663.

1650 ▪ **Anne Bradstreet** (1612-1672) was the first American woman to become a published poet. Without Bradstreet's knowledge, a collection of her verse called *The Tenth Muse Lately Sprung up in America* was published in London, England, by Bradstreet's brother-in-law. This collection was the first volume of original poetry to be written in New England.

Source: James, Edward T., and others, *Notable American Women, 1607-1950: A Biographical Dictionary*. Cambridge: Harvard University Press, 1971, pp. 222-23.

c. 1667 ▪ **Katherine Fowler Philips** (1631-1664) was the first female English poet whose work was published. Printed secretly in 1663, Philips's poems were publicly released in 1667, three years after her death. Known as "The matchless Orinda," Philips founded a London literary salon called the Society of Friendship, which was frequented by such important literary figures as British writer Jeremy Taylor (c. 1613-1667) and Welsh poet Henry Vaughan (1621-1695).

Source: Parry, Melanie, ed., *Larousse Dictionary of Women.* New York: Larousse Kingfisher Chambers, Inc., 1995, p. 525.

c. 1671 ▪ **Aphra Behn** (1640-1689) was the first professional female writer in England. Behn grew up in Surinam, where she lived with the family of the British governor of the colony. During the second Anglo-Dutch War (1664-1667), Behn worked without pay in Antwerp, Belgium, as a British spy. When she returned penniless to England, Behn briefly served time in debtors' prison before becoming a writer to support herself. Behn's plays and novels were highly popular in the late seventeenth century. Among her most notable works are the novel *Oroonoko* (1688) and the plays *The Forced Marriage* (1670) and *The Rover* (1678).

Source: Parry, Melanie, ed., *Larousse Dictionary of Women.* New York: Larousse Kingfisher Chambers, Inc., 1995, p. 66.

1682 ▪ **Mary White Rowlandson** (c. 1635-c. 1678) wrote the first book published in the American colonies. In *The Narrative of the Captivity and Restoration of Mrs. Mary Rowlandson—* which was anonymously published in Cambridge, Massachusetts—Rowlandson writes about being captured by Narragansett Indians in 1676. During her captivity she witnessed the death of one of her daughters. Rowlandson was ransomed after three months of marching through the wilderness.

Source: Read, Phyllis J., and Bernard L. Witlieb, *The Book of Women's Firsts.* New York: Random House, 1992, pp. 382-83.

1711 ▪ **Mary de la Rivière Manley** (1663-1724) was named the first female editor of *The Tory Examiner,* a political journal. The previous *Tory* editor was Jonathan Swift (1667-1745), the Anglo-Irish writer and satirist. Manley is also remembered for her plays and novels, as well as her collaboration with Swift on Tory (conservative political party) pamphlets.

Source: Magnusson, Magnus, *Larousse Biographical Dictionary.* Edinburgh: Larousse Kingfisher Chambers, Inc., 1994, p. 963.

1740s ▪ **Hannah Allgood Glasse** (1708-1770) wrote *The Art of Cooking Made Plain and Simple,* the first guide to cooking and meal planning for the English housewife. The tenth edition of the book was published in 1784, and it remained in print until 1824.

Source: Uglow, Jennifer S., ed., *The Continuum Dictionary of Women's Biography.* New York: Continuum, 1989, p. 227.

c. 1750 ▪ **Hedwig Nordenflycht** (1718-1763) became one of the first female Swedish writers to earn a living from her work. Nordenflycht gained national prominence with her poems, which she published from 1744 to 1750 in "yearbooks" under the title *Qvinligit Tankespel* ("A Woman's Thoughts"). Nordenflycht was also a leading member of the "Society of Thought Builders," a literary group in Stockholm.

Source: Parry, Melanie, ed., *Larousse Dictionary of Women.* New York: Larousse Kingfisher Chambers, Inc., 1995, p. 497.

1769 ▪ **Frances Brooke** (1723-1789), considered the first Canadian novelist, published *The History of Emily Montague.* Through the story of a woman living in Quebec during the mid-eighteenth century, the novel explored the role of women in Canada and England. Brooke also wrote plays and translated Italian and French works into English.

Source: Parry, Melanie, ed., *Larousse Dictionary of Women.* New York: Larousse Kingfisher Chambers, Inc., 1995, p. 102.

1783 ▪ **Ekaterina Romanovna Dashkova** (1743-1810), a Russian princess and educator, was appointed the first president of the Russian Academy. (The academy was originally founded for the preservation and study of the Russian language.) In the same year, Dashkova also became the director of the Academy of Arts and Sciences in St. Petersburg. A favorite of Empress Catherine II (also called "Catherine the Great"; reigned 1762-1796), Dashkova had helped bring about Catherine's rise to power by dressing as a soldier and leading troops in the overthrow of the empress's husband, Peter III, in 1762. Dashkova then asked to be put in command of the Imperial Guards, but Catherine denied her request.

Source: Uglow, Jennifer S., ed., *The Continuum Dictionary of Women's Biography.* New York: Continuum, 1989, p. 148.

1783 ▪ Phillis Wheatley (1753-1784) became the first published African-American poet with *Poems on Various Subjects, Religious and Moral.* When she was eight years old, Wheatley arrived in the United States aboard a slave ship; she was purchased immediately by Mrs. John Wheatley, who taught Phillis to read and write. Wheatley's *Collected Works* was published in 1988.

Source: Parry, Melanie, ed., *Larousse Dictionary of Women.* New York: Larousse Kingfisher Chambers, Inc., 1995, p. 686.

1789 ▪ Charlotte Brooke (1740-1793), an Anglo-Irish scholar, published *Reliques of Irish Poetry.* A collection of translations of Irish songs, odes (poems of praise), elegies (tributes to the dead), and lyrics (songs), *Reliques* is considered the first work of Irish literary scholarship. Brooke's book was an important contribution to the revival of Irish-language literature, which had been suppressed by the British government since the seventeenth century. In addition to *Reliques,* Brooke wrote *School for Christians* (1791) and *Account of Henry Brooke* (1792), a biography of her father, who was a well-known author and playwright.

Source: Deane, Seamus, ed., *The Field Day Anthology of Irish Writing.* Derry, Northern Ireland: Field Day Publications, 1994, pp. 980-81.

c. 1791 ▪ Hannah Adams (1755-1831) was the first American woman to support herself by writing. Adams's first publications were *View of Religions: An Alphabetical Compendium of the Various Sects* (1784) and *A Summary History of New England* (1799). By 1791 the second edition of *Views of Religion,* which was also printed in Great Britain, was successful enough to provide Adams with a comfortable income. She also wrote three religious works: *The Truth and Excellence of the Christian Religion Exhibited* (1804), *History of the Jews* (1812), and *Letters on the Gospels* (1824). Adams's autobiography was published after her death in order to provide a small income for her sister.

Source: James, Edward T., and others, *Notable American Women, 1607-1950: A Biographical Dictionary.* Cambridge: Harvard University Press, 1971, pp. 9-11.

1808 ▪ Jane Aiken (1764-1832) was the first American woman to print an edition of the Bible. Aiken was a professional printer, bookbinder, and bookseller in Philadelphia, Pennsylvania. In 1808 she published the four-volume Thompson Bible, the first English translation of the Septuagint (the Greek version of the Jewish Scriptures).

Source: James, Edward T., and others, *Notable American Women, 1607-1950: A Biographical Dictionary.* Cambridge: Harvard University Press, 1971, p. 26.

Hannah Adams was the first American woman to support herself through writing.

1826 ▪ Lydia Maria Child (1802-1880), an American writer, founded *Juvenile Miscellany,* the first American periodical for children. Child is also known for her novels, *Hobomok* (1824) and *The Rebels* (1825), which described life in the American colonies. A committed social and political reformer, Child published essays on abolition (the effort to end slavery) and women's rights which had a major impact on American life in the mid-nineteenth century.

Source: Read, Phyllis J., and Bernard L. Witlieb, *The Book of Women's Firsts.* New York: Random House, 1992, pp. 88-89.

1839 ▪ Caroline Matilda Stansbury Kirkland (1801-1864), an American writer, was the first author to publish realistic fiction about the American frontier. Kirkland based her novels and stories on the experiences of her family, pioneers in Livingston

County, Michigan, from 1836 to 1843. Kirkland's first novel, *A New Home-Who'll Follow? or, Glimpses of Western Life,* was published in 1839. Her second book, *Forest Life,* appeared in 1842. Throughout the 1850s Kirkland's work continued to appear in many eastern periodicals.

Source: James, Edward T., and others, *Notable American Women, 1607-1950: A Biographical Dictionary.* Cambridge: Harvard University Press, 1971, pp. 337-39.

1854 ▪ Charlotte Helen Spence (1825-1910) wrote *Clare Morrison: A Tale of South Australia During the Gold Fever,* the first novel about Australian life written by a woman. While also working as a journalist for newspapers in South Australia and Victoria, Spence continued to write fiction for the next 30 years. She also founded the Effective Voting League (1895) and, in 1897, became the first woman in Australia to run for elected office.

Source: Uglow, Jennifer S., ed., *The Continuum Dictionary of Women's Biography.* New York: Continuum, 1989, pp. 509-10.

c. 1860 ▪ Sappho Leontias (1832-1900), a Greek feminist and teacher, was founder and first editor of the literary periodical *Euridice.* In addition to encouraging women to contribute, Leontias emphasized works written in vernacular Greek (the commonly spoken form of the language). Committed to the education of women as a means of improving their status in society, she headed girls' schools on the Greek islands of Samos and Smyrna for many years. Leontias was also a renowned lecturer and translator of classical literature.

Source: Uglow, Jennifer S., ed., *The Continuum Dictionary of Women's Biography.* New York: Continuum, 1989, p. 323.

1867 ▪ Lucy McKim Garrison (1842-1877) was the first person to collect American slave songs. After visiting the South Carolina Sea Islands in 1862, Garrison began writing down the songs she heard sung by freed slaves who lived on the islands.

With the assistance of William Francis Allen and Charles Pickard Ware, Garrison annotated these lyrics (provided critical or explanatory notes). *Slave Songs of the United States,* the first collection of its kind, was published in 1867.

Source: Uglow, Jennifer S., ed., *The Continuum Dictionary of Women's Biography.* New York: Continuum, 1989, p. 220.

1873 ▪ Mary Elizabeth Mapes Dodge (1831-1905), an American author and editor, was the first editor of the highly influential children's magazine, *St. Nicholas.* Publishing the work of leading American and British writers and artists, Dodge made the magazine an impressive literary and financial success. Dodge is also remembered as the author of *Hans Brinker; or, The Silver Skates* (1858), a classic children's book.

Source: James, Edward T., and others, *Notable American Women, 1607-1950: A Biographical Dictionary.* Cambridge: Harvard University Press, 1971, pp. 495-96.

1878 ▪ Anna Katherine Green (1846-1935), an American mystery writer, published *The Leavenworth Case,* the first detective story written by a woman. An immediate success and a long-time best-seller, the book featured the adventures of detective Ebenezer Gryce. Gryce and his occasional assistant, Amelia Butterworth, appeared in several of Green's other novels. Green also created the female detective Violet Strange.

Source: Uglow, Jennifer S., ed., *The Continuum Dictionary of Women's Biography.* New York: Continuum, 1989, p. 235.

1890 ▪ Mabel Loomis Todd, an American author, coedited and published the first collection of poems by Emily Dickinson (1830-1886). A neighbor of Dickinson in Amherst, Massachusetts, Todd had an interesting friendship with the poet. Although Todd frequently played the piano and sang in Dickinson's home, the two women never met face to face. A famous eccentric and recluse (one who avoids the company of other people), Dickinson stayed out of sight while Todd performed. In gratitude for the entertainment, Dickinson sent Todd numerous poems. In 1890 Todd and Thomas Wentworth Higginson coedited and published *The Poems,* a collection of

Frances Ellen Watkins Harper wrote Iola Leroy, or Shadows Uplifted, the first novel by an African American.

several of the more than eight hundred of Dickinson's poems that were discovered after her death in 1886. The collection was so successful that Todd and Higginson released two more series in 1891 and 1896.

Source: James, Edward T., and others, *Notable American Women, 1607-1950: A Biographical Dictionary.* Cambridge: Harvard University Press, 1971, pp. 468-69.

1892 ▪ Frances Ellen Watkins Harper (1825-1911), an American writer, published *Iola Leroy, or Shadows Uplifted,* the first novel by an African American. The daughter of freed slaves, Harper worked for the abolition (elimination) of slavery. Following the Civil War (1861-1865), she campaigned for African-American civil rights, helping to found the National Association of Colored Women in 1896.

Source: James, Edward T., and others, *Notable American Women, 1607-1950: A Biographical Dictionary.* Cambridge: Harvard University Press, 1971, pp. 136-37.

1894 ▪ Constance Garnett (1861-1946), an English translator, was the first person to translate major Russian writers into English. Garnett began teaching herself Russian while recovering from a difficult childbirth in 1892. Her translations of the novels of Ivan Turgenev (1818-1883), Leo Tolstoy (1828-1910), Fyodor Dostoyevsky (1821-1881), Anton Chekhov (1860-1904), and Nikolay Gogol (1809-1852) appeared between 1894 and 1928.

Source: Parry, Melanie, ed., *Larousse Dictionary of Women.* New York: Larousse Kingfisher Chambers, Inc., 1995, p. 259.

1908 ▪ Julia Ward Howe (1819-1910), an American writer and reformer, was the first woman elected to the American Academy of Arts and Letters. (She was also the only female member until 1930.) Howe is remembered as the author of "The Battle Hymn of the Republic" (1862), which was popular in the North during the Civil War (1861-1865).

Source: Read, Phyllis J., and Bernard L. Witlieb, *The Book of Women's Firsts.* New York: Random House, 1992, p. 218.

Julia Ward Howe is remembered as the author of "The Battle Hymn of the Republic," a popular song in the North during the Civil War.

1908 ▪ **Ethel Florence Lindesay Robertson** (1870-1946), an Australian author whose male pseudonym (pen name) was Henry Handel Richardson, published *Maurice Guest*, widely considered the first novel in England to feature homosexuality as a major theme.

Source: Uglow, Jennifer S., ed., *The Continuum Dictionary of Women's Biography.* New York: Continuum, 1989, p. 457.

1909 ▪ **Selma Lagerlöf** (1858-1940), a Swedish novelist, was the first woman to receive the Nobel Prize for literature. Lagerlöf led a sheltered childhood because she was disabled. Most of her novels are based on the tales and legends of Värmland, where she grew up. Among Lagerlöf's best-known works are a series of three novels titled *The Rings of the Lowenskolds* (1931) and the children's classic *The Wonderful Adventures of*

Selma Lagerlöf was the first woman to receive the Nobel Prize for literature.

Nils (1906-1907). Lagerlöf used her Nobel Prize money to buy back her childhood home, which her family had been forced to sell in the late nineteenth century. She was the first woman to be inducted into the Swedish Academy (1914).

Source: Parry, Melanie, ed., *Larousse Dictionary of Women.* New York: Larousse Kingfisher Chambers, Inc., 1995, p. 380.

1910 ▪ **Anna Akhmatova** (1889-1967), a Russian poet, cofounded the Acmeist movement with her husband Nicholas Gumilov. The Acmeists wrote poetry that emphasized Russian traditions; the group was reacting against Symbolism (a modern poetry movement that used symbols to represent ideas). Gumilov was executed for being a counter-revolutionary (a person who did not support the Communist Revolution of 1917) in 1921. Although Akhmatova had remained neutral during the revolution, she was officially forbidden to publish her work. In the 1950s she was restored to favor by the government, and she continued writing poetry. *The Complete Poems of Anna Akhmatova* was published in 1993.

Source: Parry, Melanie, ed., *Larousse Dictionary of Women.* New York: Larousse Kingfisher Chambers, Inc., 1995, p. 11.

1912 ▪ **Harriet Monroe** (1860-1936) founded *Poetry: Magazine of Verse,* the first journal devoted solely to modern poetry, in Chicago, Illinois. A champion of modernist causes (attempts to break from the past and establish new artistic forms), Monroe was the first person to publish the works of Imagist poets, including Hilda Doolittle (1886-1961), Richard Aldington (1892-1962), F. S. Flint (1885-1960), and Ezra Pound (1885-1972), who served for a period as her "foreign correspondent."

Source: James, Edward T., and others, *Notable American Women, 1607-1950: A Biographical Dictionary.* Cambridge: Harvard University Press, 1971, pp. 562-64.

c. 1912 ▪ **Margit Kaffka** (1880-1918) was the first recognized female Hungarian writer. A feminist and pacifist (a person who is strongly opposed to war), Kaffka started writing fiction in 1912. In her pioneering work, she explored the thoughts and emotions of her main characters, particularly women who were unhappy with their traditional roles. Kaffka's novels are still popular in Hungary. Among the best known are *Mária évei* (1913; "Mary's Years"), *Két nyár* (1916; "Two Summers," and *Hangyaboly* (1917; "Anthill"). Kaffka died during the influenza (flu) epidemic that followed World War I (1914-1918).

Source: Uglow, Jennifer S., ed., *The Continuum Dictionary of Women's Biography.* New York: Continuum, 1989, p. 290.

Japanese Novelist Honored

Higuchi Ichiyo (1872-1896), a Japanese novelist known for her moving portraits of the emotional life of women and children, was the first and only woman represented in the Museum of Contemporary Literature in Yokohama, Japan. Ichiyo grew up in poverty in Tokyo and died at an early age of tuberculosis.

1915 ▪ **Dorothy Richardson** (1873-1957) originated the modernist "stream-of-consciousness" novel with *Painted Roofs.* (Stream of consciousness is a literary technique by which the writer "records" thoughts as they occur to the character in a story or novel.) *Painted Roofs* was the first of a 12-volume series titled *Pilgrimage,* which Richardson completed in 1938. Stream of consciousness was later made famous by British writer Virginia Woolf (1882-1941).

Source: Uglow, Jennifer S., ed., *The Continuum Dictionary of Women's Biography.* New York: Continuum, 1989, pp. 456-57.

1916 ▪ **Alfonsina Storni** (1892-1938), an Argentine poet, published her first volume of verse, *La inquietud del rosal* ("The Solitude of the Rosebush"). Storni is considered the first writer in Argentina to compose from a woman's point of view. Among her other works are *Languidez* (1921; "Langor"), which won several prizes; and *Hombre pequeñito* ("Little Man"), her most famous poem, which is about hatred of men.

Source: Chicago, Judy, *The Dinner Party.* New York: Anchor, 1979, p. 210.

1916 ▪ **Maud Howe Elliot** (1854-1948) and **Laura Howe Richards** (1850-1943) were the first women to win the

Pulitzer Prize for biography. The duo was honored for a biography of their mother, American reformer and writer **Julia Ward Howe** (1819-1910), which was published in 1915.

Source: Read, Phyllis J., and Bernard L. Witlieb, *The Book of Women's Firsts.* New York: Random House, 1992, p. 143.

1917 ▪ Virginia Woolf (1882-1941), a British writer, cofounded Hogarth Press in London, England, with her husband Leonard Woolf (1880-1969). Hogarth published nearly all of Woolf's work as well as that of friends, among them T. S. Eliot (1888-1965) and Katherine Mansfield (1888-1923). Woolf is particularly remembered for her novels, which utilize stream-of-consciousness techniques. (Stream of consciousness is a literary device by which the writer "records" thoughts as they occur to the character being depicted.) Considered one of the greatest novelists of the twentieth century, Woolf is most famous for *Mrs. Dalloway* (1925), *To the Lighthouse* (1927), and *The Waves* (1931). She also wrote two important feminist book-length essays, *A Room of One's Own* (1929) and *Three Guineas* (1938).

Source: Uglow, Jennifer S., ed., *The Continuum Dictionary of Women's Biography.* New York: Continuum, 1989, pp. 589-90.

1917 ▪ Katherine Mansfield (1888-1923), a New Zealand short-story writer, was the first woman to have work published by the prestigious Hogarth Press in London, England. (Hogarth Press was founded by novelist Virginia Woolf (1882-1941) and her husband Leonard Woolf (1880-1969). Mansfield's story collection, *Prelude,* which is based on her childhood in New Zealand, is considered her best work.

Source: Uglow, Jennifer S., ed., *The Continuum Dictionary of Women's Biography.* New York: Continuum, 1989, pp. 352-53.

1921 ▪ Edith Newbold Jones Wharton (1862-1937), an American novelist, was the first woman to receive the Pulitzer Prize for fiction. Wharton was honored for her novel *The Age of Innocence* (1920; *The Age of Innocence* served as the basis for a 1993 motion picture directed by Martin Scorsese). She was also the author of more than fifty other works, including travel books and poetry. Among Wharton's other best-known novels are *The House of Mirth* (1905) and *Ethan Frome* (1911), also adapted to film (1992).

Source: James, Edward T., and others, *Notable American Women, 1607-1950: A Biographical Dictionary*. Cambridge: Harvard University Press, 1971, pp. 570-73.

1921 ▪ **Zona Gale** (1874-1938), an American playwright and novelist, was the first woman to win the Pulitzer Prize for drama. Gale was honored for her play *Miss Lulu Bett,* which depicted life in the Midwest and opened on Broadway in 1920. Among Gale's other works are the novel *Portage, Wisconsin* (1928), which was set in the author's hometown, and *Yellow Gentians and Blue* (1927), a collection of poetry.

Source: Read, Phyllis J., and Bernard L. Witlieb, *The Book of Women's Firsts.* New York: Random House, 1992, p. 171.

Edith Wharton was the first woman to receive the Pulitzer Prize for fiction.

1923 ▪ **Edna St. Vincent Millay** (1892-1950), an American poet, was the first woman to receive the Pulitzer Prize for poetry. Millay was honored for her fourth book of verse, *The Ballad of the Harp-Weaver* (1923). She is remembered particularly for her sonnets (a form of verse consisting of 14 lines and a fixed rhyme pattern).

Source: Read, Phyllis J., and Bernard L. Witlieb, *The Book of Women's Firsts.* New York: Random House, 1992, pp. 290-91.

1926 ▪ **Marianne Craig Moore** (1887-1972), an American poet, was the first woman to serve as editor of *The Dial.* Based in New York City, this publication was an important literary journal that published modernist poetry (new forms of verse that rejected traditional patterns). Moore is credited with giving the journal an international and lasting influence.

Source: Magnusson, Magnus, *Larousse Biographical Dictionary*. Edinburgh: Larousse Kingfisher Chambers, Inc., 1994, p. 1037.

Pearl S. Buck was the first American woman to win a Nobel Prize for literature.

1928 ▪ **(Marguerite) Radclyffe Hall** (1886-1943), a British author, published *The Well of Loneliness,* the first book judged obscene because of its sympathetic portrayal of lesbian love (or love between two women). Hall's novel was found obscene by an English judge in a famous London trial. Among Hall's defenders were British writers Virginia Woolf (1882-1941) and Richard Aldington (1892-1962).

Source: Chicago, Judy, *The Dinner Party.* New York: Anchor, 1979, p. 205.

1931 ▪ **Victoria Ocampo** (1890-1978), an Argentine writer, founded the important literary periodical *Sur* in Buenos Aires. Ocampo is remembered for her vigorous support of modern writers in Argentina, most notably Jorge Luis Borges (1899-1986). Through her feminist interests and her friendships with prominent figures such as the modern British writer Virginia Woolf (1882-1941), Ocampo introduced Argentine readers to new ideas in contemporary literature.

Source: Uglow, Jennifer S., ed., *The Continuum Dictionary of Women's Biography.* New York: Continuum, 1989, p. 410.

1935 ▪ **Pearl Sydenstricker Buck** (1892-1973), an American author, was the first American woman to win a Nobel Prize for literature. Buck received this honor in recognition of her novels that vividly depicted Chinese life, the most famous of which was *The Good Earth,* published in 1931.

Source: Magnusson, Magnus, *Larousse Biographical Dictionary.* Edinburgh: Larousse Kingfisher Chambers, Inc., 1994, p. 224.

c. 1935 ▪ **Bing Xin (Xie Wanying)** (1902-) was the first twentieth-century Chinese woman to become a successful writer. After publishing her first work at the age of 17, Bing Xin became known for her poetry and prose for both children and adults. By 1935 her famous collection of stories for children, *Letters to Young Readers,* had gone through 20 printings. Among Bing Xin's other works are *After Returning Home* (1958) and *We Awakened Spring* (1960). Her subjects included social oppression, particularly among women. Bing Xin was named vice chairman of the Chinese Federation of Literature and Art in 1979 and was elected to the Praesidium of the Central Committee (the main governing body in China). Since 1989 she has served as honorary president of the Prose Society.

Source: Uglow, Jennifer S., ed., *The Continuum Dictionary of Women's Biography.* New York: Continuum, 1989, p. 66.

1939 ▪ **(Margaret) Storm Jameson** (1891-1986), an English writer, was the first woman to serve as president of the British section of PEN, an international society of authors. Known for her journalism as well as her novels, Jameson served throughout World War II (1939-1945). During this period, in addition to supervising the club's regular activities, she worked on behalf of refugee writers from war-torn European countries.

Source: Uglow, Jennifer S., ed., *The Continuum Dictionary of Women's Biography.* New York: Continuum, 1989, pp. 280-81.

Gabriela Mistral was noted for her children's literature, much of which was translated into English in the book Frogs.

1945 ▪ **Gabriela Mistral (Lucila Godoy de Acayaga)** (1889-1957), founder of the modern poetry movement in Chile, received the Nobel Prize for literature. A teacher, Mistral also worked in the Chilean government. She was noted particularly for her children's literature, much of which was translated into English in the book *Frogs* (1972).

Source: Parry, Melanie, ed., *Larousse Dictionary of Women.* New York: Larousse Kingfisher Chambers, Inc., 1995, p. 464.

1945 ▪ **Louise Bogan** (1897-1970), an American poet, was the first woman appointed by the Library of Congress in Washing-

French novelist Colette was the first woman elected to the Académie Goncourt in France.

ton, D.C., as consultant in poetry in English. A distinguished poet, Bogan also wrote literary criticism and an autobiography, *Journey Around My Room,* which was published posthumously (after Bogan's death) in 1981.

Source: Read, Phyllis J., and Bernard L. Witlieb, *The Book of Women's Firsts.* New York: Random House, 1992, pp. 58-59.

1945 ▪ Sidonie Gabrielle Claudine Colette (1873-1954), a French novelist, was the first woman elected to the Académie Goncourt. Colette published her early novels under the name of her first husband, Henri Gauthier-Villars. After the couple divorced in 1904, Colette continued writing under her last name. She became famous not only for her novels and stories about animals and rural life, but also for her flamboyant personality. She had several love affairs and marriages and worked as an actress, editor, newspaper columnist, and beautician. Among her best-known novels are *Chéri* (1920) and *La fin de Chéri* (1926; "The Last of Chéri"). Beloved by the French people, Colette was given a state funeral attended by thousands of mourners.

Source: Briggs, Asa, *A Dictionary of 20th Century Biography.* Oxford, England: Oxford University Press, 1992, pp. 128-29.

1950 ▪ Gwendolyn Brooks (1917-), an American poet, was the first African-American writer to win a Pulitzer Prize for poetry. Brooks was honored for her second volume of verse, *Annie Allen,* which tells the story of an African-American woman's experience with racism. Her autobiography, *Report from Part One,* appeared in 1971.

Source: Parry, Melanie, ed., *Larousse Dictionary of Women.* New York: Larousse Kingfisher Chambers, Inc., p. 103.

1959 ▪ Lorraine Hansberry (1930-1965), an American playwright, was the first African-American writer to have a play produced on Broadway in New York City. Her work, *A Raisin* *in the Sun,* opened in 1959. The drama explores the problems faced by an African-American family when they try to move into a white neighborhood. The first production by a black writer to receive the New York Drama Critics Circle Award, *A Raisin in the Sun* was also adapted as a musical, *Raisin,* in 1973. Hansberry's other plays include *The Sign in Sidney Brustein's Window* (1964).

Source: Parry, Melanie, ed., *Larousse Dictionary of Women.* New York: Larousse Kingfisher Chambers, Inc., 1995, p. 298.

1960 ▪ **Esther Forbes** (1891-1967), an American novelist and historian, was honored for her life's work when she became the first woman elected to the American Antiquarian Society. The author of many historical novels, Forbes is perhaps best known for her children's novel, *Johnny Tremain* (1943).

Source: Read, Phyllis J., and Bernard L. Witlieb, *The Book of Women's Firsts,* New York: Random House, 1992, pp. 161-62.

1960 ▪ **Hilda Doolittle** (1886-1961), an American writer known as "H. D.," was the first woman to receive an award from the American Academy of Arts and Letters. Doolittle was recognized for her contributions to literature, beginning with her Imagist poems in 1912. (The Imagists wrote poems in free verse, using clear, precise words to evoke ideas and emotions.) H. D. is known for her war poems in *Trilogy* (1944-1946) and her epic poem *Helen in Egypt* (1961). Her autobiographical novel, *Bid Me to Live,* was published in 1960.

Source: Magnusson, Magnus, *Larousse Biographical Dictionary.* Edinburgh: Larousse Kingfisher Chambers, Inc., 1994, p. 431.

1963 ▪ **Barbara Wertheim Tuchman** (1912-1989) was the first woman to receive the Pulitzer Prize for general nonfiction. Tuchman was honored for *The Guns of August,* a history of the period before World War I (1914-1918). In recognition of her illustrious career, Tuchman was the first woman to be elected president of the American Academy and Institute of Arts and Letters in 1979.

Source: Read, Phyllis J., and Bernard L. Witlieb, *The Book of Women's Firsts.* New York: Random House, 1992, p. 452.

1967 ▪ **Anita Brookner** (1928-), an English novelist and art historian, was the first woman to hold the Slade Professorship at Cambridge University in England. An international authority on eighteenth-century painting, Brookner was the author of *Watteau* (1968), *The Genius of the Future* (1971), and *Jacques-Louis David* (1981). She won the Booker Prize for literary achievement for her novel *Hotel du Lac* in 1986. Brookner's other works of fiction include *Family and Friends* (1985) and *Friends from England* (1987).

Source: Parry, Melanie, ed., *Larousse Dictionary of Women.* New York: Larousse Kingfisher Chambers, Inc., pp. 102- 03.

c. 1971 ▪ **Bessie Head** (1937-1986), a South African- born Botswanian novelist, was considered the first "colored" South African writer to establish an international reputation. The daughter of a white mother and a native African father, Head was a victim of apartheid (racial segregation) and fled South Africa for Botswana (a republic in south central Africa) in her early twenties. After settling in Botswana Head wrote novels about apartheid. Among her best-known works are *When Rain Clouds Gather* (1969), *Maru* (1971), and *Question of Power* (1973).

Source: Parry, Melanie, ed., *Larousse Dictionary of Women.* New York: Larousse Kingfisher Chambers, Inc., 1995, p. 307.

1972 ▪ **Carmen Thérèse Callil** (1938-), an Australian publisher, founded Virago Press with Ursula Owen and Rosie Boycott in London, England. A powerful force in modern British feminism, Virago Press promoted the works of such writers as American novelists Maya Angelou (1928-) and Edith Wharton (1862-1937), and the Canadian novelist Margaret Atwood (1939-).

Source: Uglow, Jennifer S., ed., *The Continuum Dictionary of Women's Biography.* New York: Continuum, 1989, pp. 103-04.

1980 ▪ **Marguerite Yourcenar** (1903-1987), a Belgian-born French writer, was the first woman writer elected to the prestigious Académie Française. She was honored for her long literary career, during which she wrote novels, plays, poems, and essays. Yourcenar's most famous works include *Mémoires d'Hadrien* (1951; "Memoirs of Hadrian") and *L'oeuvre au noir* (1968; "The Abyss").

Source: Read, Phyllis J., and Bernard L. Witlieb, *The Book of Women's Firsts.* New York: Random House, 1992, p. 501.

1983 ▪ Alice Walker (1944-), an American novelist, was the first African-American woman to receive a Pulitzer Prize for fiction. Walker was honored for her novel *The Color Purple* (1982), which also won the American Book Award in 1983. The story of two sisters living in the segregated American South, *The Color Purple* was made into a successful motion picture in 1985.

Source: Parry, Melanie, ed., *Larousse Dictionary of Women.* New York: Larousse Kingfisher Chambers, Inc., 1995, pp. 672-73.

1993 ▪ Toni Morrison (1931-), an American novelist, was the first African-American woman to win the Nobel Prize for literature. Morrison also received a Pulitzer Prize in 1988 for her novel *Beloved* (1987).

Source: Parry, Melanie, ed., *Larousse Dictionary of Women.* New York: Larousse Kingfisher Chambers, Inc., 1995, pp. 479-80.

1993 ▪ Maya Angelou (1928-), an African-American poet, was the first female poet to read from her work at the inauguration of a U.S. president. For the inauguration (official swearing in) of President Bill Clinton (elected in 1992) she read "On the Pulse of Morning," a piece she composed especially for the occasion. Angelou is perhaps best known for her award-winning autobiography, *I Know Why the Caged Bird Sings* (1970).

Source: Parry, Melanie, ed., *Larousse Dictionary of Women.* New York: Larousse Kingfisher Chambers, Inc., 1995, p. 23.

1993 ▪ Rita Dove (1952-), an American poet, was the first African-American named poet laureate (most important or respected poet) of the United States. At age 40, Dove was also the youngest person ever chosen for the post, which she held until 1995. In 1987 Dove received a Pulitzer Prize for her book of poetry, *Thomas and Beulah* (1986), the story of the lives of

her grandparents. Dove's most recent works include the novel *Through the Ivory Gate* (1992) and the verse drama *Darker Face of the Earth* (1994).

Source: Parry, Melanie, ed., *Larousse Dictionary of Women.* New York: Larousse Kingfisher Chambers, Inc., 1995, p. 196.

Fashion Design

c. 1150 B.C. ▪ According to legend, the Greek woman **Arachne** was the first weaver and cloth designer. Arachne could make nets and weave cloth so beautifully that her work inspired the jealousy of the goddess Athena, who destroyed it. When Arachne hanged herself in despair, Athena took pity on her and turned her into a spider.

Source: Chicago, Judy, *The Dinner Party.* New York: Anchor, 1979, p. 112.

In 1920 Coco Chanel introduced the very popular chemise dress.

1920 ▪ **Coco Chanel** (1883-1971), a French couturier (fashion designer), was the first person to introduce the chemise dress (a loose, straight-hanging dress), in Paris. In 1924 Chanel created the famous perfume, Chanel No.5.

Source: Uglow, Jennifer S., ed., *The Continuum Dictionary of Women's Biography.* New York: Continuum, 1989, pp. 117-18.

1931 ▪ **Elsa Schiaparelli** (1890-1973), an Italian-born fashion designer, was the first woman to design clothing with padded shoulders. Settling in Paris, France, in the 1920s, she showed her innovation during the 1931-32 fashion season. In 1939 Schiaparelli introduced her trademark color, "shocking pink."

Source: Uglow, Jennifer S., ed., *The Continuum Dictionary of Women's Biography.* New York: Continuum, 1989, p. 483.

c. 1943 ▪ **Claire McCardell,** an American fashion designer, invented the stretch leotard and other practical items. World War II (1939-1945) greatly contributed to McCardell's design influence. Because of labor and material shortages, McCardell's ready-to-wear line became popular with women who had entered the labor force. Her first design, the leotard, was named after the nineteenth-century French acrobat Jules Leotard. It was originally made for female college students who needed to stay warm in dormitories that were not heated due to wartime fuel shortages.

McCardell also introduced the idea of "separates" so that women on a limited budget could mix and match clothing items. Her breakthrough garment was the tent dress modeled after a Moroccan robe. At first ignored by fashion buyers, the tent dress caught on only when a buyer saw it hanging in McCardell's office; the buyer ordered one hundred copies. "The Monastic," as it was named, helped create the casual and functional post-war "American Look."

Source: Vare, Ethlie Ann, and Greg Ptacek, *Mothers of Invention: From the Bra to the Bomb, Forgotten Women and Their Unforgettable Ideas.* New York: William Morrow, 1988, pp. 74-76.

1965 ▪ **Mary Quant** (1934-), a British designer, popularized the miniskirt (a woman's short skirt). Working in London, England, in the 1960s, she became internationally famous and produced over twenty collections a year by the end of the decade. Since 1970 Quant has been a member of the fashion establishment and has diversified her interests, moving from clothing to cosmetics.

Source: O'Neill, Lois Decker, *The Women's Book of World Records and Achievements.* Garden City, New York: Doubleday, 1979, p. 249.

1970 ▪ **Anna Kalso,** a Danish shoe designer, introduced the "Earth Shoe." Kaslo got the idea for her comfortable shoe in the 1950s while traveling in Africa. Observing the easy movement of people who walked barefoot, Kalso noted the impression their feet left in soft soil or sand: the heel print was lower than that made by the toes. She then compared the bare-foot print to the Western practice of building up the heels of shoes. She concluded that Westerners were forcing their bodies into unnatural postures while walking. Using the natural footprint as a model, Kalso designed the Earth Shoe with a large,

Mary Quant, a British designer, popularized the miniskirt during the 1960s.

chunky sole that cushioned the heel at a level below the ball of the foot. Although the result was unattractive by Western standards, the shoe was an immediate success.

Source: Vare, Ethlie Ann, and Greg Ptacek, *Mothers of Invention: From the Bra to the Bomb, Forgotten Women and Their Unforgettable Ideas.* New York: William Morrow, 1988, p. 78.

1973 ▪ **Rei Kawakubo** (1942-), a Japanese fashion designer, established "Comme des Garçons," her own brand of clothing. One of the most influential fashion designers of the late twentieth century, she is known as the founder of "raven fashion." Kawakubo's work is untraditional and emphasizes such elements as holes, asymmetry, rug-like textures, and simple lines.

Source: Parry, Melanie, ed., *Larousse Dictionary of Women.* New York: Larousse Kingfisher Chambers, Inc., 1995, p. 360.

Painting and Sculpture

c. 975 ▪ **Ende,** a Spanish artist, was the first woman to paint an extensive cycle of miniatures (a series of pictures done in reduced scale on a related theme). Ende was also instrumental in painting *The Commentary on the Apocalypse of St. John by Beatus of Liebana,* which is located in Gerona, Spain.

Source: Chicago, Judy, *The Dinner Party.* New York: Anchor, 1979, p. 138.

c. 12th century ▪ **Guda,** a twelfth-century German writer and artist, was the first woman in the West whose self-portrait is still in existence. Guda signed her discourse on morality with a picture of herself; her manuscript is now in Frankfurt, Germany.

Source: Chicago, Judy, *The Dinner Party.* New York: Anchor, 1979, p. 136.

c. Late 1400s ▪ **Honorata Rodiana** (1472-?) was the first female fresco painter (an artist who paints on freshly spread moist lime plaster with water-based pigments). She worked for the ruler of Cremona in Italy until one of his courtiers attempted to rape her. Rodiana fled disguised as a man.

Source: Chicago, Judy, *The Dinner Party.* New York: Anchor, 1979, p. 161.

c. 1550 ▪ **Caterina van Hemessen** (1528-1587) was the first female Flemish artist. She began her career in Antwerp, Belgium, where she was born. Between 1556 and 1558 she worked in Spain under the patronage of Queen Mary of Hungary, former Regent of the Netherlands.

Source: Uglow, Jennifer S., ed., *The Continuum Dictionary of Women's Biography.* New York: Continuum, 1989, p. 254.

1559 ▪ **Sofonisba Anguissola** (1535?-1625), an Italian artist, was the first woman to become a famous professional painter. She studied with Bernardo Campi (1522-1591?), then established her own studio. In 1559 Anguissola was invited to serve as court portrait painter to Phillip II of Italy. Her work focuses on domestic life and her example is thought to have inspired other female artists.

Source: Chicago, Judy, *The Dinner Party.* New York: Anchor, 1979, p. 160.

1608 ▪ **Clara Peeters** (1594-1657?) was the first Dutch woman to paint still lifes (the depiction of inanimate objects, such as food or flowers). Peeters specialized in scenes of food and tableware and was particularly skilled in depicting reflected light.

Source: Uglow, Jennifer S., ed., *The Continuum Dictionary of Women's Biography.* New York: Continuum, 1989, p. 428.

c. 1620 ▪ **Artemisia Gentileschi** (1590-1652) was the first established female artist to paint from a woman's point of view. Gentileschi was known for her portraits of seventeenth-century figures, as well as for her religious and historical works. She was eventually honored by admission to the Academy of Design in Florence.

Source: Chicago, Judy, *The Dinner Party.* New York: Anchor, 1979, pp. 81-82.

1631 ▪ **Judith Leyster** (1609-1660) was the first female Dutch artist to portray sexual harassment. Leyster's best work focuses on everyday life. The painter was especially adept at recording the lives of women and children in domestic (household) settings. Leyster's work depicting men forcing their unwanted sexual attention on women is called *The Proposition,* painted in 1631.

Source: Uglow, Jennifer S., ed., *The Continuum Dictionary of Women's Biography.* New York: Continuum, 1989, pp. 325-26.

1769 ▪ **Angelica Kauffman** (1741-1807), a Swiss painter who worked widely throughout Europe, was a cofounder of the

Royal Academy in London, England. Kauffman was an original painter; her feminine and graceful compositions were much admired by her contemporaries. Her work became well known through engravings by artist Francesco Bartolozzi.

Source: Magnusson, Magnus, *Larousse Biographical Dictionary.* Edinburgh: Larousse Kingfisher Chambers, Inc., 1994, p. 811.

1795 ▪ **Adelaide Labille-Guiard** (1749-1803), a French portrait painter renowned for her pastel (pale in light and color) masterpiece *Portrait of the Sculptor Pajou,* was the first woman to obtain an apartment in the Louvre, the famous French palace that was converted into an art museum in the eighteenth century. A distinguished professional in her field, Labille-Guiard worked continuously for greater opportunities for female artists.

Source: Uglow, Jennifer S., ed., *The Continuum Dictionary of Women's Biography.* New York: Continuum, 1989, p. 308.

1833 ▪ **Anne Hall** (1792-1863), an American painter, was the first woman elected to full membership in the National Academy of Design. She was honored for her work as a miniaturist. (Miniaturists paint things on a very small scale.)

Source: Read, Phyllis J., and Bernard L. Witlieb, *The Book of Women's Firsts.* New York: Random House, 1992, p. 193.

1847 ▪ **Frances Flora Bond Palmer** (1812-1876) was the first woman to establish a reputation as a lithographer (a person who practices a special process of printing) in the United States. Born and trained in England, Palmer settled in New York City in the 1840s and opened a lithographic printing and publishing business with her husband. By 1847 she had established herself as the foremost lithographer in America. A creative lithographer, Palmer drew directly on stone, doing her best work in the 1850s. She was remembered particularly for her landscapes.

Source: James, Edward T., and others, *Notable American Women, 1607-1950: A Biographical Dictionary.* Cambridge, Massachusetts: Harvard University Press, 1971, pp. 10-11.

1852 ▪ Rosa Marie Rosalie Bonheur (1822-1899), the French artist known for the vivid depiction of animals in her paintings, was the first woman granted official police permission to wear male attire in Paris, France. Bonheur initially dressed as a man in order to be allowed to observe anatomy at Paris slaughter houses, but her male attire later became a trademark. Bonheur's work was first exhibited in the Fine Arts Exhibition of 1841. In 1853 her work was judged to be of such quality that she was automatically admitted to juried exhibitions without having to first submit works to the examining committee. According to French tradition, this entitled Bonheur to receive the Legion of Honor (an honor later denied to the artist because she was a woman).

Source: Uglow, Jennifer S., ed., *The Continuum Dictionary of Women's Biography.* New York: Continuum, 1989, p. 77.

Rosa Bonheur was the first woman granted official police permission to wear male clothing in Paris, France.

c. 1853 ▪ Elizabeth Ney (1833-1907) was the first woman to attend the Munich Art Academy in Germany. Ney married and emigrated to the United States, deferring her career in sculpture for 20 years after the birth of her son. In 1893 she resumed her art when she produced a commissioned statue for the Columbian Exhibition in Chicago.

Source: Chicago, Judy, *The Dinner Party.* New York: Anchor, 1979, p. 213.

1873 ▪ Louisine Waldron Elder Havemeyer (1855-1929) was the first American patron (financial supporter) of the French Impressionist painter Edgar Degas (1834-1917; Impressionist painters were concerned with the general impression of a scene or image, especially the play of light and color). While still in boarding school in Paris in 1873, Havemeyer was introduced to Degas by painter Mary Cassatt (1844-1929). Havemeyer was remembered as an art collector who donated a large part of her holdings to the Metropolitan Museum of Art in New York City.

Source: James, Edward T., and others, *Notable American Women, 1607-1950: A Biographical Dictionary.* Cambridge, Massachusetts: Harvard University Press, 1971, pp. 156-58.

1876 ▪ Mary Cassatt (1844-1929), an American artist who studied and worked in France, was the first person to exhibit Impressionist paintings in the United States. (Impressionist painters were concerned with the general impression of a scene or image, especially the play of light and color. The Impressionist movement came out of France in the later decades of the 1800s.) In 1879 a number of Cassatt's paintings received wide exposure when they appeared through the support of the newly formed Society of American Artists. Cassatt is particularly well known for her sensitive portraits of women and children in domestic (household) settings.

Source: James, Edward T., and others, *Notable American Women, 1607-1950: A Biographical Dictionary.* Cambridge, Massachusetts: Harvard University Press, 1971, pp. 303-05.

1898 ▪ Florence Nightingale Levy (1870-1947), an American supporter of the arts, was the founder of the influential *American Art Annual* in New York City. This periodical quickly became a standard and valued reference guide to schools, museums, galleries, and art societies. It also provided biographical listings of artists and a yearly record of exhibits.

Source: James, Edward T., and others, *Notable American Women, 1607-1950: A Biographical Dictionary.* Cambridge, Massachusetts: Harvard University Press, 1971, pp. 395-97.

c. 1900 ▪ Hannah Höch (1889-1971), a German artist, was the coinventor, with artist Raoul Hauseman, of photomontage (an arrangement of photographic images). Throughout her life, Höch created collages (artistic compositions made of various materials) from lace, buttons, and bits of fabric, often focusing on female experience.

Source: O'Neill, Lois Decker, *The Women's Book of World Records and Achievements.* Garden City, New York: Doubleday, 1979, p. 599.

1901 ▪ May Wilson Preston (1873-1949), an American artist, was the first female member of the Society of Illustrators, which she joined shortly after its establishment in New York

City. Founded by the Ashcan School of artists, illustrators, and painters, who favored documentary realism in their work, the society included Robert Henri, John Sloan, George B. Luks, and Preston's husband, James Preston.

Source: James, Edward T., and others, *Notable American Women, 1607-1950: A Biographical Dictionary.* Cambridge, Massachusetts: Harvard University Press, 1971, pp. 98-100.

1909 ▪ Natalia Sergeyevna Goncharova (1881-1962), a Russian painter of international reputation, cofounded the Rayonnist movement with her husband in Moscow. The Rayonnists' style of painting was based on the manipulation of invisible "rays" emanating from all objects, giving the artists' work a futuristic look.

Source: Uglow, Jennifer S., ed., *The Continuum Dictionary of Women's Biography.* New York: Continuum, 1989, p. 230.

1909 ▪ Gabriele Munter (1877-1962), a German painter, cofounded the New Artists Association of Munich with the Russian painter Wassily Kandinsky (1866-1944). Munter completed her most original paintings in her youth and was remembered for her brilliant work with color and for her studies of women.

Source: Uglow, Jennifer S., ed., *The Continuum Dictionary of Women's Biography.* New York: Continuum, 1989, pp. 391-92.

1910 ▪ Cornelia B. Sage Quinton (1879-1936), an American curator (a person who oversees a collection), became the first woman to head an art museum when she was appointed director of the Albright Art Museum and Gallery in Buffalo, New York. Quinton held this position until 1924.

Source: Read, Phyllis J., and Bernard L. Witlieb, *The Book of Women's Firsts.* New York: Random House, 1992, pp. 354-55.

1921 ▪ Angeliki Hatzimichali (1895-1956), a Greek writer and folklorist (a person who studies the customs and traditions of a culture), was the first person to present an exhibit of folk art in Greece. Concerned that traditional folkways and artistic cultural expression were being eclipsed by modern life, she

mounted a show in Athens in 1921. Hatzimichali also wrote extensively about folk art and Greek crafts.

Source: Uglow, Jennifer S., ed., *The Continuum Dictionary of Women's Biography.* New York: Continuum, 1989, p. 250.

1927 ▪ Anna Charlotte Rice Cooke (1853-1934), the daughter of American missionaries, was the founder of the Honolulu Academy of Arts. More than a traditional art museum of the time, the academy sought to establish links with the community through a variety of educational programs and constantly changing exhibits.

Source: James, Edward T., and others, *Notable American Women, 1607-1950: A Biographical Dictionary.* Cambridge, Massachusetts: Harvard University Press, 1971, pp. 377-78.

1930 ▪ Juliana Rieser Force (1876-1948) devoted her life to the visual arts. She assisted Gertrude Vanderbilt Whitney (1875-1942) in managing the Whitney Studio, a New York

Gertrude Vanderbilt Whitney was the driving force behind the Whitney Studio, an avant-garde New York City gallery managed by Juliana Force.

City gallery that championed avant-garde American artists (artists who experiment with new ideas and techniques). When the gallery became the Whitney Museum in 1930, Force served as its first director, a position she held until her death.

Source: Read, Phyllis J., and Bernard L. Witlieb, *The Book of Women's Firsts.* New York: Random House, 1992, pp. 162-63.

1934 ▪ **Peggy Guggenheim** (1898-1980), an American art collector, founded the Guggenheim-Jeune Art Gallery in Paris, France, with the support of her friend, French-born American artist Marcel Duchamp (1887-1968). In 1940 Guggenheim founded another gallery in New York City called "Art of This Century."

Source: Uglow, Jennifer S., ed., *The Continuum Dictionary of Women's Biography.* New York: Continuum, 1989, pp. 239-40.

1959 ▪ **May Massee** (1881-1966) became the first female member of the American Institute of Graphic Arts in 1959. That same year Massee became the first woman to receive this organization's gold medal in honor of her work in the field of children's books.

Source: Read, Phyllis J., and Bernard L. Witlieb, *The Book of Women's Firsts.* New York: Random House, 1992, pp. 271-72.

c. Early 1960s ▪ **Helen Kalvak** (1901-1984), an artist who began drawing in her late sixties, was one of the first Inuit woman to chronicle (to record) the life of her people in her art. (The Inuits are a Native American tribal group.) Traveling throughout Canada's Northwest Territories, Kalvak created over 3,000 pictures that vividly convey the traditional culture and activities of the Copper Inuit, stressing their spiritual life, legends, and ceremonies. She was honored in 1975 with membership in the Royal Canadian Academy of Arts.

Source: Uglow, Jennifer S., ed., *The Continuum Dictionary of Women's Biography.* New York: Continuum, 1989, p. 291.

1964 ▪ **Sonia Delaunay** (1885-1979), a Russian-born artist, was the first woman to have an exhibition at the Louvre museum in Paris, France, during her lifetime. Delaunay was a pioneer abstractionist (a person who paints images that do not represent familiar objects or recognizable space).

Source: Chicago, Judy, *The Dinner Party*. New York: Anchor, 1979, p. 212.

1969 ▪ Frances Hodgkins (1869-1947), a New Zealand artist of international reputation who settled in England, was the first woman to be the subject of a centenary exhibition at the Auckland City Art Gallery. Hodgkins was honored in her own country—which had neglected the artist's achievement during her lifetime—for her paintings in both watercolors and oils. Hodgkins's early work is in the style of post-impressionism (a movement in art that revolted against impressionism. Impressionist painters were concerned with the general impression of a scene or image, especially the play of light and color).

Source: Uglow, Jennifer S., ed., *The Continuum Dictionary of Women's Biography*. New York: Continuum, 1989, pp. 261-62.

1974 ▪ Magdelena Abakanowicz (1930-) was the first Polish woman to receive an honorary doctorate from the Royal College of Art in London, England. Known in her native Poland and around the world for her sculpture and her weaving, Abakanowicz used her art to express her views of the world and the human body.

Source: Uglow, Jennifer S., ed., *The Continuum Dictionary of Women's Biography*. New York: Continuum, 1989, p. 1.

1981 ▪ Wilhelmina Cole Holladay (1922-), an American art collector, was the founder and first president of the National Museum of Women in the Arts. Drawing on her own collection of art, Holladay founded the museum in 1981; in 1987 the museum opened in its own building in Washington, D.C.

Source: Read, Phyllis J., and Bernard L. Witlieb, *The Book of Women's Firsts*. New York: Random House, 1992, pp. 211-13.

Knight Joined Academy

In 1967 Laura Knight (1877-1970), an English painter known for her depictions of circus life, the ballet, and landscapes, was the first woman allowed to attend the annual members' banquet of the Royal Academy in London, England. Knight had been a full member of the academy since 1936.

1982 ▪ **Lucie Rie** (1902-1995), an Austrian-born British potter, was the first female potter to have a retrospective exhibition of her work at the Victoria and Albert Museum in London, England. Rie worked in her own studios in Vienna and London and was known as an influential artist and teacher.

Source: Uglow, Jennifer S., ed., *The Continuum Dictionary of Women's Biography.* New York: Continuum, 1989, p. 459.

1982 ▪ **Susan Kare,** an American artist, designed the first icons (symbols or pictures that serve as labels for particular computer functions or programs) for the original Macintosh computer. While working at the Apple company, which made the Macintosh, Kare designed several icons. Among these icons were the smiling computer terminal signifying the computer was booted (had reached full power), a trash can showing deleted files, and a moving watch indicating that functions were being executed. In 1985 Kare opened her own design business in San Francisco, California.

Source: *Working Woman.* November/December, 1996, p. 50.

Business

Banking
Business Management
Entrepreneurship
Inventors

Banking

1903 ▪ **Maggie Lena Walker** (1867-1934) was the first woman—and also the first African-American woman—to become a bank president when she founded the St. Luke Penny Savings Bank in Richmond, Virginia. Walker had the help of the Independent Order of St. Luke, an African-American insurance cooperative formed in 1867 by a former slave to support health care and funeral arrangements for its members. After becoming a highly successful institution, the St. Luke Penny Savings Bank absorbed other African-American banks in Richmond, eventually reorganizing as the "Consolidated Bank and Trust Company" in 1929. Walker served as chair of the board of directors until her death.

Source: O'Neill, Lois Decker, ed., *The Women's Book of World Records and Achievements.* New York: Doubleday, 1979, p. 526.

1917 ▪ **Kate Gleason** (1865-1933) became the first woman to serve as president of a national bank when she was appointed

Margaret Rudkin founded Pepperidge Farm, a nationwide bakery of premium bread and pastries. (See "Business Management" entry dated 1938.)

head of the First National Bank of Rochester in Rochester, New York. The previous male president resigned to enter military service during World War I (1914-1918).

Source: Read, Phyllis J., and Bernard L. Witlieb, *The Book of Women's Firsts*. New York: Random House, 1992, pp. 176-77.

c. 1919 ▪ **Brenda Vineyard Runyon** was the first woman bank president to employ an all-female staff, including the janitor. The bank was highly successful for seven years, until Runyon was forced to resign due to illness. With no one willing to assume her role, Runyon's staff liquidated (closed out) their assets, and on June 8, 1926, merged with the First Trust and Savings Bank of Clarksville.

Source: McCullough, Joan, *First of All: Significant "Firsts" by American Women*. New York: Holt, 1980, p. 61.

1949 ▪ **Claire Giannini Hoffman** (1904-) was the first female director of the world's largest bank, the Bank of America (later BankAmerica). Hoffman assumed this position in 1949 after the death of her father, the bank's founder and first president.

Source: Read, Phyllis J., and Bernard L. Witlieb, *The Book of Women's Firsts*. New York: Random House, 1992, pp. 210-21.

1975 ▪ **Madeleine McWhinney** (1922-) was the first president of the First Women's Bank and Trust Company, an organization committed to providing banking services on a nondiscriminatory (equal opportunity) basis in New York City. In 1965 McWhinney was named the first woman assistant vice president of the Federal Reserve System. From 1957 to 1959 McWhinney served as the first woman president of the New York University Graduate School of Business.

Source: Read, Phyllis J., and Bernard L. Witlieb, *The Book of Women's Firsts*. New York: Random House, 1992, p. 285.

Business Management

1735 ▪ **Ann Smith Franklin** (1696-1763) was the first female printer in New England. She took over her husband's printing business in Boston, Massachusetts, at the time of his death. Franklin ran the business until her son took over in 1748, though she continued to be an active printer until 1757.

Source: James, Edward T., and others., *Notable American Women, 1607-1950: A Biographical Dictionary.* Cambridge, Massachusetts: Harvard University Press, 1971, pp. 662-63.

c. 1761 ▪ Hester Needham Bateman

(1709-1794) was the first female silversmith (an artisan who makes silverware) to register her own hallmark, "H.B." (A hallmark is an official stamp that attests to an item's purity or quality.) Bateman worked with her husband until his death in 1760, then carried on his business as her own. She is now regarded as one of the greatest eighteenth-century silversmiths.

Source: Raven, Susan, and Alison Weir, *Women of Achievement: Thirty-Five Centuries of History.* New York: Harmony Books, 1981, p. 192.

Ivers Managed Studio

Julia Crawford Ivers (?-1930) was the first woman to serve as general manager of a film studio. In 1915 Ivers took on this job at the Bosworth Company, where she was in charge of production and day-to-day business. Ivers occasionally assumed the responsibilities of directing and screenwriting.

1929 ▪ Rose Markward Knox (1857-1950), an American

businesswoman, was the first woman elected to the board of directors of the American Grocery Manufacturers' Association. She was head of the Knox Company, which is still famous for its gelatin (an edible jelly used in making desserts and other dishes). Knox took over the business at the time of her husband's death in 1908 and built it into a major enterprise with plants in Johnstown, New York, and Camden, New Jersey.

Source: James, Edward T., and others, *Notable American Women, 1607-1950: A Biographical Dictionary.* Cambridge, Massachusetts: Harvard University Press, 1971, pp. 343-44.

1929 ▪ Gertrude Battles Lane (1874-1941) was the first

female vice-president of the Crowell Publishing Company in New York City. Lane established her reputation as an editor of the *Woman's Home Companion,* serving on the board of the magazine from 1903 until 1937.

Source: James, Edward T., and others, *Notable American Women, 1607-1950: A Biographical Dictionary.* Cambridge, Massachusetts: Harvard University Press, 1971, pp. 363-65.

1938 ▪ **Margaret Fogarty Rudkin** (1897-1967), an American businesswoman, founded Pepperidge Farm, a nationwide bakery of premium bread and pastries, in Fairfield, Connecticut. Rudkin began baking at the age of forty in order to produce a healthy bread without additives for her children with asthma. Under Rudkin's leadership, Pepperidge Farm expanded rapidly, becoming a multi-million-dollar operation that remains one of the largest baking companies in the United States.

Source: Uglow, Jennifer S., ed., *The Continuum Dictionary of Women's Biography.* New York: Continuum, 1989, p. 467.

c. 1949 ▪ **Mirabel Topham** (?-1980) was the first woman to own the Aintree Racecourse, site of the Grand National, the world's most famous steeplechase (a horse race over a closed course with obstacles such as hedges and walls). Topham purchased the racecourse outright in 1949. The course had been in her husband's family since 1843; she was the first woman to serve on its board (in 1935) and the first woman to manage the company (in 1936). Topham sold the course in 1973 for three million pounds.

Source: Uglow, Jennifer S., ed., *The Continuum Dictionary of Women's Biography.* New York: Continuum, 1989, p. 542.

1951 ▪ **Armi Ratia** (1912-1979), a Finnish designer, was cofounder (with her husband) of Marimekko, a textile design firm. (Marimekko means "Mary's dress.") Becoming a successful international business, Marimekko was exporting clothing to over twenty countries by 1970. In 1968 Ratia was the first Finnish woman to be awarded the American Neiman Marcus Award in recognition for her art and business success. She also received the Order of the White Rose, First Class, the highest Finnish honor.

Source: Uglow, Jennifer S., ed., *The Continuum Dictionary of Women's Biography.* New York: Continuum, 1989, pp. 449-50.

1963 ▪ **Katharine Graham** (1917-) became president of the Washington Post Company, which published the *Washington Post* newspaper and *Newsweek* magazine. In assuming the position after the death of her husband, Philip Graham, Katherine became the first woman to head a Fortune 500 company (the Fortune 500 is a list of the largest corporations in the United States).

Graham's most famous act as publisher of the *Washington Post* was her 1971 decision to publish the "Pentagon Papers," which revealed previously hidden information regarding the nature and planning of U. S. military activities during the Vietnam War (1965-1973). She also supported *Post* reporters Bob Woodward and Carl Bernstein in their investigation of the Watergate scandal, which led to the resignation of President Richard M. Nixon (began term in 1969) in 1974. That same year Graham became the first female member of the Associated Press. In 1973 she was the first person to receive the John Peter Zenger Award, which honors service in behalf of freedom of the press.

Source: Read, Phyllis J., and Bernard L. Witlieb, *The Book of Women's Firsts.* New York: Random House, 1992, p. 182.

1965 ▪ **Giuliana Benetton** (1937-), together with her three brothers—Luciano, Gilberto, and Carlo—was the founder of Benetton, the world's largest knitwear company. Giuliana started the business in Treviso, Italy, a town near Venice, Italy,

Together with her three brothers, Giuliana Benetton founded Benetton, the world's largest knitwear company.

where she grew up. By 1996 the company had 7,000 outlets in 120 countries, making it the world's largest manufacturer of knitwear and the greatest consumer of virgin (pure) wool.

Source: Uglow, Jennifer S., ed., *The Continuum Dictionary of Women's Biography.* New York: Continuum, 1989, p. 61.

1966 ▪ **Mary Wells Lawrence** (1928-), an American advertising executive, was the founder, first chairperson, and first chief executive of Wells, Rich, Greene, Inc., a prestigious advertising firm. Lawrence is said to have rejected a ten-year, million-dollar contract to found the company in New York City in 1966 ("Wells" was then her married name). By 1971 Lawrence was chair of the board and chief executive officer. In the 1980s she was reputed to be the most powerful woman in the advertising industry as well as the highest paid advertising executive in the United States. Lawrence started her advertising career in Youngstown, Ohio, where she worked from 1951 to 1952 at McKelvey's Department Store.

Source: O'Neill, Lois Decker, ed., *The Women's Book of World Records and Achievements.* Garden City, New York: Doubleday, 1979, p. 516.

1977 ▪ **Maria Pia Esmeralda Matarazzo** inherited Brazil's tenth largest private company, Industrious Reunidas F. Matarazzo, from her father when she was 35. The inheritance made Matarazzo the only woman chief executive officer of a major enterprise in Brazil. When Matarazzo took over the company, it had 76 factories and employed 21,000 workers.

Source: O'Neill, Lois Decker, ed., *The Women's Book of World Records and Achievements.* Garden City, New York: Doubleday, 1979, p. 525.

c. late 1970s ▪ **Cecilia Danieli** (1943-), an Italian business executive, is the first woman to head Danieli of Buttrio, the steel company founded by her grandfather in 1914. Danieli began work at the company as assistant to her father in 1965 and is known as "Italy's first lady of steel."

Source: Uglow, Jennifer S., ed., *The Continuum Dictionary of Women's Biography,* New York: Continuum, 1989, p. 147.

1980 ▪ Sherry Lee Lansing (1944-) was the first woman to head a major film studio. In 1980 Lansing was appointed president of the feature-film division of Twentieth Century-Fox, a position she held until 1982, when she left to cofound Jaffe-Lansing Productions with Stanley R. Jaffe. In 1992 Lansing was named chair of Paramount Pictures, which has made successful films such as *Forest Gump* (1996).

Source: Parry, Melanie, ed., *Larousse Dictionary of Women.* New York: Larousse Kingfisher Chambers, Inc., 1995, p. 383.

1987 ▪ Dawn Steel (1946-) became the first woman to head a motion picture corporation in 1987 when she took over Columbia Pictures. In addition to overseeing production, marketing, and distribution for Columbia itself, Steel was also responsible for Tri-Star and other Columbia subsidiaries.

Source: Parry, Melanie, ed., *Larousse Dictionary of Women.* New York: Larousse Kingfisher Chambers, Inc., 1995, p. 619.

Sherry Lansing was the first woman to head a major film studio.

1994 ▪ Linda Warren, an American entertainment executive, was the first female general manager of Epcot, a theme park operated by Walt Disney World in Orlando, Florida. In 1995 Warren was appointed senior vice president of marketing for product and brand management for Walt Disney World. She began her Disney career as a cast member greeting tourists in Tomorrowland at Epcot.

Source: *Working Woman.* November/December, 1996.

1997 ▪ Jill Barad, an American executive, was the first female chief executive officer (CEO) of a Fortune 500 company to obtain a position through her own initiative. In 1992 she was appointed the first female president and chief operating officer at Mattel, a toy company. During her fifteen-year career at Mattel, Barad held numerous positions, including product manager, marketing director for the "Barbie" doll, vice president, and senior vice president.

Source: "Letter from Barbie," *Working Woman.* November/December, 1996, p. 109.

Entrepreneurs

c. 1817 ▪ Elizabeth Veale Macarthur (1766-1850) was the first person to establish New South Wales, Australia, as a wool producing area. Elizabeth left England for Australia with her husband John Macarthur in 1789, and is regarded as the first cultured, or educated, woman to settle in Botany Bay. When her husband fled the country in 1809 after the "Rum Rebellion" against Governor William Bligh, she took over the management of their property. Macarthur worked the sheep farm, known as Elizabeth Farm, for eight years. She introduced merino sheep and developed an English market for Australian wool. After her husband's death in 1834, she passed on to her sons the wool empire she had started.

Source: Parry, Melanie, ed., *Larousse Dictionary of Women.* New York: Larousse Kingfisher Chambers, Inc., 1995, pp. 416-17.

1860 ▪ Ellen Louise Curtis Demorest (1824-1898), an American entrepreneur, originated the use of accurate tissue-paper dress patterns in New York City. Demorest's husband, a dry goods merchant, ran a quarterly magazine called *Mme. Demorest's Mirror of Fashions.* In 1860 he stapled a paper pattern into each issue of the magazine. The success of the patterns and later fashion ventures made the Demorests wealthy entrepreneurs.

Source: James, Edward T., and others, *Notable American Women, 1607-1950: A Biographical Dictionary.* Cambridge, Massachusetts: Harvard University Press, 1971, pp. 459-60.

1875 ▪ Lydia Estes Pinkham (1819-1883), an entrepreneur in Boston, Massachusetts, was the first American woman to make money by selling patent (over-the-counter) medicine. Pinkham decided to combat her family's poverty by selling an herbal mixture for "female complaints" (symptoms usually associated with menstrual periods), which she called "Lydia E. Pinkham's Vegetable Compound." Although the mixture had no evident curative powers, it became the most widely advertised merchandise in the United States by 1898 and earned its maker fame and prosperity.

Source: James, Edward T., and others, *Notable American Women, 1607-1950: A Biographical Dictionary*. Cambridge, Massachusetts: Harvard University Press, 1971, pp. 71-73.

1906 ▪ Sarah Breedlove Walker (1867-1919), better known as Madam C. J. Walker, was the first person to make a career out of developing and selling hair straightener. Beginning in St. Louis, Missouri, in 1905, Walker experimented with hair products for African Americans, especially women. She moved her business to Denver, Colorado, in 1906. Walker eventually built up a huge mail-order business, establishing an office in Pittsburgh, Pennsylvania, in 1908 and founding laboratories in Indianapolis, Indiana, in 1910.

Source: James, Edward T., and others, *Notable American Women, 1607-1950: A Biographical Dictionary*. Cambridge, Massachusetts: Harvard University Press, 1971, pp. 533-35.

1968 ▪ Laura Mountney Ashley (1925-1985), an English designer and businesswoman, founded a worldwide corporation to market her own fashion designs. Ashley began her career in 1953 by designing silk-screened scarves at home under her own name. By the 1960s Ashley and her husband, Bernard Ashley, had formed a design corporation and opened a shop in London under the name Ashley Mountney, Ltd. (The firm became Laura Ashley, Ltd. in 1968.) At the time of Laura Ashley's death, the design business included eleven factories and 225 shops and employed a staff of over four thousand people.

Source: Magnusson, Magnus, *Larousse Biographical Dictionary*. Edinburgh: Larousse Kingfisher Chambers, Inc., 1994, p. 70.

Haughery Established Bakery

Margaret Gaffney Haughery (1814-1882) was the first woman to establish a steam bakery in the American South when she opened the D'Aquin Bakery in New Orleans, Louisiana, in 1858. D'Aquin Bakery soon became the city's largest export business. Haughery is remembered not only as a successful entrepreneur, but also as a generous supporter of the city, where she established a number of orphanages. Each year New Orleans celebrates February 9 as "Margaret Day."

Inventors

1715 ▪ **Sybilla Masters** (?-1720), an American inventor, patented a device for cleaning and curing American corn. Since the American colonies were governed by England at the time, Sybilla and her husband, Thomas Masters, traveled to London in 1715, where they were granted a patent (a special license under their own name) for the invention. Sybilla Masters's device differed from existing grinding processes in that it stamped corn with a wooden structure powered by a water wheel or by horses. Masters called her corn meal "Tuscarora Rice" and sold it in her home city of Philadelphia, Pennsylvania. While she was in London, Masters also received a patent—again in her husband's name—for making hats and bonnets from palmetto leaves imported from the West Indies. She briefly ran a shop that sold these items in London before returning to Philadelphia.

Source: James, Edward T., and others, *Notable American Women, 1607-1950: A Biographical Dictionary.* Cambridge, Massachusetts: Harvard University Press, 1971, pp. 508-09.

c. 1809 ▪ **Mary Kies** (1752-18?) was the first woman to receive a patent in the United States. In 1809, she patented a new method for weaving straw with silk or thread to make bonnets.

Source: Vare, Ethlie Ann, and Greg Ptacek, *Mothers of Invention: From the Bra to the Bomb, Forgotten Women and Their Unforgettable Ideas.* New York: William Morrow, 1988, pp. 30-31.

1870 ▪ **Margaret Knight** (1838-1914), an American inventor, was the first person to find a way to fold and seal the bottoms of paper bags in one operation. Her process, which she sold to the Eastern Paper Bag Company, was patented in 1870.

Source: Uglow, Jennifer S., ed., *The Continuum Dictionary of Women's Biography.* New York: Continuum, 1989, p. 301.

1872 ▪ **Jane Wells,** an American inventor, patented (licensed the design under her own name) the baby jumper, which has remained largely unchanged for more than a century. In her patent application, Wells described the advantages of the swing-like device that is suspended from springs: "This machine may be operated by an infant from the time it can sit erect until it walks, giving it the ability to dance, swing, and turn itself in any direction, affording it healthy and safe amusement, and relieving parents and nurses from much care and labor."

The first baby jumpers were manufactured by Occidental Manufacturing Co., which employed Wells's husband. The jumpers themselves were assembled by women.

Source: Vare, Ethlie Ann, and Greg Ptacek, *Mothers of Invention: From the Bra to the Bomb, Forgotten Women and Their Unforgettable Ideas.* New York: William Morrow, 1988, p. 46.

1905 ▪ **Mary E. H. Greenewalt**(1871-19?), an American musician, patented (licensed the design under her own name) the rheostat, a device that varies the intensity of light produced by an incandescent bulb. (In an incandescent bulb, light is produced by intense heat.) A pianist who toured with the Pittsburgh and Philadelphia symphony orchestras, Greenewalt was famous for her interpretations of works by the Polish pianist and composer Frédéric Chopin (1810-1849). Greenewalt was interested in how color affected a listener, so she investigated the relationship between the beat of the metronome (a device that marks time with a regular ticking sound) and the human heart. She also analyzed the connection between the colors on the light spectrum (a range of colors that appear when a beam of white light is passed through a prism) and the seven notes of the diatonic musical scale (a major or minor scale composed of five whole steps and two half steps).

Greenewalt speculated that the listening experience could be enhanced if joined with the mathematical equivalents of light and color. With the invention of the rheostat in 1905, she became a pioneer in relating music to color and light. She went on to invent the Sarabet, a "light-and-color player," which she demonstrated in 1916. Consisting of a series of on-off switches and rheostats arranged like a piano keyboard, the instrument allowed the operator to manipulate color and light intensity in an auditorium. Although the Sarabet soon became obsolete, Greenewalt is widely considered as the first multi-media artist.

Source: Vare, Ethlie Ann, and Greg Ptacek, *Mothers of Invention: From the Bra to the Bomb, Forgotten Women and Their Unforgettable Ideas.* New York: William Morrow, 1988, pp. 81- 82.

1908 ▪ **Melitta Bentz,** a German inventor, developed the coffee filtration system. A housewife who was tired of drinking bitter coffee, Bentz thought that if the coffee grounds were placed on the top of a filter and the boiling water poured over it, the bitter taste could be avoided. She then took a sheet of blotting paper from her son's schoolbook, cut it into a circle, and placed it in the bottom of a brass pot poked with holes. The method worked, producing a fresh-tasting coffee brew. After a tinsmith fabricated a new pot to Bentz's specifications, she introduced her new device as the Melitta coffee maker at the 1909 Leipzig trade fair. By 1912 Melitta was manufacturing a line of coffee filters, although the original disk-shaped filter was replaced with a cone-shaped design that is still popular. In time porcelain pots were replaced by metal, which eventually evolved into the plastic funnels that are currently in use. Today, most Americans prefer the drip preparation method when brewing coffee.

Source: Vare, Ethlie Ann, and Greg Ptacek, *Mothers of Invention: From the Bra to the Bomb, Forgotten Women and Their Unforgettable Ideas.* New York: William Morrow, 1988, pp. 42- 43.

1908 ▪ **E. L. Todd** was the first woman to invent an airplane. In 1908 Todd filed a patent for her new invention, a collapsible airplane that folded up to a third of its full size. Todd exhibited a working model of the airplane at an air show in Brooklyn, New York.

Source: Read, Phyllis J., and Bernard L. Witlieb, *The Book of Women's Firsts.* New York: Random House, 1992, pp. 446-47.

1912 ▪ **Rose O'Neill** (1874-1944), an American entrepreneur, patented the "Kewpie doll," which she named after Cupid (the Roman god of love). "Kewpies" became a very popular toy, eventually earning O'Neill more than a million dollars. O'Neill first presented the Kewpies—chubby infants with wings, perky faces, and curly hair—in a series of illustrations that accompanied verse stories in the *Ladies' Home Journal* magazine. According to these tales, the Kewpies woke the flowers, kept birds' eggs warm, and found lost babies. The dolls' popularity was capitalized on in many forms, including salt and pepper shakers, figurines, buttons, and decorations for stationery, fabric, and greeting cards. Kewpies reached their height of popularity in 1912.

Source: James, Edward T., and others, *Notable American Women, 1607-1950: A Biographical Dictionary.* Cambridge, Massachusetts: Harvard University Press, 1971, pp. 650-51.

1924 ▪ **Gertrude Muller,** an American inventor, patented the "Toidy Seat." The idea of the Toidy Seat was suggested to Muller by her sister. At the time Muller was working for a plumbing company, and her sister approached her about getting the company to build a smaller, portable toilet for Muller's niece. Muller designed the seat, the plumbing company made it, and her sister's child tested it. In 1924 Muller established her own business, the Juvenile Wood Products Company. When the company started making the seats from plastic, the name was shortened to the Toidy Company.

Source: Vare, Ethlie Ann, and Greg Ptacek, *Mothers of Invention: From the Bra to the Bomb, Forgotten Women and Their Unforgettable Ideas.* New York: William Morrow, 1988, p. 47.

1933 ▪ **Ruth Graves Wakefield,** an American restaurateur (a person who operates a restaurant), baked the first batch of chocolate chip cookies by accident. Wakefield and her husband Ralph owned the Toll House Inn in Whitman, Massachusetts. The couple added a restaurant in 1930. While making a batch of chocolate butter drop cookies for the restaurant menu, Ruth Wakefield decided not to melt the chocolate first in order to save time. Assuming it would melt as the cookies baked, she mixed chunks of chocolate into the batter. However, the chunks remained solid.

Deciding to serve the cookies anyway, Wakefield called her new creation the "Toll House cookie." By 1939 the Nestlé candy company was making chocolate bits specifically for Wakefield's recipe. Nestlé eventually bought the rights to the Toll House name from Wakefield, supplying her with free chocolate. A Toll House cookie recipe is now in the public domain (the rights are not owned by Nestlé, and the recipe is available to anyone who wants to use it).

Source: Vare, Ethlie Ann, and Greg Ptacek, *Mothers of Invention: From the Bra to the Bomb, Forgotten Women and Their Unforgettable Ideas.* New York: William Morrow, 1988, pp. 90-92.

A Famous Relation

Bette Nesmith Graham, inventor of Liquid Paper, is also the mother of musician and actor Michael Nesmith. As one of television's original *Monkees,* Michael Nesmith enjoyed great popularity with teens during the late 1960s. In recent years, the *Monkees* have enjoyed a popular revival, with repeats of their television show being televised on stations such as VH-1.

1951 ▪ Marion Donovan, an American inventor, designed the disposable diaper. During the postwar American baby boom (1946-1964), Donovan wondered why there was no alternative to the cloth diaper that could be thrown away after one use. Her solution was to create a disposable diaper that she called the "Boater." Donovan made the first "Boater" out of a shower curtain and absorbent padding. Manufacturers showed no interest in Donovan's invention, however, labeling it too costly. Donovan finally manufactured the diaper herself, selling the popular item to department stores. She sold her company for one million dollars prior to the mass introduction of disposable diapers.

Source: Vare, Ethlie Ann, and Greg Ptacek, *Mothers of Invention: From the Bra to the Bomb, Forgotten Women and Their Unforgettable Ideas.* New York: William Morrow, 1988, pp. 43- 44.

1956 ▪ Bette Nesmith Graham (1924-1980), an American entrepreneur, received a patent for Liquid Paper. Graham invented the correction fluid in 1951 after she took her first job as a secretary and became frustrated when she tried to erase errors on her typewriter. Applying water-base white paint to her mistakes with a watercolor brush, she kept her method a secret until 1956. Somehow her co-workers found out about Graham's unique idea and asked to borrow the correction fluid. She then began marketing the product as "Mistake Out." Graham changed the name to Liquid Paper, Inc., and by 1978 she had a million-dollar business that produced 10 thousand bottles a day. In 1979 the Gillette Corporation bought the company. Graham's estate continues to earn a royalty on every bottle of Liquid Paper that is sold until the year 2000.

Source: Vare, Ethlie Ann, and Greg Ptacek, *Mothers of Invention: From the Bra to the Bomb, Forgotten Women and Their Unforgettable Ideas.* New York: William Morrow, 1988, pp. 38- 42.

1959 ▪ Ruth Handler, an American entrepreneur, invented the Barbie doll. In 1946 Handler and her husband Elliot founded Mattel Creations, a toy company. Six years later Mattel became the first toy company to use television to advertise its products when it aired commercials on the *Mickey Mouse Club* program. The Barbie doll, however, was the product that brought Mattel worldwide attention and profits. Handler conceived the idea for the doll when she noticed that her daughter preferred to play with teenage doll cutouts over baby dolls. This led Handler to design Barbie—which she named after her daughter—as a young mature woman with adult clothes and accessories. Handler introduced her invention at the New York Toy Show in 1959, where its potential success was questioned by industry insiders. Proving the critics wrong within its first eight years, Barbie grossed five hundred million dollars in sales. The actual Barbie patent was granted in the name of Mattel employees who fabricated the toy.

Barbie's Changes

Over the years, Mattel's Barbie doll has changed to reflect the times. First sold as a "dress up" toy with lots of fashions, accessories, and glamorous friends, Barbie has more recently become a member of the work force. Her many careers have included nurse, doctor, veterinarian, and teacher. In 1997 Mattel introduced—amid some controversy—the first handicapped Barbie, a doll that used a wheelchair.

Source: Vare, Ethlie Ann, and Greg Ptacek, *Mothers of Invention: From the Bra to the Bomb, Forgotten Women and Their Unforgettable Ideas.* New York: William Morrow, 1988, pp. 87- 90.

1977 ▪ Ann Moore, an American inventor, originated the Snugli. While serving in the Peace Corps in the early 1960s in Togo (formerly French West Africa), Moore noticed mothers carrying babies in pouches that fit across a woman's upper body. Moore liked the idea because it allowed the mothers to take their babies to work and continue the bonding process. (Bonding is the link that is formed between a caregiver and a baby during the early months following birth.) When Moore had her first child she tried to devise her own carrier, but was unsuccessful. With the help of her baby's grandmother, Lucy Aukerman, Moore made a pouch from a sheet with back straps and holes in front for the child's arms and legs. Successful word-of-mouth business led Moore to start a mail order company, which led to the birth of the Snugli baby carrier. Patented in 1977, the Snugli was grossing six million dollars within six years.

Source: Vare, Ethlie Ann, and Greg Ptacek, *Mothers of Invention: From the Bra to the Bomb, Forgotten Women and Their Unforgettable Ideas.* New York: William Morrow, 1988, pp. 44- 45.

1988 ▪ **Sally Fox** (1956-), an American biologist, developed FoxFibre. A natural color cotton fiber that is free of chemical coloring agents and pesticides, FoxFibre is also fire resistant. Fox discovered the fiber when she was testing the pest resistance of cotton seeds; she soon began developing natural brown cotton for hand-spinners and weavers. In 1988 Fox established Natural Cotton Colours. The company sells FoxFibre, which comes in a range of colors from reddish-brown to olive green, to major commercial manufacturers that make it into a variety of products such as clothing, towels, upholstery fabric, table linens, and hosiery. Fox has also worked on a non-flammable cotton for children's sleepwear.

Source: *Discover.* October, 1994, p. 72.

Education

Higher Education
Secondary and Primary Education

Higher Education

C. A.D. 440 ▪ **Eudocia** (401?-460) was the founder of the University at Constantinople. A scholar, writer, and patron of education, Eudocia encouraged the study of Greek literature. In part because of a power struggle with her sister-in-law, Pulcheria, Eudocia was exiled to Jerusalem in 443. Eudocia built a number of churches in the Holy Land, including St. Stephen, where she is buried.

Source: Chicago, Judy, *The Dinner Party*. New York: Anchor, 1979, pp. 69-70.

1505 ▪ **Margaret Beaufort** (1441-1509), the mother of Henry VII (1457-1509), founded Christ's College of Cambridge University in England. Popularly known as "Lady Margaret," Beaufort lectured on divinity at both Oxford and Cambridge Universities. She left most of her fortune as an endowment (gift) to St. John's College, Cambridge, in 1508.

Source: Chicago, Judy, *The Dinner Party*. New York: Anchor, 1979, p. 151.

In 1814 Emma Hart Willard established the first institution for the higher education of women. (See "Secondary and Primary Education" entry dated 1814.)

Margaret Founded College

In 1465 Margaret of Anjou (1430-1482), cofounded Queen's College, Cambridge, with Elizabeth Woodward (1437-1472). Margaret was the wife of Henry VI and a powerful ruler in her own right (particularly after her husband went insane in the 1450s). Woodward was the wife of Edward IV.

1678 ▪ **Helen Cornaro** (1646-1684), an Italian scholar, was the first woman to receive the degree of doctor of philosophy (also known as a "Ph.D."). Cornaro presented her dissertation (a highly detailed written analysis of a particular subject) at the University of Padua, Italy, and was awarded her degree.

Source: Chicago, Judy, *The Dinner Party*. New York: Anchor, 1979, pp. 163-64.

1768 ▪ **Selina Huntingdon,** the Countess of Huntingdon (1707-1791), an ardent Calvinist-Methodist (a member of a Protestant religious denomination), was the founder of Trevecca College in Brecknockshire, England. Intended for the training of evangelical (Christian) clergy, the college moved after the Countess's death to Hertfordshire and then to Cambridge in 1904.

Source: Uglow, Jennifer S., ed., *The Continuum Dictionary of Women's Biography*. New York: Continuum, 1989, p. 269.

1837 ▪ **Mary Lyon** (1797-1849), a pioneer in women's education in America, was the founder of Mount Holyoke Seminary for Women, the first women's college in the United States. Lyon spent four years soliciting funds for the founding of the college despite public criticism; she later became the school's first director. Because Lyon was technically Mount Holyoke's principal and not its president, Frances Willard (1839-1898)— named president of the Evanston (Illinois) College for Ladies in 1871— is widely considered the first female college president.

Source: Chicago, Judy, *The Dinner Party*. New York: Anchor, 1979, p. 196.

1848 ▪ **Sarah Anne Worthington King Peter** (1800-1877), an American civic leader and churchwoman, was the founder of the Philadelphia School of Design for Women. A pioneering school for industrial art in the United States, the institution began with one teacher in Peter's home and continued until

1932, when it merged with the Moore Institute of Art, Science, and Industry. Peter also founded the Protestant Orphan Asylum in Cincinnati, Ohio, as well as the Women's Museum Association and hospitals in Cincinnati and Covington, Kentucky.

Source: James, Edward T., and others, *Notable American Women, 1607-1950: A Biographical Dictionary*. Cambridge, Massachusetts: Harvard University Press, 1971, pp. 54-56.

1850 ▪ **Lucy Ann Stanton** was the first African-American woman to graduate from college when she received a bachelor of literature degree from Oberlin College in Oberlin, Ohio.

Source: Kane, Nathan Joseph, *Famous First Facts*. New York: Wilson, 1981, p. 186.

Medical College Admitted Women

The first medical institution in the United States to admit women was Central Medical College in Syracuse, New York. The school opened its doors to female students in the 1840s. Lydia Folger Fowler, the second American woman to receive a medical degree, graduated from this school and taught there briefly before the college closed in 1852.

1852 ▪ **Barbara Leigh-Smith Bodichon** (1827-1891), an English feminist, was the founder of Portman Hall School in London, England. Committed to gaining rights for women, Bodichon was a pioneer in woman's education. She was also instrumental in founding and endowing (providing money for) Girton College, Cambridge, in 1873.

Source: Uglow, Jennifer S., ed., *The Continuum Dictionary of Women's Biography*. New York: Continuum, 1989, pp. 74-75.

1852 ▪ **Anna Peck Sill** (1816-1889), an American educator, was the founder of Rockford Female Seminary in Rockford, Illinois. An outgrowth of a private school for girls founded by Sill in 1849, the seminary was modeled on Mary Lyon's Mount Holyoke Seminary (established in 1837) in Massachusetts. Sill served as first principal of Rockford Seminary until her retirement in 1884, two years after the institution began to grant bachelor degrees. The school became Rockford College in 1892.

Source: James, Edward T., and others, *Notable American Women, 1607-1950: A Biographical Dictionary*. Cambridge: Harvard University Press, 1971, pp. 290-91.

First Sorority Formed

In 1851 sixteen women at Wesleyan College in Macon, Georgia, formed the first sorority. The group's motto was "We live for one another." Originally calling themselves the "Adelphian Society," the sorority sisters voted in 1904 to change their name to Alpha Delta Phi and, in 1913, to Alpha Delta Pi.

1860 ▪ Julie-Victoire Daubie (1824-1874) was the first woman to take and pass the French *baccalaureat* exam before a jury from the Faculté des Lettres of Lyon, France. Daubie went on to become the first woman to pass the advanced exam, the *licence,* in 1871.

Source: Uglow, Jennifer S., ed., *The Continuum Dictionary of Women's Biography.* New York: Continuum, 1989, p. 148.

1866 ▪ Ann Preston (1813-1872) was the first dean of the first women's medical college in the United States. In 1866 she was promoted from professor of physiology and hygiene to the new position of dean at the Female Medical College in Philadelphia, Pennsylvania.

Source: Read, Phyllis J., and Bernard L. Witlieb, *The Book of Women's Firsts.* New York: Random House, 1992, pp. 349-50.

1866 ▪ Lucy Beaman Hobbs (1833-1910), an American dentist, became the first woman to graduate from an U.S. dental school when she received her degree from the Ohio College of Dental Surgery in Cincinnati, Ohio. Five years earlier, Hobbs had been rejected by that school on the basis of her sex. After opening her own practice and gaining the respect of her fellow dentists, Hobbs reapplied to the college; she was admitted into the senior class and was graduated after only four months of study.

Source: Read, Phyllis J., and Bernard L. Witlieb, *The Book of Women's Firsts.* New York: Random House, 1992, p. 207.

c. early 1870s ▪ Nadezhda Stasova (1822-1895), a Russian feminist, was the first director of the Bestuzehv Advanced Courses, the first advanced-level university courses open to women in Russia. Women were first formally admitted to the University of St. Petersburg in 1869, in large measure because of the efforts of Stasova and her two colleagues, Anna Filosova and Mariya Trubnikova. The three friends were known as "the female triumvirate" (a triumvirate is a group of three) and together were responsible for the founding of Russia's first feminist organizations, in the 1860s.

Source: Uglow, Jennifer S., ed., *The Continuum Dictionary of Women's Biography.* New York: Continuum, 1989, p. 515.

1871 ▪ Frances Elizabeth Willard (1839-1898) is widely considered the first female college president. In 1871 she was chosen president of Evanston College for Ladies in Evanston, Illinois. Two years later, the college became the Woman's College of Northwestern University. Willard became dean of women there, a position she held for a year. The state of Illinois has placed a statue of Frances Willard in Statuary Hall at the Capitol building in Washington, D.C.

Source: James, Edward T., and others, *Notable American Women, 1607-1950: A Biographical Dictionary.* Cambridge, Massachusetts: Harvard University Press, 1971, pp. 613-18.

Frances E. Willard is widely considered the first female college president.

1871 ▪ Learmonth White Dalrymple (1827-1906), a New Zealand feminist, was the first woman to petition for the admission of women to the University of New Zealand. An ardent feminist, Dalrymple campaigned for women's education throughout her life. By 1873 more than half of university students in New Zealand were women.

Source: Uglow, Jennifer S., ed., *The Continuum Dictionary of Women's Biography.* New York: Continuum, 1989, p. 145.

1874 ▪ Abbie Park Ferguson (1837-1919) and **Anna Elvira Bliss** (1843-1925) were the founders and first directors of the Huguenot Seminary (later Huguenot College) in Wellington, South Africa. Graduates of Mount Holyoke Seminary in Massachusetts, both women felt the need to establish similar schools elsewhere. In 1916 Huguenot College was incorporat-

Medical School Opened Doors

In 1870 the University of Michigan in Ann Arbor was the first state university to open its medical school to female students. The university awarded its first medical diploma to Amanda Sanford, who had trained extensively in Philadelphia, Pennsylvania, and Boston, Massachusetts.

ed as part of the new University of South Africa. Ferguson served as president of the college until 1910, when Bliss took the position. Bliss remained in the post until 1920.

Source: James, Edward T., and others, *Notable American Women, 1607-1950: A Biographical Dictionary.* Cambridge, Massachusetts: Harvard University Press, 1971, pp. 607-10.

1874 ▪ Sarah Emily Davies (1830-1921), an English feminist and lifelong advocate of higher education for women, was the founder of Girton College in Cambridge, England. In 1859 Davies founded the Northumberland and Durham Branch of the Society for Promoting the Employment of Women. In 1863 Davies was the first woman to persuade Cambridge University to hold an experimental examination for girls, a test that was later made permanent.

Source: Parry, Melanie, ed., *Larousse Dictionary of Women.* New York: Larousse Kingfisher Chambers, Inc., 1995, p. 177.

1877 ▪ Kate Edger was the first woman to graduate from the University of New Zealand, earning a degree in mathematics. By 1893 over half the students at New Zealand universities were women.

Source: Uglow, Jennifer S., ed., *The Continuum Dictionary of Women's Biography.* New York: Continuum, 1989, p. 145.

1877 ▪ Helen Magill White (1853-1944) became the first woman to earn a doctoral degree from an American university when she received a doctorate in classics from Boston University in Boston, Massachusetts.

Source: Read, Phyllis J., and Bernard L. Witlieb, *The Book of Women's Firsts.* New York: Random House, 1992, p. 265.

1878 ▪ Christine Ladd-Franklin (1847-1930), an American psychologist, was the first female graduate student at Johns Hopkins University in Baltimore, Maryland. An 1869 gradu-

Main Building

ate of Vassar College, Ladd-Franklin was unofficially admitted to graduate study at Johns Hopkins in 1878 and awarded an unofficial fellowship in 1879. Although she completed all of the requirements for a doctorate in 1882, Ladd-Franklin was not awarded a degree because of her gender. She went on to study in Germany and had a distinguished career in psychological research.

Source: James, Edward T., and others, *Notable American Women, 1607-1950: A Biographical Dictionary.* Cambridge, Massachusetts: Harvard University Press, 1971, pp. 354-56.

Vassar College was the undergraduate institution attended by psychologist Christine Ladd-Franklin.

1879 ▪ Mary Elizabeth Mahoney (1845-1926) was the first African-American woman to earn a degree in nursing. In 1879 Mahoney graduated from the nursing program at the New England Hospital for Women and Children in Boston, Massachusetts.

Source: James, Edward T., and others, *Notable American Women, 1607-1950: A Biographical Dictionary.* Cambridge, Massachusetts: Harvard University Press, 1971, p. 486.

Sophia B. Packard founded Spelman College in 1881.

1879 ▪ Mary Foot Seymour (1846-1893) became the founder of the first secretarial school for women in America when she opened the Union School of Stenography in New York City.

Source: Read, Phyllis J., and Bernard L. Witlieb, *The Book of Women's Firsts*. New York: Random House, 1992, pp. 403-04.

c. 1880 ▪ Henrietta Szold (1860-1945) was the first woman to attend the Jewish Theological Society—though she was admitted only on the condition that she promise not to become a rabbi (the official leader of a Jewish congregation). A Zionist throughout her life, Szold was also active in the women's rights movement. (Zionism was an international movement started in the late nineteenth century that originally sought the establishment of a Jewish national and religious homeland in Palestine; later, the term came to be applied to support for modern Israel.) Szold became the first Secretary for Health, Education and Welfare of Jewish Palestine (an area now divided between Israel and Jordan in the Middle East). She is also remembered as the founder of the first night school where immigrants could learn English and American history, an institution opened in New York City in November, 1889. Szold was also the founder and first president of Hadassah (a women's Zionist organization), in New York City on February 24, 1912. In May of 1930, she became the first woman to receive the honorary degree of Doctor of Hebrew Letters from the Jewish Institute of Religion.

Source: James, Edward T., and others, *Notable American Women, 1607-1950: A Biographical Dictionary*. Cambridge, Massachusetts: Harvard University Press, 1971, pp. 417-20.

1880 ▪ Anne Clough (1820-1892) was the first principal of Newnham College of Cambridge University (England). Newnham was the first British college to offer women university-level education. Clough served as principal until her death.

Source: Chicago, Judy, *The Dinner Party*. New York: Anchor, 1979, p. 196.

1881 ▪ **Sophia B. Packard** (1824-1891), an American teacher, was the founder of Spelman College. Started as a school for African-American women in Atlanta, Georgia, the college became Spelman Seminary in 1888, with Packard serving as the first president. The first nursing school for African-American women was opened at Spelman in 1886 and remained open until 1921. **Dr. Sophia Jones,** a graduate of the University of Michigan Medical College in Ann Arbor, was the first African-American female to join the faculty. Jones taught nurses' training until 1888. Endowed by John D. Rockefeller, the seminary was reorganized as Spelman College in 1924 and has served an important need in educating young African-American women.

Source: James, Edward T., and others, *Notable American Women, 1607-1950: A Biographical Dictionary.* Cambridge, Massachusetts: Harvard University Press, 1971, pp. 2-4.

Dr. Sophia Jones was the first African-American woman to join the faculty of Spelman Seminary's nursing school.

1882 ▪ **Alice Elvira Freeman Palmer** (1855-1902) was the first active president of Wellesley College in Wellesley, Massachusetts. Preceded by Ada L. Howard, Palmer took over as acting president in 1881 and formally assumed the post in 1882. She served in this capacity until her marriage in 1887. In 1892 Palmer became the first dean of women at the University of Chicago, Illinois, a position she held until 1895.

Source: James, Edward T., and others, *Notable American Women, 1607-1950: A Biographical Dictionary.* Cambridge, Massachusetts: Harvard University Press, 1971, pp. 4-8.

1885 ▪ **Dorothea Beale** (1831-1906) was the founder of Saint Hilda's College in Cheltenham, England. Established to train teachers, Saint Hilda's later became one of the colleges at Oxford University in 1893. Devoted throughout her life to the education of women, Beale was also an active advocate of women's suffrage (the right to vote).

First Women's State College

The Mississippi Industrial Institute and College for the Education of White Girls of the State of Mississippi was the first state college for women. Founded in 1884, the institution later became Mississippi State College for Women.

Source: Parry, Melanie, ed., *Larousse Dictionary of Women*. New York: Larousse Kingfisher Chambers, Inc., 1995, p. 62.

1887 ▪ Jane Marie Bancroft Robinson (1847-1932), an American scholar, was the first woman to be admitted to the Ecole Pratiques des Hautes Etudes of the University of Paris (France). With a doctorate in history from the University of Syracuse, Robinson became a professor of French language and literature at Northwestern University in Chicago, Illinois, and was the founder of the Western Association of Collegiate Alumnae in 1883 in Evanston, Illinois. This organization was a forerunner of the American Association of University Women (AAUW).

Source: James, Edward T., and others, *Notable American Women, 1607-1950: A Biographical Dictionary*. Cambridge, Massachusetts: Harvard University Press, 1971, pp. 183-84.

1889 ▪ Annie Nathan Mayer (1867-1951), an American writer, was instrumental in founding Barnard College of Columbia University in New York City. Mayer is remembered for her commitment to women's education and to the women's suffrage movement.

Source: Trager, James, *The Women's Chronology*. New York: Holt, 1994, p. 234.

1890 ▪ Susan Lincoln Tolman Mills (1825-1912), an American educator, became the first president of the oldest women's college on the Pacific coast when she was elected president of Mills College in Oakland, California. This school, which she and her husband Cyrus established as a seminary in 1871, followed the model of Mount Holyoke in Massachusetts, from which Susan Mills had graduated in 1845. Susan Mills held the position of president until her retirement at the age of 84 in 1909.

Source: James, Edward T., and others, *Notable American Women, 1607-1950: A Biographical Dictionary*. Cambridge, Massachusetts: Harvard University Press, 1971, pp. 546-47.

Mead Headed College

Elizabeth Mead (1832-1917) was the first president of Mount Holyoke College (originally founded as Mount Holyoke Seminary in 1837). Mary Ann Brigham (1824-1889) was actually the first woman appointed president of Mount Holyoke, but she was killed in a railroad accident a few days before she was to take over the job. In 1893 Mount Holyoke was authorized by the state of Massachusetts to adopt the name Mount Holyoke College.

1890 ▪ **Mary Mills Patrick** (1850-1940), a missionary educator, was the first president of the American College for Girls in Istanbul, Turkey. She assumed her position when the American High School for Girls in that city—where she had taught since 1875—was chartered as a college in 1890 by the Commonwealth of Massachusetts. Patrick served the college in this capacity until her retirement in 1924.

Elizabeth Mead was the first president of Mount Holyoke College, originally founded as Mount Holyoke Seminary.

Source: James, Edward T., and others, *Notable American Women, 1607-1950: A Biographical Dictionary.* Cambridge, Massachusetts: Harvard University Press, 1971, pp. 25-26.

1894 ▪ **Elizabeth Cabot Cary Agassiz** (1822-1907) served as the first president of Radcliffe College in Cambridge, Massachusetts, from 1893 through 1903. Instrumental in founding this female counterpart of Harvard University, Agassiz believed that women should have the same educational opportunities as men.

Source: Ogilvie, Marilyn Bailey, *Women in Science: Antiquity through the Nineteenth Century.* Cambridge, Massachusetts: M.I.T. Press, 1986, pp. 23-25.

1894 ▪ **Martha Carey Thomas** (1857-1935) became the first female president of Bryn Mawr College, a position she held until 1922. Thomas was appointed a professor and a dean of Bryn Mawr College in Bryn Mawr, Pennsylvania, when it opened in 1885. In addition, Thomas was the first woman to earn a doctoral degree from the University of Zurich (Switzerland) in 1882.

Source: Read, Phyllis J., and Bernard L. Witlieb, *The Book of Women's Firsts.* New York: Random House, 1992, p. 442.

1895 ▪ **Cecilia Beaux** (1855-1942), an American portrait painter, was the first female instructor at the Pennsylvania Academy of the Fine Arts in Philadelphia.

Source: James, Edward T., and others, *Notable American Women, 1607-1950: A Biographical Dictionary.* Cambridge, Massachusetts: Harvard University Press, 1971, pp. 119-21.

1896 ▪ **Lucy Wheelock** (1857-1946), a leader in the American kindergarten movement, was the founder of Wheelock College in Boston, Massachusetts. (Kindergarten is often referred to as "pre-school" instruction.) The institution began as Wheelock Kindergarten Training School with Wheelock as its first head, a position she maintained as the school expanded until her retirement in 1939. In 1941, Wheelock Kindergarten Training School formally became Wheelock College.

Source: James, Edward T., and others, *Notable American Women, 1607-1950: A Biographical Dictionary.* Cambridge, Massachusetts: Harvard University Press, 1971, pp. 577-78.

1898 ▪ **Ellen Spencer Mussey** (1850-1936), an American lawyer and feminist, was the first dean of the Washington College of Law, a school she helped found with her friend and colleague, Emma M. Gillett, in Washington, D.C. The coeducational school was incorporated in 1898. While maintaining an active private law practice, Mussey continued in the position of dean until 1913. In 1949 the Washington College of Law, keeping its name, merged with American University.

Source: James, Edward T., and others, *Notable American Women, 1607-1950: A Biographical Dictionary.* Cambridge, Massachusetts: Harvard University Press, 1971, pp. 606-07.

1898 ▪ Annie Besant (1847-1933) was the founder of the Hindu College in Benares, India. Born in England, Besant was an ardent socialist (a person who advocates collective or government control over the production and distribution of goods) who was active both politically and as a writer. Besant later traveled to India where she became involved in Indian politics. During her later years she devoted much energy to theosophy (which promotes teaching about God and the world through mystical insight; theosophy is also the name of a religious movement begun in the United States in 1875 that advocates the Buddhist doctrines of pantheism, the belief that equates God with the forces and laws of nature, and reincarnation, the belief that after death one's soul is reborn in a new body or form). Besant also learned Sanskrit (an ancient Indo-Aryan language) so that she could translate the *Bhagavadgītā* (c. 400-c. 200 B.C.; pronounced "bog-a-vod-'ghee-ta," this work is a poem of 18 songs and 700 verses that is part of the larger epic poem *Mahābhārata,* believed to have been written by Vyāsa).

Source: *Who Was Who, 1929-1940.* London: A. C. Black, 1941, p. 104.

1900 ▪ Sarah Whiting (1847-1927), an American physicist and astronomer educated at the Massachusetts Institute of Technology (MIT), was the first director of the Whiting Observatory at Wellesley College in Massachusetts. (An astronomer studies stars and other celestial bodies.) Whiting served in this capacity beginning in 1900, when the building was completed, until 1916. A teacher at Wellesley from 1876 until 1912, Whiting was also the first person to introduce "applied physics" (astronomy) at the college (in 1880).

Source: Uglow, Jennifer S., ed., *The Continuum Dictionary of Women's Biography.* New York: Continuum, 1989, p. 579.

1903 ▪ Maria Kraus-Boelté (1836-1918), a kindergarten developer, was the first person to teach a university course in kindergarten education, at New York University in New York City. (Kindergarten is often referred to as "pre-school" instruction.) Born in Germany, Kraus-Boelté and her American husband, John Kraus, worked to bring the Froebel tradition of early childhood education to the United States. In 1873 the couple founded the New York Seminary for Kindergarteners, a teacher-training institute that they directed together until Kraus's death in 1896, after which time Kraus-Boelté served as sole principal until her retirement in 1913.

Source: James, Edward T., and others, *Notable American Women, 1607-1950: A Biographical Dictionary*. Cambridge, Massachusetts: Harvard University Press, 1971, pp. 346-48.

1904 ▪ **Fanny Bullock Workman** (1859-1925) was the first American woman to lecture at the Sorbonne in Paris. In 1904 Workman lectured on the topic of her own scientific explorations, including accounts of mountain climbing expeditions with her family.

Source: Read, Phyllis and Bernard L. Witlieb, *The Book of Women's Firsts*. New York: Random House, 1992, p. 496.

1905 ▪ **Sarah Luella Miner** (1861-1935), an American Congregational missionary and educator, was the organizer and first president of the first college for women in China. Miner founded the North China Union Women's College in Tungchow, near Beijing, in 1905. She served as head of the college until it merged with Yenching University in Beijing in 1920. Miner was also the first person to write a geology text in Chinese in the 1880s, a book she and other teachers used for 25 years. (Geology involves the study of rocks, minerals, and the structure of the Earth.)

Source: James, Edward T., and others, *Notable American Women, 1607-1950: A Biographical Dictionary*. Cambridge, Massachusetts: Harvard University Press, 1971, pp. 548-50.

1907 ▪ **Mary Emma Woolley** (1863-1947) was the first female senator of Phi Beta Kappa, an honor society for university students. Wooley was elected to serve in this capacity while she was president of Mount Holyoke College in South Hadley, Massachusetts, a position she held from 1901 until her retirement in 1937. In 1894 Woolley and Annie Weeden were the first women to receive bachelor of arts degrees from Brown University, in Rhode Island.

Source: Read, Phyllis J., and Bernard L. Witlieb, *The Book of Women's Firsts*. New York: Random House, 1992, p. 495.

1908 ▪ **Isabel Bevier** (1860-1942) became the first woman to establish a home economics laboratory on a college campus when she headed the Department of Household Science at the University of Illinois, Champaign-Urbana.

Source: James, Edward T., and others, *Notable American Women, 1607-1950: A Biographical Dictionary*. Cambridge, Massachusetts: Harvard University Press, 1971, pp. 141-42.

1915 ▪ **Amalie Emmy Noether** (1882-1935), a German mathematician, was the first woman to attempt a lecture at Göttingen University. Noether was denied status as a teacher on the basis of her gender; for the next seven years she could instruct only as an "assistant" to a professor. In 1922 Noether was finally permitted to teach as a lecturer on her own, but her "special" salary was well below that of male professors.

Source: Ogilvie, Marilyn Bailey, *Women in Science: Antiquity through the Nineteenth Century*. Cambridge, Massachusetts: M.I.T. Press, 1986, pp. 140-41.

1916 ▪ **Clara Damrosch Mannes** (1869-1948), a pianist and teacher, was the cofounder and codirector (with her husband David Mannes, a famous violinist) of the David Mannes Music School in New York City. In 1953 the prestigious school became the Mannes College of Music, offering a five-year course leading to a bachelor of science degree.

Source: James, Edward T., and others, *Notable American Women, 1607-1950: A Biographical Dictionary*. Cambridge, Massachusetts: Harvard University Press, 1971, pp. 490-91.

1918 ▪ **Ida Sophia Scudder** (1870-1960), an American physician and medical missionary, was the founder of the Vellore Christian Medical College in Vellore, India, in 1918. Scudder's purpose was to train Indian women to be doctors in areas where *purdah,* the Hindu practice of secluding women from public observation, was practiced. (Hinduism is the national religion of India.)

Source: Uglow, Jennifer S., ed., *The Continuum Dictionary of Women's Biography,* New York: Continuum, 1989, pp. 489-90.

1918 ▪ **Mabel Smith Douglass** (1877-1933) was the founder and first dean of the New Jersey College for Women in New Brunswick, New Jersey. In 1955 the college was renamed Douglass College of Rutgers University in her honor. Douglass served as dean until her retirement in 1933. Shortly thereafter, despondent over the suicide of her 16-year-old son, she took her own life in what initially was regarded as a drowning accident on Lake Placid, New York. Her body was not recovered for 30 years.

Source: James, Edward T., and others, *Notable American Women, 1607-1950: A Biographical Dictionary.* Cambridge, Massachusetts: Harvard University Press, 1971, pp. 510-11.

1921 ▪ **Ruth Wheeler** (1877-1948), an American home economist and dietician (a specialist in preparing nutritious diets), introduced professional training for dietitians at the College of Medicine at the State University of Iowa at Ames. In the same year Wheeler became the first female professor and the first head of the department of nutrition at the College of Medicine. She also established the first one-year dietetic internship course leading to a master's degree at Iowa State University.

Source: James, Edward T., and others, *Notable American Women, 1607-1950: A Biographical Dictionary.* Cambridge, Massachusetts: Harvard University Press, 1971, pp. 576-77.

1922 ▪ **Lizzie Pitts Merrill Palmer** (1838-1916), an American philanthropist (a person who promotes human welfare, usually by donating large sums of money to worthy causes), was founded the Merrill-Palmer Institute of Human Development and Family Life, which opened its doors in Detroit, Michigan, in 1922. Made possible by her bequest of over $3 million, the school stressed home economics and teacher training.

Source: James, Edward T., and others, *Notable American Women, 1607-1950: A Biographical Dictionary.* Cambridge, Massachusetts: Harvard University Press, 1971, pp. 11-12.

1922 ▪ **Patty Smith Hill** (1868-1946), an American educator, was the first person to introduce the area of nursery school education at Columbia University's Teachers College in New York

City. Hill taught at Columbia from 1906 until 1935. She is also remembered—along with her sister, Mildred J. Hill—as the composer of the song "Happy Birthday to You." Patty wrote the lyrics and Mildred wrote the music. The song was first published in the sisters' *Song Stories for the Kindergarten* (1893).

Source: James, Edward T., and others, *Notable American Women, 1607-1950: A Biographical Dictionary.* Cambridge, Massachusetts: Harvard University Press, 1971, pp. 194-95.

1923 ▪ Ada Comstock (Notestein; 1876-1973) became the first full-time president of Radcliffe College in Cambridge, Massachusetts:, a position she held until 1943. Devoting her life to teaching and educational administration, Comstock was also the first president of the American Association of University Women (AAUW).

Source: Read, Phyllis J., and Bernard L. Witlieb, *The Book of Women's Firsts.* New York: Random House, 1992, pp. 98-99.

1923 ▪ Lucy Diggs Slowe (1885-1937), an American educator dedicated to the advancement of African-American women, was the first president of the National Association of College Women, a position she held until 1929. In 1919 Slowe was also named the first principal of Shaw Junior High School in Washington, D.C. After entering Howard University in 1904, Slowe was one of the founders and the first vice-president of Alpha Kappa Alpha, the first sorority among African-American college women. Slowe received a master's degree from Columbia University in 1915 and went on to become dean of women at Howard University in 1922.

Source: James, Edward T., and others, *Notable American Women, 1607-1950: A Biographical Dictionary.* Cambridge, Massachusetts: Harvard University Press, 1971, pp. 299-00.

1927 ▪ Ellen Browning Scripps (1836-1932), an American journalist and philanthropist (a person who promotes human welfare, usually by donating large sums of money to worthy causes), was the founder of Scripps College for Women in Claremont, California. The driving force in her family's newspaper empire from its earliest days in Detroit, Michigan, in the

1860s, Scripps settled in La Jolla, California, in 1897. She and her half-brother, E. W. Scripps, established the Marine Biological Association of San Diego in 1903, a society that became part of the University of California in 1912. Scripps is remembered for her generosity and for her lively mind and wide range of interests.

Source: James, Edward T., and others, *Notable American Women, 1607-1950: A Biographical Dictionary.* Cambridge, Massachusetts: Harvard University Press, 1971, pp. 250-52.

1930 ▪ Dorothy Weeks (1893-1990) was the first woman to earn a doctorate in mathematics from the Massachusetts Institute of Technology (MIT) in Cambridge, Massachusetts. Weeks established her career in industry and university teaching; her specialty was physics.

Source: Read, Phyllis J., and Bernard L. Witlieb, *The Book of Women's Firsts.* New York: Random House, 1992, p. 474.

Dorothy Weeks was the first woman to earn a doctorate in mathematics from the Massachusetts Institute of Technology (MIT).

1939 ▪ Dorothy Garrod (1892-1968) was the first female professor at Cambridge University in England. Garrod was elected professor of archaeology (the scientific study of material remains of past human life) even before women students were allowed to receive degrees. Her explorations from 1929 to 1934 in Gibraltar, Mount Carmel (Israel), Kurdistan, and Beirut, Lebanon, revolutionized the understanding of early Stone Age chronology and culture.

Source: Magnusson, Magnus, *Larousse Biographical Dictionary.* New York: Larousse Kingfisher Chambers, 1994, p. 568.

1944 ▪ Ludmilla B. Turkevich, an expert in Russian language and literature, was the first woman to become a teacher at Princeton University in New Jersey. Turkevich remained on the faculty for 17 years as a lecturer in Russian and Spanish literature until Rutgers University offered her a full professorship at Douglass College, its women's division, in 1961. She spent 18 years as chair of the Russian department there.

Source: *The New York Times.* April 16, 1995.

1956 ▪ **Cecelia Payne Gaposhkin** (1900-1979) was the first woman to become a tenured professor at Harvard University in Cambridge, Massachusetts. (Becoming tenured usually means that a person becomes a fully-vested member of the faculty for the balance of his or her professional career.) During the same year, she was the first woman to chair the department of astronomy (the study of stars and other celestial objects), a position she held until 1960.

Source: Read, Phyllis J., and Bernard L. Witlieb, *The Book of Women's Firsts.* New York: Random House, 1992, p. 334.

1967 ▪ **Iffat** (1910-), wife of King Faisal of Saudi Arabia, was the founder of the College of Education, an institution designed to train girls as teachers. A lifelong advocate of education, Iffat also founded a government boys' school called "Dar al Hanam" in 1942.

Source: Uglow, Jennifer S., ed., *The Continuum Dictionary of Women's Biography,* New York: Continuum, 1989, p. 273.

1970 ▪ **Graciela Olivarez,** an American lawyer, was the first woman to graduate from the Notre Dame University Law School in South Bend, Indiana. In the early 1970s she went on to become the first woman to serve as chair of the board of the Mexican-American Legal Defense Educational Fund. Olivarez was appointed head of the U.S. Community Services Administration in 1977.

Source: O'Neill, Lois Decker, ed., *The Women's Book of World Records and Achievements.* New York: Doubleday, 1979, p. 716.

1971 ▪ **Margery Ann Tabankin** (1948-), became the first female president of the National Student Association in 1972, the year after she graduated from the University of Wisconsin at Madison. Tabankin was also an anti-war activist during the years of America's heaviest involvement in the Vietnam War (1963-1975).

Source: O'Neill, Lois Decker, ed., *The Women's Book of World Records and Achievements.* Garden City, New York: Doubleday, 1979, p. 726.

1974 ▪ **Pauline Jewett** (1922-), who received a doctorate from Harvard University, was the first woman to serve as a college president in Canada when she was named president of Simon Fraser College in 1974.

Source: O'Neill, Lois Decker, ed., *The Women's Book of World Records and Achievements.* Garden City, New York: Doubleday, 1979, p. 407.

1975 ▪ **Jill Ker Conway** (1934-) became the first female president of Smith College in Northampton, Massachusetts, on the hundredth anniversary of the institution. A native of Australia, Conway wrote about her experiences growing up there and about the challenges faced by women scholars in two autobiographical works, *The Road from Coorain* (1990) and *True North: A Memoir* (1994).

Source: Read, Phyllis J., and Bernard L. Witlieb, *The Book of Women's Firsts.* New York: Random House, 1992, p. 412.

1975 ▪ **Rosemary Murray,** a British educator who had previously been president of New Hall, Cambridge, was the first woman to serve as vice-chancellor (assistant chief executive officer) of Cambridge University (England). The position, which is equivalent to the presidency of an American university, was established in 1412.

Source: O'Neill, Lois Decker, ed., *The Women's Book of World Records and Achievements.* Garden City, New York: Doubleday, 1979, p. 407.

1976 ▪ **Hélène Ahrweiler** (1916-), a French historian, was the first woman to become president of the Sorbonne in Paris. Ahrweiler held the post until her retirement in 1981, when she

Female Rhodes Scholars

In 1977 24 women from several former British colonies were selected as Rhodes Scholars. This was the first time women were permitted to receive this honor, which offers students scholarships for graduate study at Oxford University in England.

began a seven-year term as chancellor (chief executive officer) of the Universities of Paris.

Source: Uglow, Jennifer S., ed., *The Continuum Dictionary of Women's Biography.* New York: Continuum, 1989, pp. 9-10.

Andrea Hollen graduated at the top of her West Point class in 1980.

1986 ▪ **Niara Sudarkasa (Gloria Marshall)** (1939-) was named the first female president of Lincoln University in Jefferson City, Missouri. Sudarkasa earned a doctorate in anthropology (the study of the origins and social history of human beings) from Columbia University in New York City. Before taking the position of president at Lincoln University, she was a tenured professor and associate vice president of academic affairs at the University of Michigan in Ann Arbor.

Source: *Jet.* October 27, 1986, p. 22.

1988 ▪ **Donna Shalala** (1942-) was appointed chancellor (chief executive officer) of the University of Wisconsin at Madison. She was the first woman to hold the post and the first woman to head a Big Ten university. Shalala, an energetic and assertive leader, once worked in Iran for the Peace Corps, spent time as the president of Hunter College in New York City, and was appointed assistant secretary of housing and urban develop-

ment under President Jimmy Carter (served in office 1977-1981). In 1993, she left the University of Wisconsin-Madison to become Secretary of Health and Human Services in President Bill Clinton's administration.

Source: *The New Yorker.* April 26, 1993, pp. 53- 62.

1993 ▪ **Joann Horton** (1932-) was named the first female president of Texas Southern University in Houston, Texas. Horton earned her bachelor and master's degrees in French from Appalachian State University in Boone, North Carolina, and her doctorate in higher education administration from Ohio State University. Before being named president of Texas Southern University, Horton worked as the administrator of community colleges for the Iowa Department of Education in Des Moines.

Source: *Jet.* August 23, 1993, p. 16.

Judith Rodin was the first female president of an Ivy League school.

1993 ▪ **Judith Rodin** (1945-) was appointed president of the University of Pennsylvania, becoming the first woman to head an Ivy League school. (The Ivy League is a group of long-established schools in the eastern United States that are widely regarded as representing the highest in scholastic status and social prestige.) Other women had held the position of acting president, but Rodin was the first to receive a full appointment. A University of Pennsylvania alumna (female graduate), she was the president of the Women's Student Government during her undergraduate years. Rodin felt that it was archaic (old-fashioned, or backward-thinking) to have separate men's and women's student governments, so before she left, she merged the two.

Source: *The Chronicle of Higher Education.* December 15, 1993, p. A20.

1994 ▪ **Gillian Beer** (1935-) became the first woman to serve as president of Clare Hall, a college of Cambridge University in England which educates both men and women. Beer was also the first woman of a wife-and-husband team who both held chairs at Cambridge University. Educated at Oxford and Girton College, Cambridge, Beer was appointed professor of English at Cambridge in 1989 and served as King Edward VII Professor of English Literature. Beer was particularly interested in the connections between literature and science.

Source: *Clare Hall Newsletter (Cambridge), 1993- 1994.*

1994 ▪ Dorothy Yancy (1944-) was elected the twelfth president of Johnson C. Smith University in Charlotte, North Carolina, becoming the first woman to be named to the post. Yancy earned a bachelor's degree in history from Johnson C. Smith University in 1964, a master of arts from the University of Massachusetts at Amherst, and a doctorate in political science from Atlanta University.

Source: *Jet.* November 21, 1994, p. 22.

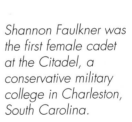

Shannon Faulkner was the first female cadet at the Citadel, a conservative military college in Charleston, South Carolina.

1994 ▪ Shannon Faulkner (1975-) was the first female cadet at the Citadel, a conservative military college in Charleston, South Carolina. After a year-long legal battle, a federal judge ordered the college to accept women on July 22, 1994. Faulkner brought the successful suit, using her own experience as a test case, so that she could attend the college beginning in the 1994-1995 academic year. Although Faulkner left the Citadel during her first year, she is credited with having paved the way for women to attend previously all-male military institutions.

Source: *The New York Times.* July 23, 1994.

1997 ▪ Ioana Dumitriu (1957-), a Romanian college student, was the first woman to win the William Lowell Putnam Mathematical Competition. Considered the "Olympics of college mathematics," the competition was founded in 1941 for students in the United States and Canada. For the previous 56 years all of the winners had been men. Dumitriu, a native of Romania, was a sophomore at New York University.

Source: *The New York Times.* May 1, 1997.

Secondary and Primary Education

1686 ▪ **Françoise de Maintenon** (1635-1719), a Frenchwoman influential at the court of Louis XIV (reigned 1643-1715), founded the Maison Royale de St. Louis in St. Cyr, France, a progressive school for impoverished (penniless) aristocratic girls. The school, where students aged 6 through 19 studied economics and literature, became popular throughout Europe.

Source: Uglow, Jennifer S., ed., *The Continuum Dictionary of Women's Biography.* New York: Continuum, 1989, p. 157.

c. 1800 ▪ **Jeanne Campan** (1753-1822) founded the first secular (non-religious) school in France to offer a liberal education to girls. Campan also published several books on the subject of education.

Source: Chicago, Judy, *The Dinner Party.* New York: Anchor, 1979, p. 178.

1814 ▪ **Emma Hart Willard** (1787-1870) organized the first institution for the higher education of women when she opened the Middlebury Female Seminary in Middlebury, Vermont. Willard went on to found the Troy Female Seminary in 1821, which was renamed the Emma Willard School in 1895. The institution still operates as a prestigious boarding school for girls in Troy, New York.

Source: Read, Phyllis J., and Bernard L. Witlieb, *The Book of Women's Firsts.* New York: Random House, 1992, p. 482.

1816 ▪ **Joanna Graham Bethune** (1770-1860), an American educator and philanthropist (a person who promotes human welfare, usually by donating large sums of money to worthy causes), was the first woman to lead the Sunday school movement in the United States. In New York City, she organized the

Female Union Society for the Promotion of Sabbath Schools. Drawing on her knowledge of the movement in Scotland, Bethune worked to set up Sunday schools that would teach basic reading and writing skills to poor children and adults. Her society later merged with the American Sunday-School Union, founded in 1824.

Source: James, Edward T., and others, *Notable American Women, 1607-1950: A Biographical Dictionary.* Cambridge, Massachusetts: Harvard University Press, 1971, pp. 138-40.

c. 1837 ▪ Charlotte Fowler Wells (1814-1901), an American phrenologist and publisher, was the first person in the United States to teach a regular class in phrenology (the belief that the shape of the skull indicates personality traits). Working with her brothers at their phrenology center in New York City beginning in 1837, Wells taught classes in this subject throughout the rest of her life.

Source: James, Edward T., and others, *Notable American Women, 1607-1950: A Biographical Dictionary.* Cambridge, Massachusetts: Harvard University Press, 1971, pp. 560-61.

1837 ▪ Laura Dewey Bridgman (1829-1889), who lost her sight and hearing at age eighteen months due to scarlet fever, became the first blind, deaf, and mute person to receive a formal education. As a student at the Perkins Institution, a school for the blind in Boston, Massachusetts, she learned to read and to communicate with others.

Source: Read, Phyllis J., and Bernard L. Witlieb, *The Book of Women's Firsts.* New York: Random House, 1992, pp. 67-68.

1843 ▪ Sarah Porter (1813-1900), an American educator, was the founder and first head of Miss Porter's School in Farmington, Connecticut. One of the oldest and best known girls' boarding schools in the country, Miss Porter's, often known simply as "Farmington," continues to have a reputation for academic excellence and social grace. Porter directed the life of the school through teaching and personal example until her death.

Source: James, Edward T., and others, *Notable American Women, 1607-1950: A Biographical Dictionary.* Cambridge, Massachusetts: Harvard University Press, 1971, pp. 88- 89.

Peabody Opened Kindergarten

In 1860 Elizabeth Palmer Peabody (1804-1894) opened the first formally organized public kindergarten in the United States in Boston, Massachusetts. (Kindergarten is often referred to as "preschool" instruction.) Influenced by the Froebels schools in Germany, Peabody was a crusader for early childhood education. The first female publisher in Boston, Peabody was also the founder and first editor of the *Kindergarten Messenger,* a post she held from 1873 through 1875.

1853 ▪ **Mary Easton Sibley** (1800-1878), an American educator, founded Lindenwood College in St. Charles, Missouri. An outgrowth of Linden Wood school for girls—which Sibley founded with her husband in 1828 and where she served as principal—Lindenwood College became formally associated with the Presbyterian Church in 1856.

Source: James, Edward T., and others, *Notable American Women, 1607-1950: A Biographical Dictionary.* Cambridge, Massachusetts: Harvard University Press, 1971, pp. 287-88.

1856 ▪ **Charlotte L. Forten Grimké** (1837-1914), a civil rights leader and educator, was the first African-American woman to teach white children, in Salem, Massachusetts. Grimké was hired as a teacher in the Epes Grammar School and held the position until 1858.

Source: James, Edward T., and others, *Notable American Women, 1607-1950: A Biographical Dictionary.* Cambridge, Massachusetts: Harvard University Press, 1971, pp. 95-97.

1857 ▪ **Margarethe Meyer Schurz** (1833-1876), a German-born educator, was the first person to operate a private kindergarten in America. (Kindergarten is often referred to as "preschool" instruction.) Following European models, Schurz opened her school in Watertown, Wisconsin, in 1857.

Source: Read, Phyllis J., and Bernard L. Witlieb, *The Book of Women's Firsts.* New York: Random House, 1992, p. 395.

1862 ▪ **Laura Matilda Towne** (1825-1901), an American teacher committed to the education of African Americans, was the founder of the Penn School on the island of St. Helena off the coast of South Carolina. The Penn School was one of the earliest and longest-lasting schools open to freed slaves. Serving as the institution's first director, Towne stressed the teaching of traditional academic subjects.

Source: James, Edward T., and others, *Notable American Women, 1607-1950: A Biographical Dictionary*. Cambridge, Massachusetts: Harvard University Press, 1971, pp. 472-74.

1863 ▪ **Anna Callender Brackett** (1836-1911) was the first woman to serve as principal of a normal school (a two-year institution for the training of elementary teachers). From 1863 until 1872 she was principal of the St. Louis Normal School in St. Louis, Missouri. Brackett went on to found a private school for girls and to serve as editor of *Women and the Higher Education* from 1893 through 1895.

Source: Read, Phyllis J., and Bernard L. Witlieb, *The Book of Women's Firsts*. New York: Random House, 1992, p. 63.

1869 ▪ **Sarah Fuller** (1836-1927) was the first principal of a day school for the deaf. Fuller served as head of the Boston School for Deaf-Mutes for 41 years from the time of its opening in Boston, Massachusetts, in 1869. In 1877 the name of the institution was changed to the Horace Mann School for the Deaf. Fuller was innovative in advocating the use of oral speech and early education for deaf children (and for admitting both residents and nonresidents of Boston).

Source: James, Edward T., and others, *Notable American Women, 1607-1950: A Biographical Dictionary*. Cambridge, Massachusetts: Harvard University Press, 1971, pp. 683-85.

1869 ▪ **Baba Petkova** (1826-1894), a Bulgarian educator, introduced a system for the education of women in Eastern Europe. Petkova began teaching in her native Bulgaria in 1859 and campaigned throughout her life, despite government objections, for access to education for women.

Source: Chicago, Judy, *The Dinner Party*. New York: Anchor, 1979, p. 196.

1869 ▪ **Amy Bradley** (1823-1904) became the first woman to supervise a public school system when she was named superintendent of the Wilmington, North Carolina, school system.

Source: Read, Phyllis J., and Bernard L. Witlieb, *The Book of Women's Firsts*. New York: Random House, 1992, pp. 63-64.

1869 ▪ Fanny Marion Jackson Coppin (1837-1913), a graduate of Oberlin College, was the first African-American woman to hold a position of independent trust in an educational institution. In 1869 she became head principal at the Institute for Colored Youth in Philadelphia. During her thirty-seven year career as a teacher and administrator at this school, she helped shape the lives of many African-American leaders and influenced the development of education for African Americans in nineteenth-century America.

Source: James, Edward T., and others, *Notable American Women, 1607-1950: A Biographical Dictionary.* Cambridge, Massachusetts: Harvard University Press, 1971, pp. 383-85.

1875 ▪ Kalliopi Kehajia (1839-1905), a Greek teacher, organized the Zappeion School for girls in Turkey and served as the first headmistress of the school from 1875 until 1890. In 1888 she traveled to the United States and, on her return to Greece, wrote articles in praise of the opportunities available to American women. Kehajia was among the first teachers to use open lectures as a means of education. Trained in London, England, she served as head of the Hill School for girls in Athens, Greece, in the 1850s. She delivered a series of 80 open lectures over two years on classical literature and social problems, focusing on the needs of women.

Source: Uglow, Jennifer S., ed., *The Continuum Dictionary of Women's Biography.* New York: Continuum, 1989, p. 294.

1875 ▪ Emily Huntington (1841-1909), an innovator in early childhood education, was the founder of the "kitchen garden" movement in New York City. Huntington introduced the teaching of domestic skills at the Wilson Industrial School for Girls in order to train poor girls to be good housekeepers and servants. Huntington also wrote *Little Lessons for Little Housekeepers,* which was published in 1875.

Source: James, Edward T., and others, *Notable American Women, 1607-1950: A Biographical Dictionary.* Cambridge, Massachusetts: Harvard University Press, 1971, pp. 239-40.

1876 ▪ **Juliet Corson** (1841-1897) was the founder of the New York Cooking School, the first cooking school in the United States. Corson published *Fifteen Cent Dinners for Families of Six* (1877) and *Family Living on $500 a Year* (1887), establishing a national reputation as an authority on cooking and domestic economy.

Source: Read, Phyllis J., and Bernard L. Witlieb, *The Book of Women's Firsts*. New York: Random House, 1992, pp. 103-4.

c. 1890s ▪ **Lida Gustava Heymann** (1867-1943), a German feminist, was the first person to found a progressive kindergarten in Germany. During the 1890s, she also started a day nursery, a lunch club for single women, an actresses' society, a women's home, and a society for female office workers. Heymann also established a school to train women as clerks. In 1902 she was one of the thirteen founders of the German Union for Women's Suffrage (the right to vote), along with her friends Minna Cauer and Anita Augsburg. In 1918, Heymann and Augsburg started the feminist periodical *Die Frau im Staat.* Heymann continued to be active on behalf of pacifism and women's rights throughout her life. (A pacifist opposes violent or aggressive actions, especially warfare.)

Source: Uglow, Jennifer S., ed., *The Continuum Dictionary of Women's Biography*. New York: Continuum, 1989, p. 258.

1896 ▪ **Alice Chipman Dewey** (1858-1927) was the cofounder—with her husband, philosopher John Dewey (1859-1952)— of the Laboratory School, an elementary school at the University of Chicago. Insisting that her husband's ideas be put into practice, Alice Dewey oversaw the work at this famous school where "learning by doing" was emphasized.

Source: James, Edward T., and others, *Notable American Women, 1607-1950: A Biographical Dictionary*. Cambridge, Massachusetts: Harvard University Press, 1971, pp. 466-67.

1897 ▪ **Alice McLellan Birney** (1858-1907) founded the National Congress of Mothers in Washington, D.C. Birney served as the first president of the organization, which she formed to unite the home, school, and community on behalf of

Trade School Established

In 1904 the Trade School for Girls, the first public vocational high school for girls in America, was established in Boston, Massachusetts. The school was designed to prepare young women for industrial jobs. The institution's first principal was Florence M. Marshall.

children and young people. Renamed the National Congress of Parents, the organization became the Parent-Teacher Association (PTA) in 1908.

Source: James, Edward T., and others, *Notable American Women, 1607-1950: A Biographical Dictionary.* Cambridge, Massachusetts: Harvard University Press, 1971, pp. 147-48.

1897 ▪ Adelaide Hunter Hoodless (1857-1910), a campaigner for women's education in domestic (related to the home) science, was the founder of the Women's Institute, a home economics school for farm women, in Stoney Creek, Ontario, Canada. Hoodless also established classes in home economics at the Young Women's Christian Association (YWCA) at Hamilton in the 1890s and at the Ontario Agricultural Institute at Guelph in 1904. The Women's Institute is now incorporated in the Associated Country Women of the World, which has over eight million members. Hoodless died on a lecture platform while seeking more funds for her work.

Source: O'Neill, Lois Decker, ed., *The Women's Book of World Records and Achievements.* Garden City, New York: Doubleday, 1979, p. 5.

1899 ▪ Ellen Swallow Richards (1842-1911) had a distinguished career in the field of chemistry and achieved many firsts throughout her life. Most notably, she was the founder of the science of home economics, a term she coined during a summer educational conference at Lake Placid, New York, in 1899. Richards was a founding member of the American Home Economics Association in 1908 and served as its first president until 1910.

Source: Ogilvie, Marilyn Bailey, *Women in Science: Antiquity through the Nineteenth Century.* Cambridge, Massachusetts: M.I.T. Press, 1986, pp. 149-52.

1907 ▪ Maria Montessori (1870-1952), an Italian educator, founded an innovative school for the education of young children. (The Montessori system involves teaching according to the educational needs of the individual child.) Montessori schools are now located throughout the world. In 1896 Montessori was also the first woman in Italy to receive a medical degree when she graduated from the University of Rome.

Source: Parry, Melanie, ed., *Larousse Dictionary of Women.* New York: Larousse Kingfisher Chambers, Inc., 1995, p. 472.

1908 ▪ **Marie Joseph Butler** (1860-1940), an Irish nun, was the founder of the Marymount schools and colleges in America and Europe. Butler started her first school in 1908 in Tarrytown, New York. In 1926, a year before she became an American citizen, she was elected Mother General of the Congregation of the Sacred Heart of Mary, the first superior to head an American Catholic congregation whose motherhouse was in Europe.

Source: James, Edward T., and others, *Notable American Women, 1607-1950: A Biographical Dictionary.* Cambridge, Massachusetts: Harvard University Press, 1971, pp. 272-73.

1910 ▪ **Ella Flagg Young** (1845-1918) was the first female president of the National Education Association (NEA). In 1910, while she was superintendent of the Chicago public schools, Flagg Young was elected to the presidency after considerable debate.

Source: James, Edward T., and others, *Notable American Women, 1607-1950: A Biographical Dictionary.* Cambridge, Massachusetts: Harvard University Press, 1971, pp. 697-99.

1916 ▪ **Emily Griffith** (1880-1947), an American teacher committed to the education of the working poor, was the founder and first principal of the Denver Opportunity School, in Denver, Colorado. Griffith served in this post until 1933, when the enrollment was 8,670 students, including both children and adults. In 1934, the school was renamed the Emily Griffith Opportunity School.

Source: James, Edward T., and others, *Notable American Women, 1607-1950: A Biographical Dictionary.* Cambridge, Massachusetts: Harvard University Press, 1971, pp. 94-95.

c. 1919 ▪ **Abala Das Bose** (1865-1951) was the first person to introduce the Montessori system of education in India. (The innovative Montessori system involves teaching according to the educational needs of the individual child.) Bose worked throughout her life on behalf of the education of women in her country, founding several service organizations and advocating school reform and innovative teaching.

Source: Uglow, Jennifer S., ed., *The Continuum Dictionary of Women's Biography.* New York: Continuum, 1989, p. 80.

1924 ▪ **Florence Rood** became the first female president of the American Federation of Teachers. Although the Federation was founded that same year in Chicago, Illinois, Rood was actually the organization's second president, serving until 1926.

Source: Read, Phyllis and Bernard L. Witlieb, *The Book of Women's Firsts.* New York: Random House, 1992, p. 378.

1963 ▪ **Princess Anne** (1950-), the only daughter of Queen Elizabeth II and Prince Philip, was the first English princess to attend school. Like her brother Prince Charles before her, Anne was initially educated at home; breaking with royal tradition, however, she was sent to boarding school at the age of 13 in 1963.

Source: Magnusson, Magnus, *Larousse Biographical Dictionary.* New York: Larousse Kingfisher Chambers, 1994, p. 49.

Government

Rulers
Presidents
Prime Ministers
Cabinet Members
Ambassadors
Representatives and Appointees

Rulers

c. 40 B.C. ▪ **Livia Drusilla** (56 B.C.-A.D. 29) was the first Roman empress. Drusilla played a significant role in governing Rome for over 70 years as the wife of Augustus Caesar (63 B.C.-A.D. 14) and mother of Tiberius (42 B.C.-A.D. 37). She struggled to assure that her son Tiberius would rule as her husband's heir.

Source: Chicago, Judy, *The Dinner Party.* New York: Anchor, 1979, p. 129.

797 ▪ **Irene the Athenian** (c.752-803) was the first woman to rule the Byzantine Empire (the eastern part of the later Roman Empire dating from A.D. 330). Irene had previously been co-ruler and regent (a person who rules) for her feeble son Constantine VI. She later imprisoned her son and may have been responsible for having him blinded. Ruling in her own right, Irene summoned the Seventh Ecumenical Council (known as the Council of Nicaea) in 787, an organization which brought peace

Sirimavo Bandaranaike became the world's first female prime minister when the Sri Lanka Freedom Party won a general election. (See "Prime Ministers" entry dated 1960.)

and stability to an empire divided by religious unrest. During her sole rule, she was addressed as "King." For her part in restoration of religion, Irene was made a saint by the Greek church.

Source: Magnusson, Magnus, *Larousse Biographical Dictionary.* New York: Larousse Kingfisher Chambers, 1994, p. 761.

1491 ▪ **Anne of Brittany** (1477-1514) succeeded her father as leader of Brittany and struggled to maintain Breton independence. When Anne was forced to marry Charles VIII of France (1470-1498), Brittany was united with France and she became queen. Anne was reportedly the first queen to give women an important place at court. Anne took over the government of France while Charles VIII was at war with Italy. A year after his death in 1498, she married his successor, Louis XII (1462-1515).

Source: Chicago, Judy, *The Dinner Party.* New York: Anchor, 1979, p. 155.

1553 ▪ **Mary Tudor** (1516-1558; also known as Queen Mary I and "Bloody Mary"), was the first woman to rule England in her own right. The daughter of Henry VIII (1491-1547) and Catherine of Aragon (1485-1536), Mary ascended to the throne after the early death of her half brother, Edward VI (1537-1553). During her five-year rule Mary struggled unsuccessfully to restore the pope in Rome as head of the church in England.

Source: Magnusson, Magnus, *Larousse Biographical Dictionary.* New York: Larousse Kingfisher Chambers, 1994, p. 276.

1558 ▪ **Elizabeth I** (1533-1603; also known as "the Virgin Queen") began her reign. Elizabeth's 45-year rule as an unmarried woman of unprecedented power brought her country prosperity and growth.

Source: Parry, Melanie, ed., *Larousse Dictionary of Women.* New York: Larousse Kingfisher Chambers, 1995, pp. 213-14.

1622 ▪ **Mbande Nzinga** (1582-1663) founded the kingdom of Matamba in Africa in reaction to Portuguese colonial repression. Nzinga was a royal princess in Ndongo, a kingdom adjoining Portuguese West Africa (present-day Angola). She attempted to declare her kingdom independent of the Portuguese in order to free her people from the horrors of the slave trade. In 1622 Nzinga was sent to negotiate with the invading Portuguese by her brother, the King of Ndongo. While Nzinga was in Portugal she converted to Christianity and was baptized Dona Aña de Souza. She then established the new kingdom, which she called Matamba. According to some historical accounts, her kingdom thrived and remained stable by acting as brokers (people who arrange transactions between buyers and sellers) for the Portuguese slave trade.

Source: Magnusson, Magnus, *Larousse Biographical Dictionary.* New York: Larousse Kingfisher Chambers, 1994, p. 1092.

c. 1675 ▪ Queen Anne (also called Totopotomoi) was the first woman to become a Native American chief. As head of the Pamunkey Tribe of Virginia, she ruled from about 1675 until 1715. Queen Anne was the widow of Chief Totopotomoi, who died in 1654 while helping the English repel an invasion by other tribes.

Source: Kane, Nathan Joseph, *Famous First Facts.* New York: Wilson, 1981, p. 17.

1689 ▪ Mary II (1662-1694) became the first woman to rule England in legal equality with her husband. The daughter of James II (1633-1701), Mary married William of Orange (1650-1702) in 1677 and settled in the Netherlands. In 1688 she and her husband returned to England and deposed (removed from power) her father in what is now known as "The Glorious Revolution." The revolution resulted in peaceful restoration of Protestant rule to England. Mary and William were crowned as joint sovereigns (equal rulers).

Source: Magnusson, Magnus, *Larousse Biographical Dictionary.* New York: Larousse Kingfisher Chambers, 1994, p. 984.

c. 1740 ▪ Maria Theresa (1717-1780) was the only woman to rule during the Habsburg (also spelled Hapsburg) era. (The Habsburgs were a royal family who ruled in Europe from the 1200s through the early 1900s.) As the last male heir of the Austrian Habsburgs, Charles VI (1685-1740) passed the Prag-

matic Sanction (1713), which allowed the female line to succeed to the throne. Maria Theresa, his daughter, ruled Austria
with her husband, Francis I (1708-1765). During her reign,
Maria Theresa achieved a remarkable unification of the diverse
parts of the Austro-Hungarian Empire and devoted her energies to making Vienna a great European capital. In the 1760s
her policy of centralization encouraged important architectural,
social, and cultural development in her native city.

Source: Magnusson, Magnus, *Larousse Biographical Dictionary.* New York:
Larousse Kingfisher Chambers, 1994, p. 971.

1875 ▪ **Rosana Chouteau** was the first female chief of the
Osage Beaver Band (a Native American tribal group). She was
elected after the death of her uncle, the previous chief.
Chouteau's situation was unusual because the Osage were a
patrilineal tribe (descent goes through the father's side of the
family).

Source: Chicago, Judy, *The Dinner Party.* New York: Anchor, 1979, p. 170.

1952 ▪ **Elizabeth II** (1926-), queen of the United Kingdom of
Great Britain and Northern Ireland, was the first queen to serve
as head of the British Commonwealth of Nations. (The Commonwealth is a voluntary alliance of 51 nations, including
Canada, Australia, India, South Africa, and New Zealand.)
Elizabeth was proclaimed queen February 6, 1952, on the
death of her father, George VI (1895-1952), and her coronation
ceremony followed on June 2, 1953.

Source: Magnusson, Magnus, *Larousse Biographical Dictionary.* New York:
Larousse Kingfisher Chambers, 1994, p. 474.

1972 ▪ **Margrethe II** (1940-) became Denmark's first queen
since A.D. 1000, when she succeeded her father Frederick IX
(1899-1972) to the throne. Margrethe's role as queen was
merely ceremonial and she spent most of her time with her
family and working in her profession, archaeology (the study
of ancient civilizations and organisms). She was also an artist
and illustrator of children's books.

Source: Magnusson, Magnus, *Larousse Biographical Dictionary.* New York:
Larousse Kingfisher Chambers, 1994, p. 970.

Presidents

1974 ▪ **Isabel Perón** (b. 1931), the widow of Juan Perón (1895-1974), president of Argentina, became the world's first female president when she took over the office on the death of her husband. Isabel Perón held this position until she was ousted during a political coup (overthrow of government) on March 24, 1976.

Source: Magnusson, Magnus, *Larousse Biographical Dictionary.* New York: Larousse Kingfisher Chambers, 1994, p. 1146.

1980 ▪ **Vigdís Finnbogadóttir** (1930-) became the world's first female head of state to be elected democratically. She was declared president of Iceland after narrowly defeating three male opponents in the election. She was returned to office in 1984, when she ran unopposed, and won reelection again in 1988. In 1972, nine years after she and her husband divorced, Finnbogadóttir adopted a daughter. This was one of the first adoptions by a single person in Iceland.

Source: Magnusson, Magnus, *Larousse Biographical Dictionary.* New York: Larousse Kingfisher Chambers, 1994, p. 516.

Vigdís Finnbogadóttir was declared president of Iceland after narrowly defeating three male opponents in a 1980 election.

1986 ▪ **Corazon Aquino** (1933-) became the first female president of the Philippines in 1986. Supported by the United States and the Roman Catholic Church, Aquino's government faced innumerable obstacles, including severe factionalism (dissension) and social problems.

Source: Briggs, Asa, *A Dictionary of 20th Century World Biography.* Oxford, England: Oxford University Press, 1992, p. 15.

1990 ▪ **Mary Robinson** (1944-), an international lawyer, activist, and Catholic, was elected the first female president of Ireland. Robinson promoted legislation that enabled women to

In 1990 Mary Robinson— an international lawyer, activist, and Catholic— was elected the first female president of Ireland.

serve on juries and gave 18-year-olds the right to vote. In 1974, while serving in the Irish legislature, she shocked her fellow country people by calling for legal sale of contraceptives (birth control).

Source: Parry, Melanie, ed., *Larousse Dictionary of Women.* New York: Larousse Kingfisher Chambers, Inc., 1995, p. 564.

Prime Ministers

1960 ▪ Sirimavo Bandaranaike (1916-), a Sri Lankan politician, became the world's first female prime minister when her party, the Sri Lanka Freedom Party, won the general election.

Source: O'Neill, Lois Decker, ed., *The Women's Book of World Records and Achievements.* Garden City, New York: Doubleday, 1979, p. 46.

1966 ▪ Indira Gandhi (1917-1984) became India's first female prime minister, serving in this position until 1977. She governed during an especially turbulent period in her nation's history and often resorted to controlling unrest by declaring a "state of emergency," which restricted constitutional freedoms and imposed strict censorship on the citizens of India. After losing the election in 1977, Gandhi was arrested and acquitted on charges of corruption; she left the Congress Parliamentary party to become leader of the newly formed Indian National Congress. Gandhi successfully ran again for prime minister in the 1980 general election. In October of 1984, she was assassinated.

Source: Magnusson, Magnus, *Larousse Biographical Dictionary.* New York: Larousse Kingfisher Chambers, 1994, p. 564.

1969 ▪ Golda Meir (1898-1978), became the first woman to serve as prime minister of Israel. A lifelong Zionist, Meir immigrated to Palestine (present-day Israel) from the United States in 1921 and devoted her life to national politics. (Zionism was an international movement started in the late nineteenth century that originally sought the establishment of a Jewish national and religious homeland in Palestine; later, the term came to be applied to support for modern Israel.) Prior to becoming prime minister, Meir served as Israeli ambassador to the Soviet Union (1948-1949), minister of labor (1949-1956), and foreign minister (1956-1966). She resigned as prime minister in 1974.

Source: Parry, Melanie, ed., *Larousse Dictionary of Women.* New York: Larousse Kingfisher Chambers, Inc., 1995, pp. 455-56.

c. 1975 ▪ Elizabeth Domitien, a politician in the Central African Republic, became her country's first prime minister. Appointed by the ruler Jean Bedel Bokassa, who had himself crowned emperor in an elaborate ceremony two years later, Domitien was essentially without power in this newly created post.

Source: Magnusson, Magnus, *Larousse Biographical Dictionary.* New York: Larousse Kingfisher Chambers, 1994, p. 1733

Indira Gandhi was India's first female prime minister, serving in this position until 1977. In October of 1984, she was assassinated.

In 1975 Margaret Thatcher was elected leader of the Conservative Party, becoming the first woman to head a British political organization.

1979 ▪ **Margaret Hilda Thatcher** (1925-) was the first woman prime minister of Britain, a post she assumed as head of the Conservative Party. In 1975 Thatcher was elected leader of the Conservative Party, becoming the first woman to head a British political organization. Thatcher served as prime minister until 1991—the longest term in British history—when she relinquished the post to fellow Conservative John Major.

Source: Magnusson, Magnus, *Larousse Biographical Dictionary.* New York: Larousse Kingfisher Chambers, 1994, p. 1445.

1980 ▪ **Mary Eugenia Charles** (1919-) became the first female prime minister of Dominica; she was also the first woman to hold the post of prime minister in the Caribbean region. Known as the "Iron Lady of the Caribbean," Charles was active in politics throughout her life. She cofounded the Dominica Freedom Party in 1968.

Source: Parry, Melanie, ed., *Larousse Dictionary of Women.* New York: Larousse Kingfisher Chambers, 1995, p. 138.

1981 ▪ **Gro Harlem Brundtland** (1939-) became Norway's first female prime minister when Odvar Nordli resigned for health reasons. As leader of the Labor Party Brundtland became prime minister a second time in 1986. She headed a cabinet of eight women and nine men, the highest number of women in a cabinet in history. Because of Brundtland's encouragement, female members comprise 34 percent of Norway's Parliament, the largest proportion of female governmental representation in the world. In 1988, Brundtland received the Third World Foundation prize for her international leadership on environmental issues.

Source: Magnusson, Magnus, *Larousse Biographical Dictionary.* New York: Larousse Kingfisher Chambers, 1994, p. 219.

1982 ▪ **Mila Planinc** (1925-), a Yugoslav politician and a dedicated follower of Yugoslav leader Josip Broz Tito, became the first female prime minister of a Communist country when she was appointed to this post in Zagreb.

Source: Uglow, Jennifer S., ed., *The Continuum Dictionary of Women's Biography*. New York: Continuum, 1989, p. 434.

1988 ▪ **Benazir Bhutto** (1953-) was the first woman to become prime minister of Pakistan, taking office on December 1, 1988. After her father, Prime Minister Zulfikar Ali Bhutto (1928-1979), was deposed and put to death, Benazir suffered imprisonment because of her family's and her own political beliefs. Bhutto rose to power as head of the Pakistan People's Party and became the group's charismatic leader in 1986.

Benazir Bhutto rose to power as head of the Pakistan People's Party. She became the party's leader in 1986.

Source: Briggs, Asa, *A Dictionary of 20th Century World Biography*. Oxford, England: Oxford University Press, 1992, pp. 61-62.

1993 ▪ **Kim Campbell** (1947-), a Canadian politician, was elected the first woman prime minister of Canada. She held the position for only four months, until October 1993, when she was defeated in elections by Jean Chretien. Earlier that year Campbell had also become Canada's first female defense minister.

Source: *Canadian Who's Who: Volume 92*. Toronto: University of Toronto Press, 1994, p. 172.

1993 ▪ **Tansu Çiller** (1946-), a former university professor, became the first female prime minister of Turkey. An economist educated in the United States, Çiller amassed a $60 million fortune in real estate speculation. Her achievements as prime minister include a loosening of restrictions on Turkish political life and running a successful campaign to bring at least some of Central Asia's oil through Turkey. She resigned

In 1993 former university professor Tansu Çiller became the first female prime minister of Turkey.

in 1995 after her coalition government lost support.

Source: Parry, Melanie, ed., *Larousse Dictionary of Women.* New York: Larousse Kingfisher Chambers, Inc., 1995, pp. 146-47.

Cabinet Members

1921 ▪ **Mary Ellen Smith** (1862-1933), an English woman who emigrated to Canada, was the first woman in the British Empire to achieve cabinet rank. (The British Empire is an historical term referring to the British Commonwealth of Nations.) Smith was appointed minister without portfolio (specific assignment) in British Columbia in 1921, a post she held until 1922. She served as a member of the legislature from 1917 until 1928.

Source: O'Neill, Lois Decker, ed., *The Women's Book of World Records and Achievements,* Garden City, New York: Doubleday, 1979, p. 50.

1927 ▪ **Miina Sillanpää** (1866-1952), a Finnish politician, was the first woman to serve as a cabinet minister in her country's government. Elected to Parliament in 1907, she became minister of the Department of Social Affairs in 1927. Sillanpää was also the first female speaker of the Finnish Parliament, from 1936 until 1947. She was remembered particularly for her commitment to improving the social conditions of working-class women and single parents.

Source: Uglow, Jennifer S., ed., *The Continuum Dictionary of Women's Biography.* New York: Continuum, 1989, pp. 498-99.

1929 ▪ **Margaret Grace Bondfield** (1873-1953) became the first female cabinet minister in England when she was appointed minister of labor. She held the post until 1931. A lifelong trade union leader, Bondfield was the first female delegate to a Trade Union Congress conference and became the first woman to serve as chair of the Trade Union Congress in 1923.

Source: Magnusson, Magnus, *Larousse Biographical Dictionary.* New York: Larousse Kingfisher Chambers, 1994, p. 176.

1933 ▪ **Frances Perkins** (1882-1965) was the first woman to serve in a presidential cabinet (an advisory council). She was appointed secretary of labor by President Franklin Delano Roosevelt (served in office 1933-1945). Perkins was one of only two cabinet members to serve for Roosevelt's entire presidency, the unprecedented fourth term of which was cut short by the president's death. Perkins sponsored legislation that included unemployment compensation; child labor, worker's compensation, and social security laws; and maximum hour and minimum wage controls.

Source: McCullough, Joan, *First of All: Significant "Firsts" by American Women.* New York: Holt, 1980, p. 81.

1946 ▪ **Maria Ulfah Santoso,** an Indonesian politician, was the first woman in her country to serve as a cabinet minister. Santoso was appointed minister of social affairs, a post she held until 1947.

Source: O'Neill, Lois Decker, ed., *The Women's Book of World Records and Achievements.* Garden City, New York: Doubleday, 1979, p. 61.

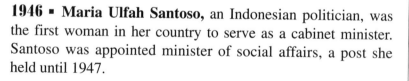

Margaret Bondfield was the first female delegate to a Trade Union Congress conference.

1947 ▪ **Rajkumari Amrit Kaur** (1889-1964) was the first woman to hold a cabinet-level position in India when she was appointed minister of health in the year her country won its independence from Great Britain. Kaur held this position until 1957. She was remembered as the founder and first president of the Indian Red Cross and as the founder of the All-India Women's Conference.

Source: O'Neill, Lois Decker, ed., *The Women's Book of World Records and Achievements.* Garden City, New York: Doubleday, 1979, p. 61.

1947 ▪ **Mabel Howard** (1893-1972) was the first female cabinet minister in both New Zealand and the British Commonwealth. Elected to Parliament in 1943, Howard was appointed minister of health and child welfare in 1947, a post she held for two years.

Source: Uglow, Jennifer S., ed., *The Continuum Dictionary of Women's Biography*. New York: Continuum, 1989, p. 267.

1950 ▪ **Olga Nuñez De Sassallow,** the first woman to receive a law degree in Nicaragua, was also the first woman to serve in a cabinet-level position in her country. De Sassallow was appointed minister of public education in 1950, a post she held until 1956.

Source: O'Neill, Lois Decker, ed., *The Women's Book of World Records and Achievements*. Garden City, New York: Doubleday, 1979, p. 61.

1960 ▪ **Esmeralda Arboleda de Cuevas Cancino,** a Colombian politician, became the first woman in Colombia to hold a cabinet-level position when she was appointed minister of transport. She held the post until 1962. Cancino was also the first Colombian woman to be elected to the Senate and, in 1966, she became her country's first female ambassador to Austria and Yugoslavia, a position she held until 1968.

Source: O'Neill, Lois Decker, ed., *The Women's Book of World Records and Achievements*. Garden City, New York: Doubleday, 1979, p. 61.

c. 1963 ▪ **Margot Honecker** (1927-), a Communist politician in the former East Germany, was the first woman to hold a cabinet-level position in her country. Honecker was appointed minister of education in Berlin, East Germany. She was the wife of Erich Honecker, the head of the East German state and president of the Communist Party.

Source: Thompson, Wayne C., Susan L. Thompson, and Juliet S. Thompson, *Historical Dictionary of Germany*. Metuchen, New Jersey: Scarecrow Press, 1994, p. 295.

1970 ▪ **Maria Teresa Carcomo Lobo,** a Portuguese politician, was the first woman in her country to hold a cabinet-level post. She was appointed under secretary of state for welfare, a position she held until 1973.

Source: O'Neill, Lois Decker, ed., *The Women's Book of World Records and Achievements*. Garden City, New York: Doubleday, 1979, p. 61.

1973 ▪ **Tan Sri Fatimah,** a Malaysian politician, became the first woman to hold a cabinet-level position in her country when she was appointed to serve as minister for social welfare.

Source: O'Neill, Lois Decker, ed., *The Women's Book of World Records and Achievements,* Garden City, New York: Doubleday, 1979, p. 61.

1975 ▪ **Toure Aissata Kane,** a feminist politician in Islamic Mauritania, was the first woman to achieve cabinet rank in her country. Kane was appointed minister for the protection of the family and for social affairs.

Source: O'Neill, Lois Decker, ed., *The Women's Book of World Records and Achievements.* Garden City, New York: Doubleday, 1979, p. 60.

Ambassadors

1918 ▪ **Rosika Schwimmer** (1877-1948), a Hungarian feminist and pacifist (a person who opposes violent acts, especially warfare), was the world's first female ambassador. She was appointed to serve her country as minister to Switzerland in October of 1918. Schwimmer served in this post for a year. Due to political unrest in Hungary, she emigrated to the United States in the 1930s. In 1948 she was nominated for the Nobel Peace Prize.

Source: Uglow, Jennifer S., ed., *The Continuum Dictionary of Women's Biography.* New York: Continuum, 1989, p. 488.

1933 ▪ **Ruth Bryan Owen** (1885-1954) was the first woman to serve as a U.S. foreign minister. The daughter of William Jennings Bryan (1860-1925; a prominent lawyer and politician), she was appointed minister to Denmark by President Franklin Delano Roosevelt (served in office 1933-1945).

Source: Read, Phyllis J., and Bernard L. Witlieb, *The Book of Women's Firsts.* New York: Random House, 1992, pp. 327-28.

1949 ▪ **Eugenie Moore Anderson** (1909-1997) of Red Wing, Minnesota, was the first woman to serve as a U.S. ambassador. She was appointed ambassador to Denmark by President Harry S Truman (served in office 1945-1953), and held

the post until 1953. Anderson was also the first woman to serve as a U.S. ambassador to Bulgaria, becoming the first woman ambassador to represent the United States in a Communist nation.

Source: Sanders, Dennis, *The First of Everything.* New York: Delacorte Press, 1981, p. 153.

1954 ▪ Liaquat Ali Khan (1905-), a Pakistani politician and an active feminist, was the first Muslim woman to serve as an ambassador when she was named ambassador to Belgium and the Netherlands; she later served as ambassador to Italy and Tunisia. Kahn founded the All-Pakistan Women's Association in 1949. In 1973 she became the first woman to govern a Pakistani province, the province of Sind. In the 1970s, Kahn was also selected as the Chancellor of the University of Karachi, and in 1978 the United Nations honored Khan with the Human Rights Award.

Eugenie Moore Anderson was the first woman to serve as a U.S. ambassador. Anderson was appointed ambassador to Denmark by President Harry S Truman.

Source: Uglow, Jennifer S., ed., *The Continuum Dictionary of Women's Biography.* New York: Continuum, 1989, p. 298.

1964 ▪ Marietta Peabody Tree (1917-1991) was the first woman to serve as a permanent ambassador to the United Nations. After three years as the U.S. representative to the Human Rights Commission and a chief U.S. delegate, Tree gained the rank of ambassador with her appointment as a U.S. representative on the Trusteeship Council.

Source: Read, Phyllis J., and Bernard L. Witlieb, *The Book of Women's Firsts.* New York: Random House, 1992, pp. 448-49.

1975 ▪ Bernadette Olowo, a Ugandan diplomat, became the first female ambassador to the Vatican (the headquarters of the Roman Catholic Church in Rome) in 1975. Her appointment broke a 900-year-old tradition that kept female envoys (government representatives) out of the Holy See (the seat of the pope).

Source: O'Neill, Lois Decker, ed., *The Women's Book of World Records and Achievements.* Garden City, New York: Doubleday, 1979, p. 42.

Representatives and Appointees

1916 ▪ **Jeanette Rankin** (1880-1973) was the first woman elected to the U.S. House of Representatives. A native of Missoula, Montana, Rankin was elected as a Republican state representative. (In Montana women were given the right to vote in state elections before national suffrage (the right to vote) was instituted in 1920.) Rankin was the only member of Congress to vote against U.S. entry into World War I (1914-1918). When Rankin ran for reelection in 1919 as a pacifist (a person who is strongly opposed to war), she was defeated. In 1941 she was successful in her campaign for a second term in the House of Representatives. On December 8, 1941, Rankin was the only member of congress to vote against entry into World War II (1939-1945). She continued her antiwar stance throughout her life—in 1968 she led the "Jeanette Rankin Brigade" to the Capitol in Washington, D.C. to protest against the United States' involvement in the Vietnam War (1965-1973).

Source: Parry, Melanie, ed., *Larousse Dictionary of Women.* New York: Larousse Kingfisher Chambers, Inc., 1995, pp. 546-47.

Montana native Jeanette Rankin was the first woman elected to the U.S. House of Representatives.

1917 ▪ **Louise McKinney** (1868-1933), a Canadian politician, was the first female member of any legislative body in the British Empire. (The British Empire is an historical term referring to the British Commonwealth of Nations.) A leading member of the Non-partisan League, McKinney was elected to the Alberta legislature. She dedicated her energies to temperance (a campaign to regulate the use and sale of alcoholic beverages) and feminist causes throughout her life.

Source: Uglow, Jennifer S., ed., *The Continuum Dictionary of Women's Biography.* New York: Continuum, 1989, p. 345.

1917 ▪ **Mrs. W. C. Tyler, Mrs. Spinks, and Mrs. Wylie,** three California suffragists (supporters of women's right to vote), were the first three women to sit in the U.S. Electoral College. (The Electoral College is the group of "electors" who vote for the president and vice president of the United States. In the United States, these offices are not elected by the popular vote of the people; when, for example, a presidential candidate "wins" the popular vote in a state, his political party sends its "electors" to the electoral college—the electors cast the votes that decide who becomes president. The number of electors a state may send is based on the number of representatives it has in Congress, which is based on population. Thus, it is possible—and has happened—that a president can win the popular vote but lose the election.) Mrs. Tyler was a delegate to the National Democratic Convention in 1916; she was also president of the Los Angeles Woman's County Democratic Committee.

Source: Read, Phyllis J., and Bernard L. Witlieb, *The Book of Women's Firsts*. New York: Random House, 1992, pp. 455-56.

c. 1918 ▪ Catherine Filene Shouse (1896-1994) became the first woman appointed to the Democratic National Committee. An active Democrat, Shouse served under President Calvin Coolidge (served in office 1923-1929) in the mid-1920s as chairwoman of the First Federal Prison for Women, where she instituted a job training and rehabilitation program. Shouse was a philanthropist (a person who promotes human welfare, usually by donating large sums of money to worthy causes) and a patron of the arts who was the founder and major benefactor of the Wolf Trap Farm Park for the Performing Arts in Virginia.

Source: *The New York Times*. December 15, 1994.

1918 ▪ Nina Bang (1866-1928), a Danish politician, was the first woman to serve as a member of the Landsting (the upper house) of the Danish Parliament. She was elected after the passage of women's suffrage (right to vote) and served in Denmark's first Social Democratic government. In 1924 Bang became minister of education. An economist by profession, she worked on behalf of the League of Nations (a former international peace organization established in 1919 after World War I, it preceded the United Nations).

Source: Uglow, Jennifer S., ed., *The Continuum Dictionary of Women's Biography*. New York: Continuum, 1989, p. 46.

1918 ▪ Anne Henrietta Martin (1875-1951) was the first woman to run for the U.S. Senate. Martin was an independent candidate in Nevada. Although she was defeated, Martin won 20 percent of the vote.

Source: Read, Phyllis J., and Bernard L. Witlieb, *The Book of Women's Firsts.* New York: Random House, 1992, pp. 269-70.

1919 ▪ **Nancy Witcher Langhorne Astor** (1879-1964) took the oath of office as the first woman member of Parliament (M.P.) in England. Born in the United States, Astor became a British subject when she married William Waldorf Astor (1879-1952), the 2nd Viscount Astor. Her husband was Conservative M.P. for Plymouth. Elected to succeed her husband as representative from Plymouth, Nancy Astor was the only female M.P. until 1921.

Source: Parry, Melanie, ed., *Larousse Dictionary of Women.* New York: Larousse Kingfisher Chambers, 1995, p. 37.

1920 ▪ **Edith Dirksey Brown Cowan** (1861-1932) became the first woman member of the Australian Parliament. Her political career began in 1915 when she became a magistrate of the state children's court. There was a legislative ban on women serving in the Australian Parliament until 1920, when Cowan and five other women ran for office. Cowan used her term in office to campaign for women's and children's rights. She sponsored the Women's Legal Status Act, which passed in 1923 and opened the legal profession to women.

Source: Arnold, John, and Deidre Morris, *Monash Biographical Dictionary of 20th Century Australia.* Port Melbourne, Australia: Reed Reference Publishing, 1994, p. 129.

1921 ▪ **Agnes Campbell McPhail** (1890-1954), a Canadian suffragist (a person who advocates the right to vote) and politician, became the first female minister of parliament in Canada when she was elected to represent the United Farmers of Ontario for Southeast Grey County. McPhail retained her seat until 1940, and for several years from 1943 until 1951 she served in the Ontario, Canada, legislature. McPhail also represented Canada in the Assembly of the League of Nations (a former international peace organization established in 1919, the League preceded the United Nations).

Source: Magnusson, Magnus, *Larousse Biographical Dictionary,* New York: Larousse Kingfisher Chambers, 1994, p. 949.

1921 ▪ **Alice M. Robertson** (1854-1931) became the first woman to preside over the U.S. House of Representatives when she was given the position of president pro tem (temporary president) as a ceremonial gesture. She announced the vote on a minor appropriations bill.

Source: Read, Phyllis J., and Bernard L. Witlieb, *The Book of Women's Firsts*. New York: Random House, 1992, pp. 373-74.

1922 ▪ Rebecca Ann Latimer Felton (1835-1930), a journalist who spoke out and worked actively for various social and feminist causes, became the first woman to serve in the United States Senate. She was appointed at the age of 87 by the governor of Georgia on November 21, 1922, to fill the post of her predecessor's unexpired term. Congress was not in session, therefore Felton served only one day. She gave an honorary speech in Washington, D.C., and then gave up her seat to Senator-elect Walter George. Felton returned to Georgia and received much national publicity for her one day as senator.

Source: O'Neill, Lois Decker, ed., *The Women's Book of World Records and Achievements*, Garden City, New York: Doubleday, 1979, pp. 65-66.

Governor "Ma" Ferguson

Nellie Taylor Ross (1876-1977) of Wyoming was the first woman elected governor of a state. Technically, she shared this honor with Miriam Amanda "Ma" Ferguson (1875-1961) of Texas, since both women were elected in November of 1924, but Ross was inaugurated three weeks before Ferguson. Both women followed their husbands into office. Ferguson succeeded her husband after he was impeached (thrown out of office) for misuse of Texas state funds in 1924. Ferguson worked for prison reform and against the power and activities of the Klu Klux Klan. She was elected to a second term as governor in 1932.

C. 1923 ▪ Jessie Duckstein became the first woman to serve as a "special agent" in the Federal Bureau of Investigation (FBI) when she was appointed by FBI director William Burns.

Source: *Parade*. June 1, 1986.

1925 ▪ Pattie Field (1902-), of Denver, Colorado, was the first woman to serve in the United States consular (embassy) service. Field was appointed vice consul (assistant to the head of the embassy) in Amsterdam, the Netherlands. She held the position until 1929.

Source: Read, Phyllis J., and Bernard L. Witlieb, *The Book of Women's Firsts*. New York: Random House, 1992, p. 155.

1928 ▪ **Ruth Shipley** (1885-1966) became the first woman to head a major division of the U.S. Department of State when she was named chief of the Passport Division. Shipley worked her way up to this position from that of clerk in the Records Department, a job she began in 1914.

Source: Read, Phyllis J., and Bernard L. Witlieb, *The Book of Women's Firsts.* New York: Random House, 1992, pp. 406-07.

1932 ▪ **Mary T. Hopkins Norton** (1875-1959) was the first woman to head a U.S. state political party when she became head of the Democratic Party in New Jersey. Norton was elected to Congress by her state in 1925 and served in this capacity until her retirement in 1951.

Source: Read, Phyllis J., and Bernard L. Witlieb, *The Book of Women's Firsts.* New York: Random House, 1992, p. 317.

1932 ▪ **Hattie Wyatt Caraway** (1878-1950) was the first woman elected to the U.S. Senate. Appointed by the governor of Louisiana to complete her dead husband's term in 1931, Caraway won the election in 1932. She became the first woman to chair a Senate committee, to preside over Senate sessions, and to conduct Senate hearings. She served for three terms (1932-1944).

Source: James, Edward T., and others, *Notable American Women, 1607-1950: A Biographical Dictionary,* Cambridge, Massachusetts: Harvard University Press, 1971, pp. 284-86.

1933 ▪ **Minnie Davenport Craig** became the first woman to serve as speaker in a state house of representatives when she was elected to that position in the North Dakota House of Representatives. Craig served for less than a year.

Source: Kane, Nathan Joseph, *Famous First Facts.* New York: Wilson, 1981, p. 348.

c. 1934 ▪ **Gertrud Scholtz-Klink** (1902-), a German and member of the Nazi party who became the spokesperson for Adolf Hitler's (1889-1945) policies towards women, was the first woman to be given the title *Reichsfrauenfürerin* ("National Women's Leader"). She also served as head of Frauenwerk, an organization of German women. In 1939 Scholtz-Klink went to England, where she was billed as the "Perfect Nazi Woman." Imprisoned as a war criminal in 1948, she was banned on her release from participation in the new German government and from professional life; she was also restricted to living in her district.

Source: Wistrich, Robert S., *Who's Who in Nazi Germany.* London: Routledge, 1982, p. 238.

1944 ▪ **Dorothy V. Bush** (1916-1991)

became the first woman to serve as an officer for either major U.S. national political party when she was appointed secretary of the national Democratic party in 1944. Bush held this post for over 40 years.

Source: Read, Phyllis J., and Bernard L. Witlieb, *The Book of Women's Firsts.* New York: Random House, 1992, pp. 77-78.

1947 ▪ **Agatha Barbara** (1923-) became

the first female member of the Maltese Parliament. On February 16, 1982, after a distinguished 35-year career in Maltese politics, Barbara was elected president of the Republic of Malta. (Malta is an island country south of Sicily in the Mediterranean.) Over the course of her political career, Barbara demonstrated particular concern for social legislation and women's rights.

Agatha Barbara was the first female member of the Maltese Parliament.

Source: Uglow, Jennifer S., ed., *The Continuum Dictionary of Women's Biography.* New York: Continuum, 1989, p. 47.

1948 ▪ **Margaret Chase Smith** (1897-1995) was the first

woman to be elected to both the U.S. House of Representatives and the U.S. Senate. When her husband, a congressman from Maine, died in 1940, Smith replaced him and served in the House for eight years—four full terms. In 1948 Chase Smith was elected to the U.S. Senate and was reelected three times, serving until 1973. When she ran for reelection in

Georgia Neese Gray was the first woman to serve as treasurer of the United States.

1960, her opponent was Democrat Lucia Marie Cormier. The contest was the first time an election for a U.S. Senate seat involved two female candidates. Chase Smith won by a vote of 255,890 to 159,809. In 1964 Chase Smith was the first woman to campaign to become a major political party candidate for president.

Source: Uglow, Jennifer S., ed., *The Continuum Dictionary of Women's Biography.* New York: Continuum, 1989, pp. 502-03.

1949 ▪ Georgia Neese Clark Gray (1900-1995) was the first woman to serve as treasurer of the United States. Her signature, then Georgia Neese Clark, appeared on $30 billion of the nation's currency during her term as the nation's 29th treasurer. She was appointed in 1949 by President Harry S Truman (served in office 1945-1953) and was unanimously approved by the Senate. Clark served as treasurer until 1953, when Dwight D. Eisenhower (served in office 1953-1961) was elected president. He appointed another woman, Utah Republican Ivy Baker Priest, to succeed Gray.

Source: Read, Phyllis J., and Bernard L. Witlieb, *The Book of Women's Firsts.* New York: Random House, 1992, p. 91.

1953 ▪ Oveta Culp Hobby (1905-1995) was appointed by President Dwight D. Eisenhower (served in office 1953-1961) to be the first woman secretary of health, education, and welfare, a position she held until 1955. A Texas lawyer and a journalist, Hobby worked for the War Department and helped in the education of a women's army corps. Appointed colonel of the Women's Army Auxiliary Corps (WAACS), Hobby retained her position in the corps when it changed to the Women's Army Corps (WACS) in 1943.

Source: McCullough, Joan, *First of All: Significant "Firsts" by American Women.* New York: Holt, 1980, pp. 82-83.

1957 ▪ **Yekaterina Alexeevna Furtseva** (1910-1974), a Russian politician, was the first woman elected a member of the Communist Party Politburo (the top policy-making and executive group) in the Soviet Union. Furtseva was one of the few women to achieve such rank and power within the Communist establishment.

Source: Parry, Melanie, ed., *Larousse Dictionary of Women*. New York: Larousse Kingfisher Chambers, Inc., 1995, p. 254.

1958 ▪ **Agda Rössel** (1910-), a Swedish diplomat, became the first woman to head a permanent delegation to the United Nations. Rössel represented her country in New York City for seven years. She was esteemed for her work on behalf of refugee children after World War II (1939-1945) and for her role as a champion of women's rights throughout the world.

Source: O'Neill, Lois Decker, ed., *The Women's Book of World Records and Achievements*. Garden City, New York: Doubleday, 1979, p. 64.

Oveta Culp Hobby (second from right) was appointed by President Dwight D. Eisenhower as the first female secretary of health, education, and welfare.

Flynn and Communism

Elizabeth Gurley Flynn (1890-1964), a lifelong political activist who joined the Communist party in 1937, was the first woman to chair the national committee of the American Communist party. Flynn was a founding member of the American Civil Liberties Union in 1920, but she was forced to resign in 1940 because of her Communist ties. The first person to be convicted of sedition (resistance to lawful authority) under the Smith Act in 1952, Flynn served three years in prison. When she died in Moscow, Russia, she was given a state funeral.

1961 ▪ **Helen Suzman** (1917-), a South African politician, became the first minister of the South African parliament to represent the Progressive party (later the Progressive Federal party). Throughout her 36-year career in parliament Suzman supported anti-apartheid legislation (laws that forbid racial segregation). She was recognized for her efforts with the United Nations Human Rights Award in 1978 and the Medallion of Heroism in 1980. Suzman was named an honorary Dame of the British Empire in 1989.

Source: Parry, Melanie, ed., *Larousse Dictionary of Women.* New York: Larousse Kingfisher Chambers, Inc., 1995, p. 631.

1965 ▪ **Patsy Mink** (1927-; some sources say 1929), a Japanese-American, was the first woman of a racial or ethnic minority to sit in the U.S. House of Representatives. A Democrat from Hawaii, Mink began the first of three terms in 1965. She was a strong supporter of equal rights for women.

Source: Sanders, Dennis, *The First of Everything.* New York: Delacorte Press, 1981, p. 150.

1966 ▪ **Constance Baker Motley** (1921-) became the first African-American female federal judge. President Lyndon B. Johnson (served in office 1963-1969) appointed Motley judge of the U.S. District Court for the Southern Division of New York. In 1964 she was the first African-American woman elected to the New York state senate. A civil rights lawyer who worked to eliminate state-enforced segregation in the South, Motley successfully argued nine civil rights cases before the U.S. Supreme Court prior to her judicial appointment. She was also the first African-American woman to serve as Manhattan borough president.

Source: McCullough, Joan, *First of All: Significant "Firsts" by American Women.* New York: Holt, 1980, pp. 90-91.

1966 ▪ **Jane Cahill Pfeiffer** (1932-) was the first woman to serve as a White House fellow. Appointed by President Lyndon B. Johnson (served in office 1963-1969), Pfeiffer took a leave of absence from her position with IBM, where she was in charge of the company's space tracking system located on the island of Bermuda. During her White House fellowship, Pfeiffer worked with Robert Wood, under secretary of the department of housing and urban development, to streamline the housing and home finance agency.

Source: Read, Phyllis J., and Bernard L. Witlieb, *The Book of Women's Firsts.* New York: Random House, 1992, pp. 343-44.

1968 ▪ **Shirley Chisholm** (b. 1924) was the first black congresswoman elected to the U.S. House of Representatives from New York. Chisholm grew up in New York City, the daughter of West Indian immigrants. Supported mainly by feminists, Chisholm was elected as a Democrat to the New York State legislature in 1964. She was a member of the House of Representatives from 1969 to 1983. In 1969 Chisholm drew national attention by pushing through a bill that guaranteed minimum wages to domestic workers, many of whom are black or minority women. In 1972, she announced her intention to run for president; at the Democratic National Convention she drew 154 delegate votes. Chisholm then ran and was re-elected to her congressional seat for second and third terms.

Source: Parry, Melanie, ed., *Larousse Dictionary of Women.* New York: Larousse Kingfisher Chambers, Inc., 1995, p. 142.

1969 ▪ **Virginia Mae Brown** (1923-1991) became the first woman to head an independent federal administrative agency when she was named director of the Interstate Commerce Commission. Brown had a host of other "firsts" to her credit: she was the first woman to serve on the Interstate Commerce Commission (1964), the first woman to be a state insurance commissioner (1961), the first woman to be executive secretary to the judicial council of West Virginia (1944), the first woman to be a West Virginia assistant attorney general (1952), and the first woman to serve on the West Virginia Public Service Commission (1962).

Source: Read, Phyllis J., and Bernard L. Witlieb, *The Book of Women's Firsts.* New York: Random House, 1992, p. 73.

Women Joined Protection Service

In 1970 the Secret Service chose seven women to join the Executive Protection Service. These seven women were the first females to serve on the White House Police Force. The group was also periodically assigned to serve at diplomatic missions in Washington, D.C.

c. Early 1970s ▪ **Jeanne Martin Cissé** (1926-), a Guinean diplomat, was the first woman to preside over the United Nations Security Council. Cissé served as Guinea's first female delegate from 1972 until 1976. She was awarded the Lenin Peace Prize in 1975.

Source: O'Neill, Lois Decker, ed., *The Women's Book of World Records and Achievements.* Garden City, New York: Doubleday, 1979, p. 65.

1972 ▪ **Jean Westwood** (1923-) was the first U.S. woman to chair a national political party. On July 14, 1972, she was elected chair of the Democratic National Committee. Westwood brought over 30 years of experience in politics to this job. In her new position, she became the first woman to cochair a presidential campaign, when she headed George McGovern's unsuccessful bid for the presidency in 1972.

Source: O'Neill, Lois Decker, ed., *The Women's Book of World Records and Achievements.* Garden City, New York: Doubleday, 1979, p. 74.

1974 ▪ **Janet Gray Hayes** (1926-) became the first woman to head a large U.S. city when she was elected mayor of San Jose, California, in a race against six male opponents. She was inaugurated in January 1974.

Source: Sanders, Dennis, *The First of Everything.* New York: Delacorte Press, 1981, p. 152.

1974 ▪ **Kathy Kozachenko** was the first lesbian elected to a city council when she won election in Ann Arbor, Michigan, in April of 1974. A senior at the University of Michigan, Kozachenko ran and was elected to the city council from a ward primarily populated by students.

Source: McCullough, Joan, *First of All: Significant "Firsts" by American Women.* New York: Holt, 1980, p. 85.

1975 ▪ **Carla Anderson Hills** (1934-) was the first woman appointed secretary of housing and urban development (HUD) in the U.S. cabinet, on March 10, 1975. Recognized as one of California's most prominent trial attorneys, Hills became assistant attorney general in the Justice Department's Civil Division in 1974. After she was appointed secretary of HUD, she remained in office until she was succeeded by the first black woman in the cabinet, Patricia Roberts Harris.

Source: McCullough, Joan, *First of All: Significant "Firsts" by American Women.* New York: Holt, 1980, p. 83.

Foley Became Mayor

Lelia Kasensia Smith Foley (1942-) was the first African-American woman elected mayor of an American city. Foley was elected mayor of Taft, Oklahoma, a predominantly African-American town of approximately 600 people, in 1973.

1976 ▪ **Lindy Boggs,** (1916-), a congressional representative from Louisiana, was the first woman to chair the national convention of a major U.S. political party. Boggs chaired the Democratic National Convention in 1976. She has been a staunch supporter of increased opportunities for women throughout her long political career.

Source: O'Neill, Lois Decker, ed., *The Women's Book of World Records and Achievements.* Garden City, New York: Doubleday, 1979, p. 75.

1976 ▪ **Shirley Temple Black** (1928-) became the first woman to serve as chief of protocol at the U.S. White House when she was named to this position by President Gerald Ford (served in office 1974-1977). Black was responsible for entertaining heads of state while they visited Washington.

Source: Sanders, Dennis, *The First of Everything.* New York: Delacorte Press, 1981, p. 154.

1977 ▪ **Juanita Morris Kreps** (1921-) was the first woman to serve as secretary of commerce in the U.S. government. She was appointed by President Jimmy Carter (served in office 1977-1981) shortly after his inauguration. Kreps had previously served as the first female director of the New York Stock Exchange (in 1972) and the first female vice president of Duke University (in 1973).

Source: McCullough, Joan, *First of All: Significant "Firsts" by American Women.* New York: Holt, 1980, p. 81.

Patricia Roberts Harris was secretary of health and human services from 1979 to 1981.

1977 ▪ Patricia Roberts Harris (1924-1985) became the first African-American woman to serve officially in a U.S. president's cabinet when Jimmy Carter (served in office 1977-1981) appointed her secretary of housing and urban development. Harris was secretary of health and human services from 1979 to 1981.

Source: Parry, Melanie, ed., *Larousse Dictionary of Women.* New York: Larousse Kingfisher Chambers, Inc., 1995, p. 301.

1977 ▪ Eleanor Holmes Norton (1937-) became the first woman to chair the Equal Employment Opportunities Commission when she was appointed in Washington, D.C., by President Jimmy Carter (served in office 1977-1981) in 1977. Norton was also the cofounder of the Black Feminist Organization in 1973.

Source: Read, Phyllis J., and Bernard L. Witlieb, *The Book of Women's Firsts.* New York: Random House, 1992, pp. 315-16.

1981 ▪ Sandra Day O'Connor (1930-) was the first woman to become an associate justice of the U.S. Supreme Court. A native of Texas, O'Connor became the first woman to serve on the high court when President Ronald Reagan (served in office 1981-1988) named her to fill the vacancy created by the retirement of Justice Potter Stewart (1915-1985). O'Connor remained the only woman on the court until 1993, when Ruth Bader Ginsburg (1933-) was appointed justice by President Bill Clinton (began term in 1992).

Source: Read, Phyllis J., and Bernard L. Witlieb, *The Book of Women's Firsts.* New York: Random House, 1992, pp. 323-24.

1984 ▪ Geraldine Anne Ferraro (1935-) was the first woman nominated by a major political party as a candidate for vice president of the United States. She was selected by Walter

Mondale, the Democratic Party's presidential candidate, to be his running mate in the 1984 campaign. Mondale and Ferraro lost the election to Ronald Reagan and his running mate George Bush, and Ferraro retired from politics.

Source: Magnusson, Magnus, *Larousse Biographical Dictionary.* New York: Larousse Kingfisher Chambers, 1994, p. 510.

1990 ▪ Antonia T. Novello (1944-) was the first woman appointed Surgeon General of the United States Public Health Service. Novello was sworn in by the first woman Supreme Court justice, Sandra Day O'Connor.

Source: Read, Phyllis J., and Bernard L. Witlieb, *The Book of Women's Firsts.* New York: Random House, 1992, pp. 317-18.

1995 ▪ Enid Waldholtz (1958-), U.S. representative from Utah, was the first woman in the U.S. Congress to give birth while still serving as a representative. Anticipating the experience, she said confidently, "There will be a playpen in my office."

Source: *Newsweek.* March 27, 1995, p. 19.

Sandra Day O'Connor remained the only woman on the Supreme Court until 1993.

1997 ▪ Madeleine Korbel Albright (1937-), a Czechoslovakian-born American diplomat, became the first woman be appointed U.S. Secretary of State. She was named to the post by President Bill Clinton (began term in 1993) in 1997. Albright was born in Czechoslovakia. In 1948 her family emigrated to the United States. Albright received a doctorate from Columbia University and became a professor of international affairs at Georgetown University in Washington, D.C. Appointed to the staff of the U.S. National Security Council during the administration of President Jimmy Carter (served in office 1977-1981), she also served as an advisor to Democratic politicians. In 1993 Albright was appointed permanent ambassador to the United Nations by President Bill Clinton and was later elevated to be a member of the president's cabinet.

Source: Parry, Melanie, ed., *Larousse Dictionary of Women.* New York: Larousse Kingfisher Chambers, Inc., 1995, p. 12.

Index

Bold type indicates main entries
Italic type indicates volume numbers
Illustrations are marked by (ill.)

Fry, Elizabeth Gurney *1:* 3
Fuldheim, Dorothy *2:* **232,** 233 (ill.)
Fuller, Fay *2:* **400**
Fuller, Loie *1:* **54**
Fuller, Sarah *1:* **175**
Furtseva, Yekaterina *1:* **203**
Gaffney, Margaret *1:* 141
Gale, Zona *1:* **113**
Gallina, Juliane *2:* 284
Gandhi, Indira *1:* **186-187,** 187 (ill.)
Gaposhkin, Cecelia Payne *1:* **167**
Garden, Mary *1:* **87**
Garland, Judy *1:* 81
Garnett, Constance *1:* **108**
Garrison, Lucy McKim *1:* **106-107**
Garrod, Dorothy *1:* 166
Gaynor, Janet *1:* **66,** 66 (ill.)
Geller, Margaret J. *2:* **348**
Gentileschi, Artemisia *1:* **124**
Gera, Berenice *2:* **392**
Gestefeld, Ursula *2:* **298**
Gibb, Roberta *2:* 376
Gibson, Althea *2:* **371-372, 377,**
    372 (ill.)
Giliani, Alessandra *2:* **251**
Gillespie, Angela *2:* **295**
Giovinco, Lucy *2:* **382**
Gipps, Ruth *1:* **96**
Girl Guides *1:* 9
Girl Scouts of America *1:* 9, 14
Glanville-Hicks, Peggy *1:* **91,** 96
Glasse, Hannah Allgood *1:* **103**
Gleason, Kate *1:* **133-134**
Glover, Jane Alison *1:* **99**
Gluck, Alma *1:* **86**
Godey's Lady's Book 2: 225
Godmarsson, Bridget *2:* **289**
Goegg, Marie *1:* **19-20**
Goeppert-Mayer, Maria *2:* **343-344**
Goldberg, Adele *2:* **353**
Goncharova, Natalia *1:* **128**
Gonne, Maud *1:* **22**
Goodall, Jane *2:* **313-314,** 313 (ill.)
Goodbody, Buzz (Mary Ann) *1:* **78**
Gordon, Gale Ann *2:* **280**
Gordon-Lazareff, Hélène *2:* **226-227**
Gourd, Emilie *1:* **50**
Graham, Katherine *1:* **136-137**
Graham, Martha *1:* **61-62,** 61 (ill.)
Gratz, Rebecca *2:* **294**
Gray, Georgia Neese *1:* **202,**
    202 (ill.)
Gray Panthers *1:* 13
Green, Anna Katherine *1:* **107**
Greenewalt, Mary E. H. *1:* **143**

Gregory, Augusta Isabella *1:* **75**
Griffith, Emily *1:* **179**
Grimké, Angelina Emily *1:* **1-2**
Grimké, Charlotte L. *1:* **174**
Grimké, Sarah Moore *1:* **1-2,** 2 (ill.)
Guda *1:* **123**
Guggenheim, Peggy *1:* **130**
Gulick, Charlotte Vetter *1:* **8,** 8 (ill.)
The Guns of August 1: 117
Guthrie, Janet *2:* **407,** 407
Guy-Blanché, Alice *1:* **62**
Hainisch, Marianne *1:* **22**
Hale, Cynthia L. *2:* 301
Hale, Sarah Josepha *2:* **225**
Hall, Anne *1:* **125**
Hall, Radclyffe *1:* **114**
Hamilton, Alice *2:* **272,** 272 (ill.)
Handler, Ruth *1:* **146-147**
Hani, Motoko *2:* 229
Hans Brinker 1: 107
Hansberry, Lorraine *1:* **116-117**
Hansteen, Hasta *1:* 18
"Happy Birthday to You" *1:* 165
Hardy, Harriet *2:* **337**
Harlem Globetrotters *2:* 395
Harper, Frances Ellen *1:* **108,**
    108 (ill.)
Harrington, Penny *2:* **244**
Harris, Barbara C. *2:* **307**
Harris, Patricia R. *1:* **208,** 208 (ill.)
Hartman, Grace *1:* **39**
Hatzimichali, Angeliki *1:* **128-129**
Hayes, Janet Gray *1:* **206**
Hayhurst, Susan *2:* **262**
Hays, Anna Mae *2:* **281**
Head, Bessie *1:* **118**
Heath, Sophia *2:* **402**
Heck, Barbara *2:* **291-292**
Hedges, Barbara *2:* **397**
Hemmings, Deon *2:* **388**
Henderlite, Rachel *2:* **304**
Henson, Lisa *2:* 227
Hepburn, Katharine *1:* **70-71**
Herman, Barbara *2:* **305**
Herman, Robin *2:* **231-232**
Herschel, Caroline *2:* **324**
Hersilia *1:* **41**
Hess, Myra *1:* **91**
Heyhoe, Rachel Flint *2:* **232**
Heymann, Lida Gustava *1:* **177**
Heyns, Penelope *2:* **387-388**
Hicks, Beatrice *2:* **351**
Higgins, Marguerite *2:* **236,** 237 (ill.)
Hilda of Whitby *2:* **287**
Hildegard of Bingen *2:* **250-251, 288**

Stopes, Marie *2:* 268-269
Storni, Alfonsina *1:* 111
Stream of consciousness *1:* 111
Streisand, Barbra *1:* 73
Stuart, Miranda *2:* 254
Sudarkasa, Niara *1:* 169
Sullivan, Kathryn D. *2:* 358
Sutherland, Joan *1:* 94
Suzman, Helen *1:* 204
Swain, Clara A. *2:* 259
Sweet, Judy *2:* 397
Switzer, Katherine *2:* 376
Swoopes, Sheryl *2:* 398
Szold, Henrietta *1:* 156
Tabankin, Margery Ann *1:* 167-168
Tabei, Junko *2:* 407
Taglioni, Marie *1:* 52-53
Tanaka, Kinuyo *1:* 67
Tarses, Jamie *2:* 235-236
Taylor, Anna Edson *2:* 400
Taylor, Susan *2:* 276
Telkes, Maria *2:* 351
Tenrikyo *2:* 295
Tent dress *1:* 121
Teresa of Ávila *2:* 290, 290 (ill.), 305
Tereshkova, Valentina *2:* 355-356, 356 (ill.)
Terpin, Mary *2:* 302
Tescon, Trinidad *2:* 264
Tettje, Clasina *2:* 331-332
Tevatron *2:* 348
Tharp, Marie *2:* 320
Tharp, Twyla *1:* 59
Thatcher, Margaret Hilda *1:* 188
Thecla *2:* 285
Theodoropoulou, Avra *1:* 25
Thiele, Geraldine *2:* 329-330
Thomas, Helen A. *2:* 231, 231 (ill.)
Thomas, Martha *1:* 160
Thompson, Mary Harris *2:* 258
Thoms, Adah B. *2:* 270
Thurman, Tracey *1:* 29
Thursby, Emma Cecilia *1:* 82
Tiamat *2:* 286
Tilley, Vesta *1:* 81
Todd, E. L. *1:* 144
Todd, Jan *2:* 383
Todd, Mabel Loomis *1:* 107-108
Toidy Seat *1:* 145
Toll House cookie *1:* 145
Tomaszewicz-Dobrska, Anna *2:* 260-261
Topham, Mirabel *1:* 136,
Tourisheva, Ludmilla *2:* 381
Towne, Laura Matilda *1:* 174

Tranchepain, Marie *2:* 291
Travell, Janet *2:* 273-274, 274 (ill.)
Tree, Marietta Peabody *1:* 194
Triathalon *2:* 387
Trotter, Mildred *2:* 342
Trotula of Salerno *2:* 250
Trout, Jennie Kidd *2:* 260
Troy Female Seminary *1:* 172
Truman, Elizabeth *2:* 274
Truth, Sojourner *2:* 359
Tuchman, Barbara *1:* 117
Tudor, Mary *1:* 182
Tufty, Esther Van Wagoner *2:* 230
Turkevich, Ludmilla B. *1:* 166-167
Twyla Tharp Dance Company *1:* 59
Tyler, Dorothy *2:* 363
Tyler, Reba C. *2:* 282
UAW (see United Auto Workers)
Underhill, Miriam *2:* 403
Unger, Karoline *1:* 79-80
United Auto Workers (UAW) *1:* 38
United Farm Workers Union *1:* 27
United Mine Workers *1:* 40, *1:* 40
United Nations *1:* 38, 194, 206, 210
Vaganova, Agrippina *1:* 58-59
Van Blarcom, Carolyn C. *2:* 267
Van Deman, Esther Boise *2:* 310
Van Dyken, Amy *2:* 388
Van Grippenberg, Alexandra *1:* 34
Van Hemessen, Caterina *1:* 123
Van Hoosen, Bertha *2:* 267-268, 267 (ill.)
Van Straten, Florence *2:* 320-321
Vassar College *1:* 155 (ill.)
Vestris, Lucia *1:* 75
Viardot-Garcia, Pauline *1:* 80
Vietnam War *1:* 195
Villa, Amelia *2:* 270
Voorhies, Marjorie *2:* 365
WAACS (see Women's Army Auxiliary Corps)
WACS (see Women's Army Corps)
Wagner, Cosima *1:* 82, 82 (ill.)
Waight, Lavinia *1:* 30
Wakefield, Ruth Graves *1:* 145
Waldholtz, Enid *1:* 209
Walker, Alice *1:* 119
Walker, Lucy *2:* 398-399
Walker, Maggie Lena *1:* 133
Walker, Mary Edwards *2:* 276-277
Walker, Sarah Breedlove *1:* 141
Walters, Barbara *2:* 225 (ill.), 232-233
Walters, Bernice R. *2:* 280
Ward, Mary Augusta *1:* 48